PURSUING PRIVACY IN COLD WAR AMERICA

Gender and Culture

Carolyn G. Heilbrun and Nancy K. Miller, editors

Gender and Culture

A SERIES OF COLUMBIA UNIVERSITY PRESS
Edited by Carolyn G. Heilbrun and Nancy K. Miller

In Dora's Case: Freud, Hysteria, Feminism
  Edited by Charles Bernheimer and Claire Kahane
Breaking the Chain: Women, Theory, and French Realist Fiction
  Naomi Schor
Between Men: English Literature and Male Homosocial Desire
  Eve Kosofsky Sedgwick
Romantic Imprisonment: Women and Other Glorified Outcasts
  Nina Auerbach
The Poetics of Gender
  Edited by Nancy K. Miller
Reading Woman: Essays in Feminist Criticism
  Mary Jacobus
Honey-Mad Women: Emancipatory Strategies in Women's Writing
  Patricia Yaeger
Subject to Change: Reading Feminist Writing
  Nancy K. Miller
Thinking Through the Body
  Jane Gallop
Gender and the Politics of History
  Joan Wallach Scott
The Dialogic and Difference: "An/Other Woman" in Virginia Woolf and Christa Wolf
  Anne Herrmann
Plotting Women: Gender and Representation in Mexico
  Jean Franco
Inspiriting Influences: Tradition, Revision, and Afro-American Women's Novels
  Michael Awkward
Hamlet's Mother and Other Women
  Carolyn G. Heilbrun
Rape and Representation
  Edited by Lynn A. Higgins and Brenda R. Silver
Shifting Scenes: Interviews on Women, Writing, and Politics in Post-'68 France
  Edited by Alice A. Jardine and Anne M. Menke
Tender Geographies: Women and the Origins of the Novel in France
  Joan DeJean

GENDER AND CULTURE READERS

Pursuing Privacy in Cold War America

DEBORAH NELSON

COLUMBIA UNIVERSITY PRESS   NEW YORK

Columbia University Press

Publishers Since 1893

New York   Chichester, West Sussex

Copyright © 2002 Columbia University Press

All rights reserved

Library of Congress Cataloging-in-Publication Data

Nelson, Deborah, 1962–

Pursuing privacy in Cold War America / Deborah Nelson.

Includes bibliographical references and index.

ISBN 0–231–11120–7 (cloth)—ISBN 0–231–11121–5 (paper)

1. American poetry—20th century—History and criticism.

2. Privacy in literature.   3. Literature and society—United States—History—20th century.

4. Privacy, Right of—United States—History—20th century.

5. Privacy—United States—History—20th century.

6. Autobiography in literature.   7. Confession in literature.

8. Cold War in literature.   9. Self in literature.   I. Title.   II. Series.

PS310.P75 N45 2001

811′.54080355—dc21   2001037260

Columbia University Press books are printed

on permanent and durable acid-free paper.

Printed in the United States of America

c 10 9 8 7 6 5 4 3 2 1

p 10 9 8 7 6 5 4 3 2 1

For Adrienne

Contents

Introduction: The Death of Privacy

Is privacy dead? By all recent accounts, we should think so. When independent counsel Kenneth Starr published on the Internet in 1998 the titillating details of President Clinton's relationship with White House intern Monica Lewinsky, there was widespread agreement that the "Starr Report" marked the death of privacy. However, it was generally forgotten, though it had occurred merely six months before the Clinton/Lewinsky scandal broke, that privacy had just died a grisly death in an underground tunnel in Paris. Princess Diana's fatal car crash while being pursued by tabloid photographers had also constituted the final proof of privacy's demise. And again, commentators on Diana's death failed to recall that privacy had died just a few weeks earlier in *Time*'s 1997 "Death of Privacy" cover story, which exposed new and previously unimagined violations enabled by the Internet. What's more, throughout this spasm of anxiety, the media's absorption in Clinton's comedy and Diana's tragedy elicited parallel "death of privacy" warnings. This time they were provoked not by the intrusion of the state, mass media, or new technology, but by the extrusion of private life in public discourse, the blurring of boundaries associated with what is often disparaged as our "confessional culture." Privacy, it seems, is not simply dead. It is dying over and over and over again.

It would be a mistake to imagine that this pattern is somehow unique to the late 1990s and the early 2000s. Such thinking merely perpetuates the amnesia that the warnings themselves display. Indeed, this sequence of obituaries belongs to a pattern that attained a measurable density some forty years prior to the most recent "deaths" of privacy. Since the end of the 1950s, the cry "the death of privacy" has rung out from a wide variety of sources: journalism, television, film, literature, law enforcement, philosophy, medical discourse, and more. One crisis after the next has seemed to prove that an unprecedented threat to privacy was about to obliterate it. The wave of apprehension about the vulnerability of privacy at the end of the twentieth century has generated a massive investigation into the changing boundaries of public and private domains that has become a central preoccupation, not to say obsession, in American political, aesthetic, and intellectual life. Predictably, under the threat of its disappearance, privacy returned triumphant as a curiously vital but deeply paradoxical concept. The problem with privacy in this country is not that we have too little privacy but that we have both too little and too much at the same time.

This ambivalence surrounding privacy lies at the heart of cold war studies in the by now ubiquitous metaphor "containment," a term that was taken from George Kennan's 1947 foreign policy directive for coping with the threat of Soviet expansion and used to describe domestic ideology and its effects on literary and mass culture. My goal is to understand the ways in which containment as a metaphor and as a material practice shaped the privacy controversy that began in the late 1950s. Extending the important insights into the dual nature of privacy that have been articulated in recent cold war scholarship, I will be tracing out the slow breakdown of containment from 1959 to 1973, when privacy emerged as a central term in a vast social debate about the dilemmas of modern citizenship. The culture of this period exhibits both a resistance to and a perpetuation of certain ideas about citizen and state, self and society, that were built into the containment project of the early cold war years. Turning to the language of containment as it reappeared in the 1980s will provide a coda to the debate over the limits and privileges of privacy that so marked the second half of the twentieth century.

The cold war scripted the privacy crisis. What I call the sudden visibility of privacy was produced by the excesses of cold war security, though of course not all the invasions or all the commentaries on this aspect of late-twentieth-century life in the United States were oriented by the cold war. What is perhaps more important is that in addition to generating a privacy crisis of its own, as we know well from histories of this period, the cold war provided a language and a narrative to the dilemma of privacy in modernity more generally. The surge of critical reflection on modernity that followed World War II made evident to the intellectual vanguard in this country that the boundaries between public and private life were highly unstable in both mass democracies and totalitarian regimes. This insight is by now familiar, as evidenced by the influence of Michel Foucault, whose account of the disciplinary technologies of modern states and the confessional structure of modern subjectivity located the interpenetration of public and private life in the founding institutions of the Enlightenment.[1]

However, the anxieties of the cold war made the idea of interpenetration, as well as any claim about the similarities between democracies and totalitarian states, difficult to assimilate. Instead, the sanctity of the private sphere was generally perceived to be the most significant point of contrast between the two regimes. The potency of American democracy in cold war rhetoric was, therefore, not its cultivation of a vibrant and free public discourse but its vigilant protection of private autonomy. Moreover, the stakes of this conviction were typically apocalyptic: either we preserved the integrity of private spaces and thus the free world, or we tolerated their penetration and took the first step toward totalitarian oppression. The very starkness of this choice manufactured the cold war's governing paradox: in the interests of preserving the space of privacy, privacy would have to be penetrated.

But if privacy was supposed to symbolize the autonomy, freedom, self-determination, and repose that the citizen of a democracy most valued, it became increasingly evident in the confessional writing of the period that privacy could also represent isolation, loneliness, domination, and routine. Moreover, it was newly obvious that these deprivations of privacy were unevenly distributed; categories of citizens—women or homosexuals—rather than unlucky individuals were banished to the deprivation, rather than the liberation, of privacy. This ambivalence suggests that the sudden visibility of privacy fractured it. Therefore, what got "lost" at the end of the 1950s was a certain fantasy of privacy as a stable and self-evident concept, "privacy as we have always known it," in the common parlance of the era. This lost privacy was also elite and patriarchal, which yoked together private property, bodily integrity, sovereignty over family members, and the proprietary interest in family name as one coherent interest. The repeated "death of privacy" warnings speak to the tenacious hold that nostalgia for this privacy has over our culture; however, this nostalgia also blinds us to the inventions of new privacies that were "found" when patriarchal privacy was lost.

What this book attempts to do is to show how this fantasy of coherent, self-evident privacy was replaced with the invention of the new privacies that emerged when patriarchal privacy began to break down. The simple binary of public and private has already been complicated by the recognition that modern society is divided into a multiplicity of public spheres; it has been less clear, however, that during the past forty years we have seen the proliferation of privacies as well.

Privacy during the latter half of this century is an extremely protean concept, something that disappeared and reappeared at the same time. As the "death of privacy" reached crisis dimensions, privacy was also more widely available than ever before in the everyday life of middle-class Americans. That is, privacy was scattered across contemporary life during this period, materializing in the mass-produced single family home, the automobile, the phone booth, even on the street. As an increasingly portable concept, privacy had to be calibrated over and over, which made it both more accessible and less familiar. Attending to this defamiliarization means probing the rhetoric of privacy, the attempts to pin it down in language when it became so unfixed in space.

In this book I concentrate primarily on two cultural and social forms—constitutional law and lyric poetry—for their particularly self-conscious engagement with the rhetoric of privacy. I contend that there is a powerful relationship between the Supreme Court's fashioning of a right to privacy and the extravagant self-disclosures of the confessional poets, a group notorious for their breach of social and poetic decorum. The self-consciousness of form in each genre allows us to perceive how the structures of privacy were transformed during the latter half of the twentieth century. The wager of this project is that the oblique connections between constitutional law and lyric poetry convey the mobility, the elasticity, and the inexhaustibility of privacy.

My investigation into the ambivalence of privacy begins with its sudden visibility, the stunning emergence of privacy as a "lost thing" at the end of the 1950s in an astonishing variety of locations: journalistic exposés, television programs, law review articles, mass-market magazines, films, Supreme Court decisions, poems, novels, autobiographies, corporate hiring manuals, scientific protocols, psychological surveys, educational records, databases, and computers. I map this visibility along two axes: the anxieties about intrusions into private life that were largely, but not exclusively, tied to the cold war; and the uneasiness about the leaking of private life into public discourse that marked the first appearance of "confessional culture." This double vision with regard to the dilemmas of privacy captures the ambivalence that marked the concept from the moment of its appearance as a central category of late-twentieth-century American culture. It was not only the cold war's intense focus on the home as a symbol of democratic liberty that sparked the interest in privacy. It was also the opening up to exposure of the sphere of intimacy, both for pleasure and in protest, which accelerated demands to establish and defend the boundaries of privacy.

Later chapters examine what sort of privacy was "found"—to borrow a term from the Supreme Court decision establishing a right to privacy—when privacy was lost. In order to understand the ways in which privacy was reinvented during this period of sudden visibility, it is necessary not only to adopt a historical perspective but also to focus on formal questions within that historical moment. This is to say that we can only understand the larger privacy crisis in the idiom of individual episodes.

During the period of sudden visibility, there occurred two parallel and extremely influential developments. One, the Supreme Court first established the "right to privacy" in *Griswold v. Connecticut* (1965),[2] and during the next twenty years it ruled on a number of landmark privacy cases, including, most famously *Roe v. Wade* (1973)[3] and *Bowers v. Hardwick* (1986).[4] I argue that the Court invented the right to privacy in this period under the pressure of privacy's sudden visibility. And two, there emerged onto the American cultural landscape a group of poets—Anne Sexton, Robert Lowell, Sylvia Plath, John Berryman, and W. D. Snodgrass—called "confessional" for their extraordinary departures from poetic and social decorum. These poets, according to Alan Williamson, were especially censured for their "socially shameful disclosures" and "their thematic interest in disclosure" itself (*Introspection* 7–8), even though they were not alone in experimenting with so-called private or intimate content. I have chosen to focus on this group because they were the best known for testing the limits of privacy.

I link constitutional law and confessional poetry not simply because they share the connection of their historical proximity; this they share with numerous other artifacts from the era. But these two traditions share more complex historical and generic similarities that make their juxtaposition illuminating. In the cross-disciplinary work of "law and literature" we are forever warned about overestimating the degree to which one illuminates the other. Whatever the limitations of disciplinary specialization during the nineteenth and twentieth centuries, a too hasty interdisciplinarity, we are told, threatens to diminish the precision, depth, complexity, or clarity that have accrued to methodological development. What I mean to suggest instead is that "law and literature" has been too quick to banish form from its debates in reaction to a now thoroughly discredited notion of the autonomy of both literary objects and legal judgments. An attention to form, and indeed to formalism itself—the rules that draw and regulate the boundaries of a field—have important contributions to make to what Brook Thomas calls "a story about American culture" (*Cross-Examinations* 15), in this case, a story about privacy. Thinking historically renews our sense of how privacy doctrine and confessional poetry expressed deep conflicts in American culture in the late twentieth century; thinking formally provides new insights into the history of a concept. Form, it seems, tells us more about the conservation of privacy than about its relentless disappearance.

Constitutional law is an obvious place to examine how the concept of privacy has been transformed. As James Boyd White has explained, in a series of Fourth Amendment cases beginning in the late nineteenth century with *Boyd v. U.S.* (1886),[5] the Supreme Court "created a language, a set of terms and assumptions and gestures in which it can talk about and dispose of the conflicts that repeatedly arise between members of police departments and investigative agencies on the one hand and those members of the public upon whom they intrude on the other. This language is itself a way of constituting and thinking about the world, a way of defining the citizen and the officer and the relation between them" (177–78). White also cautions us that the discourse of the Fourth Amendment is a set of conventions that a citizen must use if his or her grievance against the police/state is to be intelligible to the court, whether or not these conventions reflect that citizen's experience or values. Constitutional rhetoric is thus the obligatory public language by which Americans in the late twentieth century imagined their citizenship and the "terms and assumptions and gestures" that would have to be renegotiated in the crisis of privacy.

It is not at all obvious that the lyric poem constitutes an appropriate counterexample to this "universal" public language of citizenship. However, lyric subjectivity shares a profound symmetry with constitutional citizenship. The lyric was transformed in the epistemological and ontological shift that occurred after the revolutions in France and the United States at the end of the eighteenth century into the form we now regard as the lyric: in J. S. Mill's terms, the "self overheard speaking to itself." This transformation of the lyric is the nearly exclusive emphasis on the "meditative" form of lyric, which increasingly came to stand in for lyric as a whole.[6]

I want to redescribe this romantic revolution in the lyric in constitutional terms. The lyric is the form in which we witness the exhilaration—and perhaps also the terror—of autonomy and self-sovereignty. Unlike the novel, which is polyvocal and social, the lyric is the aesthetic and ideological form in which a speaker conveys the experience and/or the fantasy of his or her own privacy and unfettered self-creation. Like the Court's language of citizenship, the lyric also contains "terms and assumptions and gestures" about the nature of autonomy and privacy.

At the time of their emergence, the confessional poets were taken to be an extreme instance of romantic lyric self-absorption. However, their significance in literary history and to the changing culture of privacy lies in their exposure of limitations on lyric autonomy and constitutional sovereignty that we had not perceived the lyric subject or the constitutional citizen to suffer. In other words, the crisis of privacy unmasked the universal, abstract categories that founded both citizenship and lyric subjectivity. Confessional poetry's revolution of decorum—a social and formal revolution—like the Court's intensive negotiation of the relationship between citizen and police, created new "terms and assumptions and gestures" of both privacy and the lyric form.

What makes constitutional law and lyric poetry so illuminating to a consideration of the changing nature of privacy is that both are exceptionally self-conscious about and dependent on their own precedents. The peculiar obligations in each genre to recognize and invoke precedent—stare decisis in the law and the informal duty to precedent in poetry—allow us to see the reconfiguration of the language of privacy in tight proximity to its discarded or revised terms. This is of particular value in the curiously amnesiac rhetoric of the privacy crisis, in which each new danger is characterized as "unprecedented."

All the questions about privacy in the legal and lyric projects turn insistently back into questions about gender and sexuality. The forms of constitutional citizenship and lyric subjectivity presupposed a privacy and autonomy that were gendered. This we know from feminist legal and literary theory. But George Lakoff and Mark Johnson unwittingly suggest the extent to which the privacy crisis of the cold war was a metaphor for the crisis of masculine self-sovereignty. They could not have imagined a pregnant woman when they argued in *Metaphors We Live By* (1980) that

each of us is a container, with a bounded surface and an in-out orientation. We project our own in-out orientation onto other physical objects that are bounded by surfaces. Thus we also view them as containers with an inside and an outside. (29)

The cold war containment metaphor was not simply an expression of foreign policy, or domestic ideology, but a figure for the impossible coherence of masculine autonomy. The power and mobility of this metaphor of containment were equal only to the power and elasticity of the metaphor of intrusion—the enemy within—which conveyed the uncanny experience of finding one's borders already violated. The impossible purity of the internal space meant the perpetual breakdown and failure of the containment project.

But I would like to take this argument one step further. Law and poetry represent privacy not only in gendered metaphors but in a syntax of gender, a structural analogy that cannot be inverted: masculinity is to privacy as femininity is to exposure. To invoke any of the terms in this equation is to be situated in a matrix from which one cannot move without a transposition of terms. This grammar suggests that modern citizenship, which takes place in the condition of exposure, is feminine. Surprisingly, however, the feminizing of citizenship does not eradicate the possibility of privacy but instead offers an escape from the anxious spaces that must continually be shored up, be they homes, nations, or bodies. It is the containment metaphor that cannot survive the conditions of modernity, which does not mean that the only alternative to contained male citizenship is female exposure.

Confessional poetry, though it does not achieve the terms of self-disclosure it wills, imagines ways in which privacy can be obtained or conserved in disclosure. Having no recourse to the sovereignty of male citizen/subjects, confessional poets such as Sexton and Plath figure the possibility of new forms of privacy that reside in a multiplication of confession. Moving beyond the fantasy of a spatial privacy—the container that must be sealed tightly at all costs—suggests a new and paradoxical model of privacy in the era of generalized exposure.

The final chapter represents a coda to the extreme volatility that characterized the privacy migrations of the late 1950s to the early 1970s. The 1980s witnessed the revival of early cold war containment rhetoric, which we see in the most direct conversation between law and lyric poetry of the postwar era, that between *Bowers v. Hardwick* and Paul Monette's *Love Alone* (1988). Monette, an AIDS activist and memoirist who linked himself with the confessional poets, responded to *Hardwick*'s denial of privacy rights to gay men with a series of elegies in which he first renounced and then revalued his privacy. At first Monette models the paranoid privacy that we associate with the early cold war. After *Hardwick*, however, he gropes toward a privacy based on publicity rather than a withdrawal into contained space. In a sense, Monette is poised between the final end point of containment privacy, whose most unstable form is the closet, and a postcontainment privacy, one that we might formulate on what Jessica Benjamin calls "mutual recognition" (21). I want to suggest that Benjamin's psychoanalytic model of relational subjectivity can also be understood as a cultural project of redescription, where the breakdown of boundaries is rewritten not as pathology but as a process of disruption and repair. Without the fantasy of a "lost" coherent privacy, the porousness of boundaries between public and private would constitute not an unappeasable anxiety but a release from ambivalence.

Monette's recovery of privacy is too easily positioned as a retreat into the closet, as many attempts to resurrect the notion of privacy are labeled in the post-*Hardwick* era. I would like to take this misreading of his work as an opportunity to explain why it is important to rethink late-twentieth-century formations of privacy. I think we have understood *Hardwick's* heterosexualizing of privacy as an unavoidable structural impasse in liberal notions of privacy rather than as the breaking point of a particular model of privacy, one that is deeply stained by the cold war obsession with containment. In this I follow George Chauncey, who demonstrates that the closet is a feature of late-twentieth-century gay identity that we have inaccurately cast backward into history.[7] I am arguing that we also mistakenly project this forward. In this sense, we need to reinterpret the seminal works of queer theory, which almost always derive their sense of urgency, and their reading of privacy, from *Bowers v. Hardwick*.

Eve Kosofsky Sedgwick has opened the door to a revision of *Epistemology of the Closet* in an essay from *Novel Gazing* (1997), "Paranoid Reading, Reparative Reading," which I would like to follow by way of a conclusion. Reparative reading offers a way out of the nostalgia and paranoia of the privacy debate, the twin fears that privacy will not remain "as we have always known it" and that it will. I am hoping that a reparative reading, one mode of which is "an unhurried, undefensive, theoretically galvanized practice of close reading" (23), will demonstrate that privacy is more mobile and elastic than we have previously imagined. No era is more in need of reparative rather than paranoid reading than the cold war.

I take Sedgwick's point seriously that "to practice other than paranoid forms of knowing does *not*, in itself, entail a denial of the reality or gravity of enmity or oppression" (7). I hope that it is clear throughout this book that certain modes of privacy are grasped in extremity. They are not fabricated in the imaginative play of abundance but in the enforced ingenuity of oppression. We might find that the intolerable ambivalence of privacy is appeased somewhat by imagining the ways in which the concept is amenable to correction. But this correction may never arrive in the domain of law. Wai Chee Dimock has imagined literature as the "residue" where the dream of a perfectly commensurable justice is suspended and where the clean abstractions of the law are complicated by the messiness of experience.[8] In this sense, poetry offers the space of contradiction and ambiguity, of improvisation and paradox that privacy depends upon. If we learn nothing else from this prolonged crisis, we should learn that privacy is available to the extent that its violations reinvent it.

Acknowledgments

This book has benefited from the rigor and imagination of a great number of friends and advisers. By far the greatest debt I owe is to Nancy K. Miller, who has been at every stage in this long process an astute critic, supportive mentor, and wonderful friend. I continue to avail myself of her critical judgment, imaginative engagement, elegant editorial advice, to say nothing of her provocation, encouragement, patience, and wit. Without her guidance and example, I cannot imagine this or indeed any future work.

In addition to Nancy Miller, many of my professors at the Graduate Center were instrumental in helping me to formulate this project and develop as a scholar. Among them, I would like to thank Luke Menand, Charles Molesworth, Rachel Brownstein, and Joan Richardson. Crucial to managing and enjoying the dissertation process were my accomplished, funny, and always open-minded writing partners Jane Collins, Brian Brewer, Lorna Smedman, Mary Jo Haronian, and Jay Prosser. A special thanks goes to Victoria Rosner, an unofficial Graduate Center alum, who made a gift of her superior organizational mind and prose styling.

At the University of Chicago, friends, colleagues, and students enriched and expanded the book. I am chiefly indebted to Eric Santner and Bill Brown, who are my heroes of intellectual openness and generosity. Both of them were unstinting in their efforts to help me discover the project I wanted to do and then to do it. Many of my colleagues were willing above and beyond the call of duty to read drafts of chapters and help me to articulate and rework the arguments. I'd like to thank in particular Bob von Hallberg, Lisa Ruddick, Lauren Berlant, Jim Chandler, Richard Strier, Janice Knight, Bill Veeder, Ken Warren, Josh Scodel, Saree Makdisi, and Mark Miller. I'd also like to thank the Lesbian and Gay Studies Workshop, especially George Chauncey and Beth Povinelli, for their thoughtful criticism. David Levin, Sandra Macpherson, and Danielle Allen were essential to me in the final stages of the project. My student and friend, Fred Whiting, and research assistants, Shaleane Gee and Sarah Rivett, were enormously giving of their time and attention to detail. I would also like to thank my department chair, Elizabeth Helsinger, and the dean of the humanities, Janel Mueller, for enthusiastically supporting my year's leave to complete the book.

I am deeply grateful to the Mellon Foundation and the Center for the Humanities at Wesleyan University where I finished the book. Director of the center, Henry Abelove, not only made my tenure there productive and stimulating but also advised a chapter with his typical grace and erudition. I owe a special thanks to Shelly Rosenblum for her fine work on the notes and bibliography. I'd also like to acknowledge Pat Camden and Jackie Rich for their cheerful and efficient administrative assistance.

At Columbia University Press, I'd like to thank Jennifer Crewe for her remarkable patience and Susan Heath for her meticulous editing of the manuscript. Carolyn Heilbrun, as informal adviser and editor of the Gender and Culture Series, has read and commented on a number of drafts, and I thank her for her sharp insight and good sense.

I'd like to thank my family—Judy and Mark Nelson, Linda Siemering, Jennifer Nelson, and Amy Dansreau—for their willingness to endure my endless rehearsal of complaint and fatigue. Each of them is incredibly good at making sure I never take myself or my work too seriously, try as I might.

Finally, I dedicate this book to my partner, best friend, and most critical reader, Adrienne Hiegel, to whom I owe the origin of the project. She is truly the better craftsman and never lets me forget it.

I thank the Houghton Library at Harvard University and the Harry Ransom Library at the University of Texas for their permission to quote from Lowell's papers. Earlier versions of chapters 3 and 4 were published previously. Chapter 3 was published as "Penetrating Privacy: Confessional Poetry and the Surveillance Society" in *Home-Making: The Poetics and Politics of Home in Women's Writing*, edited by Fiona Barnes and Catherine Wiley, Garland Press, 1996. Chapter appeared as "Beyond Privacy: Confessions Between a Woman and Her Doctor" in *Feminist Studies*, Summer 1999. Many thanks to the editors of both for their criticism and advice.

PURSUING PRIVACY IN COLD WAR AMERICA

Reinventing Privacy

Part I: The Sudden Visibility of Privacy

No concept in the late twentieth century proved more generative or more volatile in more domains of social, political, and aesthetic life or for longer duration than "privacy." Studies of late-twentieth-century American culture, particularly in the cold war; surveys of American poetry; gender studies, including feminist and queer theory; and reflections on modernity all mount inquiries into the boundaries between public and private. Indeed, in the last forty years, the terms "public" and "private" became essential, maybe even mandatory categories of evaluation. This return does not always brood over the same object of anxiety; that is, if some of these critics predict the death of privacy, others envisage the death of the public sphere. These are twin anxieties and ought to be considered adjacent rather than opposed. Holding the technological, the political, the aesthetic, and the social components of privacy in tension will begin to suggest the continuity among all of these fields of inquiry.

We can locate rather precisely the emergence of privacy as a dominant concern in the United States by touching first on the Supreme Court's 1965 decision *Griswold v. Connecticut*. This case—in which the Court struck down Connecticut's law prohibiting the use (not sale) of birth control—so reshaped constitutional doctrine that the legal history of privacy can be divided into before and after *Griswold*. We can also consider this case to be broadly symbolic because though the source of tremendous controversy in the legal community, it has enjoyed since its announcement remarkably widespread popular acceptance (with the notable exception of its application in abortion rulings, a problem to which we will return). Although the words "the right to privacy" had been used in court opinions throughout the twentieth-century and even occasionally in the nineteenth, *Griswold* marks the first time the Court gave privacy a constitutional guarantee. Writing for the majority, Justice Douglas crafted the right out of what he called the "penumbra" of specific amendments of the Bill of Rights: the First, which guarantees the right to free speech and free assembly; the Third, which bars the quartering of troops in the homes of citizens; the Fourth, which protects the citizen from illegal search and seizure; the fifth, which is the "right to remain silent"; and the Ninth, which leaves powers not already enumerated in the Bill of Rights to the citizens and the states. In "finding" this right, the Court made the home a "zone of privacy" protecting the relationship that lay within it—marriage—from the scrutiny of the state through the application of fundamental constitutional guarantees. Moreover, in so doing, the right to privacy became firmly associated, not with the wiretapping or surveillance cases that surround it, but with domesticity and family, with rights of child rearing, procreation, and sexual expression.

I begin with *Griswold* not only because it so reshaped legal history but also because it marks the culmination of a major reassessment of privacy that had begun at the end of the 1950s. As a point of contrast, a 1959 case, *Frank v. Maryland*,[1] did not find a right to privacy in the home though the breach of the physical zone was much clearer than in *Griswold*. In *Griswold* the head of Planned Parenthood and the doctor at a Connecticut birth control clinic were convicted as accessories to violation of the birth control statute for giving information, instruction, and advice on contraception to married couples. When Douglas asked: "Would we allow the police to search the sacred precincts of marital bedrooms for telltale signs of the use of contraceptives?" (485), he was outraged by a vision of what might have happened in Connecticut but, in fact, did not. No "user" of birth control had ever been convicted, much less intruded upon by the police. Instead, the head of a clinic operated by Planned Parenthood and one of its staff doctors were arrested. In contrast, *Frank v. Maryland* permitted a health inspector, who did not have a warrant, to search for evidence of health code violations against the wishes of the resident. Though, as the dissent noted, mere inconvenience prevented the inspector from obtaining a warrant, the Court ruled that the state's interest in public health outweighed the citizen's interest in privacy. *Frank* concedes no "zone of privacy" protected with constitutional guarantees, and yet the literal invasion into the home appears to be a much more explicit and egregious violation of the Fourth Amendment's ban on "unreasonable search and seizure" than that in *Griswold*.

The Supreme Court's shift toward embracing a constitutionally guaranteed right to privacy correlates with the sudden emergence of privacy as an object of intense anxiety, scrutiny, investigation, and exploration in mid-1960s American culture. This widespread debate is something that legal historians have yet to come to terms with in understanding the right to privacy and that cultural historians have underestimated as a central transformation of postwar aesthetic and political life.[2] Privacy has been an important facet of cold war studies, chiefly as a paradoxical feature of "containment ideology," but it has been yoked too tightly to national security issues, which while accounting for the unique pressures of the cold war, does not allow ample enough room for the more general concern about public and private boundaries to register.[3] I would like to suggest that in addition to contributing its own pressures on privacy, the cold war *scripted* a topological crisis, a generalized anxiety about zones of sovereignty that was far more general and mobile.

While anxieties about privacy never really disappear during the latter half of the twentieth century—and remain acutely visible in the early years of this one—the debate has moments of vivid intensity, which are marked by controversy and incoherence. Moreover, each of its key moments—1965, 1973, and 1986—was centered on a different anxiety about privacy: the police state and the sanctity of the home, the woman's body, and the homosexual relationship. This chapter creates a patchwork in which the Supreme Court cases—*Griswold. v. Connecticut* (1965), *Roe v. Wade* (1973), and *Bowers v. Hardwick* (1986)—mark a particularly strong and visible moment of public reflection and offer a set of terms, metaphors, and concepts that shift the privacy debate, unsettling aspects of privacy that had rested undisturbed in earlier moments of debate. The cases provide temporal anchor points where we can see the belated expression of cultural changes wrought by the visibility of privacy at a given historical juncture.

If we are going to understand how unusual, indeed how unprecedented, the Court's endorsement of privacy rights is in *Griswold*, it is crucial to recognize the resistance to a general privacy right in the Court's rulings during the first half of the twentieth century. This history of privacy law will pivot upon three significant changes. One, the heat of this debate over privacy shifted decisively in the early 1960s from the social and commercial to the political, that is, from tort conflicts between citizens where the state intervened to protect one from the other, to constitutional disputes between the citizen and the state, where the state itself acts as both intruder and protector.[4] Moving from the social and commercial realms to the political dramatically elevated the stakes of privacy's fragility. It was no longer merely a question of how citizens treated one another, or how they were treated by the mass media; privacy violation had become a measure of the state of democracy, the health of American culture, and the future of the free world. Two, privacy became an increasingly incoherent concept, which proved both troubling and, paradoxically, very valuable. That is, violations that were not literal—i.e., transgressing space with telephone wires or telescopes, "seizing" conversation from remote locations with highly sensitive listening devices, restricting the use of birth control—were more easily adapted to the capacious and protean notion of privacy, which had little constitutional weight but enormous experiential resonance. Third, privacy would become linked to the coercion of confession; it was not simply the Fourth Amendment's protection of the sovereignty of a private home that grounded privacy, it was also the Fifth Amendment's protection against the coercion of confession. This integration of the Fourth and Fifth amendments into a right to privacy is extremely important to late-twentieth-century notions of privacy when the invasion and the confession become increasingly blurred.[5]

The reappraisal of privacy that took place in the years just prior to *Griswold* witnessed a renewed attention to the origin of tort privacy, which dates to a very specific and unusual textual source: "The Right to Privacy," by Louis Brandeis and Samuel Warren, in the *Harvard Law Review* (1890), considered the most influential law review article ever written.[6] Though the words "right to privacy" appear in state and federal court opinions prior to 1890, Brandeis and Warren are credited with devising the legal rationale that state legislatures would later employ in drafting privacy law. Arguing that changing social, political, and economic circumstances had necessitated their new right, they sought to prevent the press from "overstepping the *obvious* bounds of propriety and decency" (196; emphasis mine). Finding the law of libel and slander unsuitable paradigms for a right to privacy—after all, it is the truth of the information published that injures the party violated—Brandeis and Warren stitched copyright and English common law together into a right to withhold material from publication, which would ground the right to privacy. "The common law," they argued, "secures to each individual the right of determining, ordinarily, to what extent his thoughts, sentiments, and emotions shall be communicated to others" (198). There were, however, important qualifications. Brandeis and Warren understood the public's right to know about public figures. They also recognized that a claim to privacy is lost when the "author himself communicates his production to the public"

(199). Moreover, the trade in gossip threatened not only to infringe on the private lives of individual citizens but also to take the space of "matters of real community interest" (196), thus trivializing serious public discourse. They went to some lengths to fault the producers of yellow journalism rather than its consumers.

This new tort privacy was meant to preserve codes of behavior eroding under the pressure of two strong forces: new technologies, such as instant photography, which made intrusion effortless, and market pressures in the form of tabloid journalism, which made these photographic images valuable commodities. In the process of defining the right to privacy, Brandeis and Warren formulated a new definition of a self "beyond" person and property, which they called the "inviolable personality," a self made up of images and text, as well as even less tangible "facts." By extending the notion of the self to this more abstract realm, they were able to devise an injury (thus a tort) to the person who was not libeled but exposed. However, in one of the paradoxes of their attempt to insulate the private self from market forces, Brandeis and Warren unwittingly turned this incorporeal self into property that could be sold. By conceiving privacy as a species of property—copyright—they turned the self into a commodity.[7] This process was completed by the mid-1950s with *Haelan v. Topps* (1953),[8] in which a state court introduced the phrase "the right to publicity," and consolidated in *Hogan v. A. S. Barnes and Co., Inc.* (1957),[9] in which golfer Ben Hogan retained the rights to his image for the purposes of deriving profit from it.[10] These cases established that individuals had the right to sell their image and that use of a person's image was actionable if there was no contract or compensation. (Golfer Tiger Woods is the perfect end result of this line of reasoning: Woods protects his image not to protect himself from being viewed by the public but to maintain his proprietary interest in its use.) Brandeis and Warren foresaw the essential questions about privacy that the new technologies of mass culture would produce, but they did not foresee the extent to which the profitability, the allure, and the political capital of publicity would render so many of their arguments undecidable.

In order to understand how and why privacy was affirmed as a constitutional right during the cold war, it is also necessary to review the Court's refusal to do so prior to the 1960s. In 1928, Louis Brandeis, now a Supreme Court justice, articulated the rationale for a constitutional right to privacy brought about by new surveillance in his extremely important dissent in *Olmstead v. U.S.* (1928).[11]

Olmstead provided the first major confrontation with advances in surveillance technology, and the Court's majority was unwilling to expand the conceptual limits of the Fourth Amendment to meet these innovations. This case brought against bootleggers for conspiring to violate the National Prohibition Act revolved around the admissibility of evidence obtained by telephone wiretaps. Police had tapped the lines of the conspirators, monitoring conversations that ran to 775 typed pages, which included pages of transcript recording people with no involvement in the conspiracy. The Court faced a number of troubling questions that would be taken up in later cases. First, was there an actual intrusion into the home if the telephone lines were tapped at another location? Second, are conversations, spoken words, seizable? Third, are telephone conversations private? Fourth, what method of constitutional interpretation would allow the Court to contend with new technologies such as electronic surveillance and telephones? Chief Justice Taft, writing for the majority, let a literal interpretation of the language guide his arguments. His opinion contended that since telephone lines fall outside the home, no invasion took place; that words, unlike papers, cannot be "seized"; and that telephone conversations are not private but public communications. Law enforcement was thus granted enormous leeway in wiretapping.

Departing from Taft's literalness, Justice Brandeis created a more abstract notion of privacy, providing the constitutional rationale for the right named in *Griswold* in his oft-cited dissent in *Olmstead v. U.S.* To Brandeis, "the right to be let alone—the most comprehensive of rights and the right most valued by civilized men" (478) was jeopardized by both the state and the media, but his rhetoric marks the state's as the graver infringement of liberty. In the course of the dissent Brandeis quickly dispensed with Taft's arguments: the phone conversation, like a letter, is clearly a private communication though transmitted in the public domain; the tapping of a phone is a much more dangerous instrument of power because it violates privacy indiscriminately, intruding on everyone using the line; the literal "ransacking" of papers is deemed far too limited an interpretation because an officer no longer needs to touch the paper to read it. Finally, he argues that admitting tainted evidence into court would sanction illegal activities by law enforcement.

In addition to deliteralizing the protections of the Fourth Amendment, Brandeis affirms the link to Fifth Amendment protections against self-incrimination in his elaboration of a constitutional right to privacy. Brandeis takes up this relationship, which he finds in the most significant precedent, *Boyd v. U.S.* (1886), in his first objection in *Olmstead*. He says:

> When the Fourth and Fifth Amendments were adopted, "the form that evil had theretofore taken" had been necessarily simple. Force and violence were then the only means known to man by which a government could directly effect self-incrimination. It could compel the individual to testify—a compulsion effected, if need be, by torture. It could secure possession of his papers and other articles incident to his private life—a seizure effected, if need be, by breaking and entry. Protection against such invasion of "the sanctities of a man's home and the privacies of life" was provided in the Fourth and Fifth Amendments by specific language. But "time works changes, brings into existence new conditions and purposes." Subtler and more far-reaching means of invading privacy have become available to the government. Discovery and invention have made it possible for the government, by means far more effective than stretching upon the rack, to obtain disclosure in court of what is whispered in the closet. (473)

Brandeis asserts that modern methods of surveillance accomplish precisely the same ends that the violence of torture achieved, not only equating surveillance with torture, but also noting its superiority in obtaining the secrets of "the closet." The most cited passage from this dissent follows:

> The makers of our Constitution undertook to secure conditions favorable to the pursuit of happiness. They recognized the significance of man's spiritual nature, of his feelings and of his intellect. They knew that only a part of the pain, pleasure and satisfactions of life are to be found in material things. They sought to protect Americans in their beliefs, their thoughts, their emotions and their sensations. They conferred, as against the government, the right to be let alone—the most comprehensive of rights and the right most valued by civilized men. To protect that right, every unjustifiable intrusion by the government upon the privacy of the individual, whatever the means employed, must be deemed a violation of the Fourth Amendment. And the use, as evidence in a criminal proceeding, of facts ascertained by such intrusion must be deemed a violation of the Fifth. (478–79)

Following his line of reasoning from "The Right to Privacy," in which he states that the law originally only recognized an injury to the body of a citizen, Brandeis continues what he sees as the development of the law to extend the person of the citizen to the incorporeal, his "inviolable personality." Privacy then became a right of the personality to set the terms of its own disclosure.

The Court's interpretation of law enforcement surveillance technologies did not vary tremendously for the next three decades after *Olmstead*.[12] It was not until two cases handed down in 1961, *Mapp v. Ohio*[13] and *Poe v. Ullman*,[14] that Court watchers began to detect a sea change in privacy rulings. Using the interest in personal privacy articulated in *Boyd v. U.S.* and in Brandeis's *Olmstead* dissent, the Court extended the exclusionary rule (that is, the rule that forbids the use of evidence obtained in violation of the Constitution, which already applied in federal courts) to the states. Miss Mapp had been convicted of possessing "lewd and lascivious books and pictures" in her home. However, Miss Mapp's home was not searched in order to find this obscene material. Instead, police officers looking for information about a recent bombing entered her home without a warrant and in defiance of her express wishes. They proceeded to search indiscriminately throughout her house and seized the obscene material, which allowed them to place her under arrest. Though the case looked like a rather clear-cut violation of the Fourth Amendment's prohibitions against unreasonable search and seizure, the Court invoked privacy rights as a way to emphasize the transgression by law enforcement. At almost the same time, the Court heard *Poe v. Ullman*, a precursor to *Griswold v. Connecticut*, brought by Planned Parenthood of Connecticut on behalf of plaintiffs who were clients of the clinic, all of whom risked extreme physical and emotional distress if they were to become pregnant. (For instance, each of Mrs. Poe's three pregnancies had terminated with the death of her infant, all of whom suffered multiple congenital abnormalities.) The plaintiffs, who were seeking information on birth control, were asking for declaratory relief from Connecticut's statute, which meant that they wished the Court to rule it invalid even though none of them had been arrested for breaking the law.[15] Oddly, it would seem, given *Mapp*'s endorsement of individual privacy, the Court refused to grant relief, arguing that there was no real threat of arrest. However, Justice Harlan wrote a crucial dissent from the decision, extending and fleshing out arguments for a right to privacy for married couples. While a right to privacy was not yet constitutionally protected, it was beginning to look as though the disposition and the rationales were in place to "find" a right to privacy if the Court were pushed to do so.

During the period from 1959 to 1965 the perceived need for privacy was utterly transformed by its sudden visibility as a dying feature of modern and cold war American society. The stunning appearance of privacy as a lost thing at the end of the 1950s and first half of the 1960s[16] can be observed in an astonishing variety of locations—journalistic exposés, television programs, law review articles, mass-market magazines, films, Supreme Court decisions, poems, novels, autobiographies, corporate hiring manuals, scientific protocols, government studies, and congressional hearings—and in response to an extraordinary range of stimuli—satellites, surveillance equipment such as "spike mikes" and telephoto lenses, job testing, psychological surveys, consumer polls, educational records, databases and computers in general, psychoanalysis, suburbs, television, celebrity profiles, news reporting, and more.[17] Looming behind these multiple eruptions of concern was Hannah Arendt's *The Origins of Totalitarianism* (1951). We can understand what I would like to imagine as the *scripting* of privacy violation in the cold war by revisiting one of Arendt's important conclusions. *Origins of Totalitarianism* argued that extinguishing private space was totalitarianism's fundamental innovation in forms of domination:

> Totalitarian government, like all tyrannies, certainly could not exist without destroying the public realm of life, that is, without destroying, by isolating men, their political capacities. But totalitarian domination as a form of government is new in that it is not content with this isolation and destroys private life as well. It bases itself on loneliness, on the experience of not belonging to the world at all, which is among the most radical and desperate experiences of man. (173)

As early as 1948 Arendt had remarked in *The Partisan Review*: "an insight into the nature of totalitarian rule . . . might serve to . . . introduce the most essential political criterion for judging events of our time: will it lead to totalitarian rule or will it not?" ("Concentration Camps" 747). The privacy debate proceeded along this bifurcated narrative trajectory: either privacy was stable and the United States would remain free, or privacy was dying and the nation was headed down the road to totalitarianism. Binary logic plotted the instability of privacy and lent it apocalyptic inevitability.

Even though George Orwell's *1984* (1948) and Arendt's *Origins of Totalitarianism* were widely circulating by the mid-1950s, at the time there were very few law review articles, academic studies, or popular investigations into privacy or its violations.[18] By the end of the decade this would change swiftly and dramatically. Only a handful of general interest books on privacy had been published prior to 1964, which by all accounts is the watershed year in this era of the privacy debate. The level of surveillance in the "organized society" suddenly became a subject of media description and academic speculation. In addition to a sudden spate of articles in *Life Magazine*, the following popular and academic books are only some of the more influential of a torrent of books on the subject. In 1959 Samuel Dash, U.S. Attorney (who later played significant roles in Watergate and in Kenneth Starr's investigation of President Clinton), wrote *The Eavesdroppers*, a study of wiretap technology.[19] In 1962 Morris Ernst's *Privacy: The Right to Be Let Alone* began to define a constitutional right to privacy by tracking the tort right of privacy in the twentieth century; in 1964 two best-selling books—Myron Brenton's *The Privacy Invaders* and Vance Packard's *The Naked Society*—alerted the nation to the perils of the surveillance society; in 1967 Alan Westin's *Privacy and Freedom* took a comprehensive look at privacy from anthropological, legal, and philosophical perspectives. Many others would follow. In fact, for the next three decades, there would be a steady stream of exposés on the death of privacy, advice manuals on how to reclaim your privacy, and books outlining new legal rights to privacy or novel threats to it. These books were to become their own genre of expert advice.

There is no doubt, however, that the most important and widely read works on privacy during the 1960s were those by Vance Packard, Myron Brenton, and Alan Westin. Vance Packard, the journalist/social critic, was riding the crest of his fame after the enormous success of his first three books: *The Hidden Persuaders* (1957), *The Status Seekers* (1959), and *The Wastemakers* (1960); in 1964 *The Naked Society* also became a bestseller. With *The Naked Society*, however, Packard departed from his well-known title formula because Myron Brenton's *The Privacy Invaders* was also to be published that same year.[20] The two books, both reviewed in the *New York Times*, Packard's on the front page of the *Sunday New York Times Book Review*, focused attention on the increasing assaults on privacy in everyday life. Brenton's reported on the emerging industry of private investigators armed with ever more sophisticated surveillance equipment, but he placed these concerns amid what he perceived as a widespread assault on traditional respect for the boundaries of private life. Packard's, as was his style, attempted a comprehensive catalogue of all the invasions facing the average American, many of which, not surprisingly, were related to cold war anticommunism. Packard surveyed the personality testing of job applicants, on-the-job monitoring of employees in government and business, the surveillance of students and teachers in universities as well as secondary schools, the secret observation of public officials in local politics as well as in the State Department and the Pentagon, the wiretapping of private homes and electronic surveillance of public bathrooms, the accumulation of financial data on individuals by credit bureaus and the IRS, and, finally, the storage of all the information gathered in these various surveillance enterprises in computers, the technological development that has produced the most anxiety about privacy in the postwar era, far outweighing in intensity and longevity the fear of sophisticated electronic listening devices. The sheer volume of detailed case studies and the masses of statistics justified his contention that privacy was on the verge of extinction.

Increasingly, two fears began to emerge out of this welter of anxious musing on the death of privacy: one, that there were dangerous levels of intrusion into the most basic aspects of an individual's private life; and two, that the changing social status of self-disclosure was going to make the violation of privacy a matter of indifference to most Americans. In other words, privacy was dying because it was vulnerable to penetration from without and exposure from within. As the tabulation of privacy invasions mounted, moreover, it was becoming evident that the cold war had created a rationale for surveillance that was infinitely expandable. Defining the subversive as the "enemy within" and the "invisible threat" had an unanticipated rhetorical flexibility as has by now been well documented in cold war histories. This formulation could describe the communist in the State Department or the homosexual on the job; it could by the early sixties describe labor unions (Robert Kennedy's *Enemy Within* [1960]) or suicide (Edward Robb Ellis's *The Traitor Within* [1961]). The tone of these cautionary tales became increasingly high-pitched, sometimes apocalyptic, because the means of surveillance grew more precise as the motives for it expanded, encompassing ever-broadening areas of behavior and belief. Surveillance, though justified on the grounds of global political survival, was exercised in the ordinary realms of everyday life. This rhetorically flexible characterization of the enemy served to both multiply the sites of invasion, dispersing them across U.S. social and political life, as well as intensify them, extending surveillance deeper into regions that did not then appear to be political, such as gender, sexuality, mental health, and personality.

Feeding these debates over widespread surveillance and linking them directly to cold war anticommunism in 1964 was journalist Fred J. Cook's *The FBI Nobody Knows* (1964), a best-selling, highly critical account of J. Edgar Hoover and the FBI, which ended a fourteen-year absence of criticism of the bureau's powerful director. Chief among the litany of abuses that led Cook to announce, "The police state looms on the horizon" (394) was "Hoover's enormous and unchecked power—the clandestine wiretapping, the mail checking, and surveillance; the gossip, the rumor, the damaging of truth and half-truth that repose in the secret dossiers of the FBI" (395). Hoover's dossier system, in which the director of the FBI kept tabs on "communists," "fellow travelers," "pseudo-liberals" and "dupes," lumped together a wide spectrum of political (and nonpolitical) affiliation.[21] One of the expansions of the subversive category that most bothered Cook was the surveillance of civil rights activists and sympathizers. According to Cook, and to many others who followed, civil rights organizations, though at one period loosely associated with communist groups, were followed and recorded as if there was no distinction. Agitating for civil rights was made equivalent to undermining the "American way of life." Moreover, Hoover's absolute control over the training of new recruits meant that his vision of the American polity would be reproduced in every FBI office across the country. In *The FBI and Martin Luther King Jr.* (1981) David Garrow states that, for J. Edgar Hoover, Martin Luther King Jr. was "the most dangerous and effective Negro leader in the country today" (69), and Hoover consequently spent a great deal of FBI manpower and technical resources recording King's sex life.

That this broadening of the category of subversive would later include the National Organization of Women and other feminist groups can be predicted in the initial outburst of anxiety about privacy violation. Packard himself is aware of the flexibility of the "enemy within," and his analysis suggests the ease with which questions of national security turned into questions about normative gender and sexuality. In the realm of job testing, for instance, the ideology of cold war domestic containment mirrored the rhetorical or symbolic propaganda that has been so well analyzed with respect to Hollywood movies, television shows, and women's magazines. In these obviously intrusive tests and psychological interviews, denying job applicants employment on the basis of their deviance from conventional gender roles comprises some of the most widespread and tangible coercion of the cold war, not only proliferating the sites of interrogation but escalating that interrogation and putting under scrutiny the most ordinary behaviors, tastes, and interests. Packard quotes "business critic" Alan Harrington, who calls the test forms used by businesses a "new type of confessional": " 'Instead of confessing to God through a priest or confessing to one's self through a psychologist, the Corporate Man confesses to the Form' " (*Naked Society* 69). Any perceived oddities of behavior or opinion—for men, in particular, deviations from gender norms—were warning signs to employers that the job applicant was a potential "risk," thus blurring political and sexual deviance. In Packard's analysis of "the Form," the "*he* applicants in business would ideally be all-he; but even the testers recognize that the gal going into business as a career need not necessarily be all-she. A number of widely peddled test forms promise to ferret out the overly unmasculine male or overly unfeminine female" (70). On one scale "the true male is assumed to be interested in hunting and fishing and working with tools and to engage in other presumed he-man endeavors; the inadequate male is more cultural and sensitive in his interests" (70). It is of little consequence that these crude assessments of personality were disparaged by experts in the field of psychology since, as Packard notes, millions of Americans were subjected to them.[22]

Packard intimates that though job-screening processes had been developed to ferret out political subversives, corporations were essentially targeting homosexuals. What was originally a fear of communists had migrated toward gender anxiety, which, according to historians of the period, copied in an almost perfect rhetorical symmetry the language of political subversion. John D'Emilio was among the first historians to note that defining communists as invisible internal threats, as subversives passing as ordinary Americans, permitted a widespread surveillance of and attack on homosexuals, who were also passing as ordinary Americans, whose subversive "tendencies," a favorite word in the job-testing industry, could also only be unmasked by surveillance.[23] From the early years of the cold war, when, for example, Eisenhower issued an executive order declaring that homosexuality was sufficient grounds for disbarment from federal employment, homosexuality and political deviance were merely different species of the same crime: undermining the "American way of life." This is all to say that so-called private sexual behavior—or what we will come to understand as the privacy of heterosexual married behavior in *Griswold*—was in the cold war fraught with political significance.

This intensifying of cold war surveillance into the realms of gender and sexuality is crucial to the privacy debate because the anxieties about police surveillance are most often treated in legal history as parallel or even unrelated to the controversies over privacy in the domains of gender and sexuality that we see in *Roe* and *Hardwick* in the next two decades. However, the privacy debate of the early 1960s suggests that concerns with domestic propriety were bound up in the excesses of anticommunism; it was simply not yet apparent what the implications of this binding would be. In other words, though privacy concerns seemed to implicate the domains of gender and sexuality "beyond" political autonomy, the asymmetries of privacy for women or for homosexuals would not yet fragment the notion of privacy itself.

This reach of cold war politics into domestic life and sexual expression is what Elaine Tyler May described as containment ideology.[24] Now the governing term in studies of the cold war, "containment" helps explain the paradox of privacy in this era. Quite simply, surveillance in this period derives from an extraordinary investment in the private realm. Michael Rogin, in *Ronald Reagan, The Movie* (1987), has explained it succinctly with regard to anticommunism in mass culture in the 1950s:

> Cold war films present themselves as defending private life from Communism. Like domestic ideology, however, these movies promote the takeover of the private by the falsely private. They politicize privacy in the name of protecting it and thereby wipe it out. Domestic and cold war ideologies not only dissolve the private into the public; they also do the reverse. They depoliticize politics by blaming subversion on personal influence. (245)

This double move—the too intimate intrusion of public concerns into the private realm and the too facile assignment of political motives to personal influence—means that we cannot imagine that privacy was an unequivocal good in cold war discourse, even if it is most often mobilized as such. Counterpoised to the fears of penetration is the anxiety that private space affords sanctuary to the enemies of privacy.[25]

Packard dedicated *The Naked Society* to his agent and friend, Harriet Pilpel, which biographically connects the popular and legal controversies over the death of privacy. Pilpel, who practiced law with Morris Ernst, was a key strategist in the long series of cases brought by Planned Parenthood, including the then pending *Griswold* litigation. Packard, very likely under her tutelage, reviewed recent Court rulings on privacy in *The Naked Society*, bringing to the attention of his national audience developments in the constitutional doctrine of privacy. Suggesting that the police state was no longer simply a threat to the expression of dissident political ideas but that it was now intruding upon the cold war's ideological centerpiece—the sanctity of marriage and family—Packard claims that the Court's refusal to rule on Connecticut's birth control statute in 1960 in *Poe v. Ullman* "would require the issuing of hundreds of thousands of search warrants and officers of the law would have to march into as many bedrooms to find out what was going on" (162–63). Packard's warning would be repeated in remarkably similar language by Justice Douglas in *Griswold v. Connecticut* one year later ("Would we allow the police to search the sacred precincts of marital bedrooms for telltale signs of the use of contraceptives?" [485]). This is not to suggest an origin of the phrase but rather to show how widely it was repeated and how fluidly metaphors and images of anxiety crossed different rhetorical domains.

The invasion of private space is only one context for imagining the newfound right of privacy in *Griswold*; the place of confession—coerced or voluntary—was instrumental in rethinking the place of private life in American culture, political, legal, and aesthetic. The right to privacy named in *Griswold* also has roots in the 1950s' spellbinding frenzy of self-exposure, what Andrew Ross called "the ritual importance of televised confession" (*No Respect* 104)—from the testimony of suspected communists before the House on Un-American Activities Committee (HUAC) to Charles Van Doren's confession of his involvement in the *Twenty-One* game show scandal—as well as in its literary counterpart, the recantations of communism by noted writers and intellectuals such as Richard Wright, Arthur Koestler, André Gide, and Whittaker Chambers, which Mary McCarthy called the "penny peep[s]" of her era (*On the Contrary* 75).[26] Many legal scholars link the transformation of the Supreme Court's position on privacy rights to *NAACP v. Alabama* (1958),[27] a case that upheld the NAACP's right to keep its membership lists secret from the state of Alabama.[28] The Supreme Court decided that the "right to association," guaranteed in the First Amendment, ensured the right of groups of people to "pursue their lawful private interests privately" (450). This right of privacy in association was then extended to the married couple in *Griswold*. However, the secrecy of membership resonates powerfully with the persecution of the Communist Party in the United States during the 1950s, a group that was afforded no such rights of association, much less privacy rights in them, especially in the HUAC investigations, which always required the naming of names.[29] *NAACP v. Alabama* steers us toward a submerged connection between privacy rights and the cold war's confounding of private and public boundaries through the coercion of confession during the McCarthy-era witchhunts.

Though not named as precedent in *Griswold*, the case of *Watkins v. U.S.* (1957)[30] forges a strong relationship between cold war confession and new configurations of privacy. *Watkins* rendered judgment on the scope of the state's power to compel testimony. Chief Justice Warren, writing for a unanimous Court in *Watkins,* struck down the conviction for contempt of Congress that had been delivered upon Watkins when he failed to answer some of the House Un-American Activities Committee's questions. After testifying to his own involvement with the Communist Party, instead of pleading the Fifth (which would have guarded him against contempt charges), Watkins refused to answer HUAC's request to name former communists by declaring that the question went beyond the legitimate purposes of the committee, which was legally limited to gathering information for the purposes of drafting legislation. Anyone with even passing familiarity with the activities of this infamous committee knows that HUAC had long since overstepped this boundary. Instead, as the committee itself acknowledged, HUAC used the forum of its hearings to punish witnesses through public shaming. Despite the dubious constitutional standing of HUAC's practices, the Supreme Court throughout the 1950s had generally upheld the committee's procedures. In *Watkins* in 1957, however, the Court began to limit the committee's seemingly unbounded license to compel testimony without reaching the question of HUAC's legitimacy per se. Taking this narrower but still vital question, the Court began to articulate one component of the right to privacy: the right to remain silent, more familiar to us today from the Miranda warnings set out in 1966.

Justice Douglas's series of lectures in 1957 at Franklin and Marshall Law School (published in 1958 as *The Right of the People*) links this case to the right to privacy. Because so much of the language in the privacy lecture finds its way into Douglas's *Griswold* decision, it seems important to revisit this lecture in order to think about how the rationale for privacy was linked to cold war political concerns around the coercion of confession. Reflecting on *Watkins* during his address, Douglas noted the historical anomaly of the Senate's information gathering, stating that prior to the end of World War II, legislative inquiries had been used sparingly. In his lecture Douglas quotes liberally from Justice Warren's argument in *Watkins*, the core of which follows:

> Abuses of the investigative process may imperceptibly lead to abridgment of protected freedoms. The mere summoning of a witness and compelling him to testify, against his will, about his beliefs, expressions or associations is a measure of governmental interference. And when those forced revelations

concern matters that are unorthodox, unpopular, or even hateful to the general public, the reaction in the life of the witness may be disastrous. This effect is even harsher when it is past beliefs, expressions or associations that are disclosed and judged by current standards rather than those contemporary with the matters exposed. Nor does the witness alone suffer the consequences. Those who are identified by witnesses and thereby placed in the same glare of publicity are equally subject to public stigma, scorn and obloquy. Beyond that, there is the more subtle and immeasurable effect upon those who tend to adhere to the most orthodox and uncontroversial views and associations in order to avoid a similar fate at some future time. (104)

Douglas takes from *Watkins* that this particular period in history—the cold war—had created a problem of coerced confession unique in United States history. This case is not only about the ability of Congress to compel testimony—or, more specifically, confession—it is also about the disciplinary function of publicity, what both Warren and Douglas abhor as "exposure for exposure's sake." Warren tests the limits of inquiry and finds a right to privacy that, coupled with other freedoms explicit in the Bill of Rights, protects Watkins from unfettered inquiry:

It is manifest that despite the adverse effects which follow upon compelled disclosure of private matters, not all such inquiries are barred. . . . The critical element is the existence of, and the weight to be ascribed to, the interest of the Congress in demanding disclosures from an unwilling witness. We cannot simply assume, however, that every congressional investigation is justified by a public need that overbalances any private rights affected. To do so would be to abdicate the responsibility placed by the Constitution upon the judiciary to insure that the Congress does not unjustifiably encroach upon an individual's right to privacy nor abridge his liberty of speech, press, religion or assembly. (198–99)

Douglas rejected the tactics used by Senate anticommunists while laying out the rationale for privacy: "Much of this liberty of which we boast comes down to the right of privacy. It is reflected in the folklore, which goes back at least as far as Sir William Staunford, that 'my house is to me as my castle.' But this right extends to the right to be let alone in one's belief and in one's conscience, as well as in one's home" (90). In this widely repeated phrase—"my house is to me as my castle" (or variations thereof)—privacy remains primarily a political right, one that protects religious as well as political beliefs and that is only secondarily a domestic right.

Although privacy became with *Griswold* a right associated with domestic sanctuary, it is very important to note that the right did not originate in a validation of domesticity but in a defense against domestic police state tactics, which appeared potentially totalitarian. The freedom to speak one's mind was no longer adequate to democratic citizenship in the cold war era; it became crucial to the free citizen to be able to refrain from speaking.

At the same time that a "right to silence" was being asserted against the coercion of confession, the nation was beginning to binge on the revelation of private life in popular and, slightly later, literary culture. The commercial culture of celebrity, not cold war anticommunism, was accused of fostering a particularly corrupt appetite for private revelation. Brenton's *The Privacy Invaders* explains the danger of transgressing private life in mass market magazines such as *Confidential*:

> When it comes to concentration on the most sordid kind of gossip and the revelation of the most private acts, certainly no publication in the history of American journalism has ever surpassed that Goldfish Age product, the magazine called *Confidential*. In its heyday during the early and middle 1950s (the title was subsequently sold and the magazine is presently published by another organization), *Confidential* adopted nearly every intrusive technique imaginable in its unremitting effort to invade the privacy of Hollywood stars and other celebrities. (185)

Brenton concludes: "The greatest harm done by *Confidential*, I think, is that the shockingly widespread acceptance and sanction it received from the public for so long worked unconsciously upon our society to alienate us still further from a valuation of privacy" (188). This argument had wide currency in the privacy debate because it linked new kinds of intrusions to new social codes of self-disclosure, which blunted people's outrage at the loss of privacy. However, as the tabloid's publisher, Robert Harrison,[31] told Tom Wolfe in the late sixties: "You couldn't put out a magazine like *Confidential* again. You know why? Because all the movie stars have started writing books about *themselves*! . . . They tell all! No magazine can compete with that. That's what really finished the *Confidential* type of thing" (Wolfe 195). Harrison's commerce in gossip and voyeurism had been undone not by the strengthening of privacy laws but by the loosening of the social/cultural prohibitions against self-disclosure. In other words, the intrusions into the private life of celebrities were replaced wholesale by their confessions. This shift from intrusion to confession is one of the signal events in the transformation of privacy in the late twentieth century.

This shift toward self-disclosure presents the mirror side of the "death of privacy" debate: pronounced anxieties about the emerging culture of confession. From the beginning of the debate over privacy, fears of intrusion were met by an equally potent distrust of the shifting boundaries of self-disclosure. This relaxing of social norms cannot be separated from the perceived fears that the state was surveying private behavior because, as Brenton argued, U.S. citizens would become indifferent to their own privacy, which was measured by their willingness to offer information about themselves to strangers, whether to doctors or pollsters. The expanding limits of self-disclosure, however, were also intimately associated with assertions of individuality against a homogenizing social environment, acts that were considered antitotalitarian protests in themselves. Norman Mailer, for example, in *Advertisements for Myself* (1959), used "[his] personality as the armature of this book" (219) because he was seeking to "make a revolution in the consciousness of our time" (17) and carry out "[his] private war on American journalism, mass communications, and the totalitarianism of totally pleasant personality" (278), as he characterized his *Village Voice* column.[32] Confession, then, offered a conceptual double bind, claiming the value of the private self while simultaneously destroying the privacy that made it possible.

With national attention focused on privacy, by 1965 no fewer than three standing House committees—the Post Office, Government Operations, and the Judiciary—not to mention ad hoc committees on "data processing and informational retrieval," were hearing testimony on invasions of privacy as Congress prepared to draft new legislation. As Alan Westin researched *Privacy and Freedom* (1967), one of the most influential works on the concept of the sixties and perhaps of the cold war, he noted that the entire terrain of privacy had been shifting as he worked. The need to warn the American public about the threats to personal privacy that had motivated his book no longer existed. If alerting the nation was no longer necessary, however, Westin discovered instead an obligation to come to grips with the "nature of privacy," which, he claimed, had never before been rigorously examined.[33] Westin aimed to establish privacy as a universal human need that crosses classes within a society and individuals across cultures by arguing that privacy is not a modern invention but, instead, something that "derives first from man's animal origins" (7). Pursuing this universality, Westin creates an almost evolutionary model, beginning with animal privacy and progressing from so-called primitive societies to modern Western democracies.

This universality underwrote his proposal to secure new legal remedies for the ubiquitous invasions of the organized society and the security state. To concede the drift toward a privacyless society in light of this claim was unthinkable; the failure to reclaim privacy meant nothing less than undermining the foundations of self and civilization, perhaps life itself. Nevertheless, Westin warned that "one could compile a long list of societies, primitive and modern, that neither have nor would admire norms of privacy found in American culture" (14). Westin recognized that his argument depended on construing widely divergent practices in relation to this central term, acknowledging that his universalist claim did not in any way prescribe the norms, practices, attributes, or relative value of privacy. The universality of privacy, however, is precisely what begins to break apart after *Griswold v. Connecticut*. Westin speculates at the end of *Privacy and Freedom* about the direction privacy law should take in the next decade. He states that "a deliberate concept of balancing competing interests was at the heart of American privacy law, as in the 'reasonable man' standard for common law privacy rules and in the federal and state constitutions' ban on 'unreasonable' searches" and that "the current legal framework is now inadequate to defend the American equilibrium on privacy from new surveillance technologies" (369). In calling for more theoretical and empirical approaches to developing privacy law, Westin also unwittingly points to the direction of privacy law that he does foresee in 1967: the inadequacy of the "reasonable man" standard. What Westin does not anticipate is the extent to which privacy will become gendered.

Griswold opened the door to a range of new possibilities for privacy rights, but it also immediately suggested a limitation. If *Griswold* found a right to privacy in the home, did that leave other spaces unprotected from the prying eyes of the state? In a series of cases that followed *Griswold*, the Court began to imagine a congeries of privacy rights in and outside of the home. For example, *Griswold* provided the foundation to overturn laws that prohibited black and white citizens from marrying one another. In *Loving v. Virginia* (1967),[34] the case that over-

turned Virginia's miscegenation laws, the Court ruled that a right to privacy prohibited the states from interfering with an individual's choice of marital partner.
In a sense, this decision relied on the exceptional privacy rights of married couples. As Harlan had argued in *Poe* and again in *Griswold* (which repeated his *Poe*
dissent), while the state could regulate sexuality in many areas—adultery, for-
nication, homosexuality—the married couple had always enjoyed special rights
to make decisions regarding their intimate lives. Nevertheless, while based on
the "association" of marriage in *Griswold*, *Loving* moves autonomous decision
making toward individuals who are agreeing to enter into a marriage contract.
In other words, *Loving* moves privacy rights prior to marriage, investing individuals who are not yet married with the autonomy previously held in the marital relationship.

Griswold's "zone of privacy" quickly expanded beyond the home and domestic autonomy. In *Katz v. U.S.* (1967),[35] where law enforcement was prevented
from wiretapping public payphones, the Court ruled that individuals had a right
to privacy in public places that offered a "reasonable expectation" of it; in *Terry
v. Ohio* (1968)[36] the Court limited the extent to which a police officer could physically intrude on a suspect's bodily integrity by placing limitations on frisking;
in *Stanley v. Georgia* (1969)[37] it ruled that a person could not be arrested for reading obscene material in his own home; and finally in *Eisenstadt v. Baird* (1972)[38]
the Court broke with the exceptional privacy of married couples by ruling that
single people shared the right to use contraceptives, thereby providing sexual
autonomy to nonmarried heterosexual individuals. From the convergence of
these cases, we can see two very significant enhancements of the right to privacy that moved privacy rights toward individual citizens. Privacy was removed
from the "zone of the home" and detached from the marital bond. This meant
that privacy rights began to apply to the citizen as he/she moved about in the
world, which suggested that privacy rights attached to persons, not places, and
were thus mobile and contextual. This mobility had the effect of proliferating
privacy into spaces that might never have been thought inviolate before.

These cases form the crucial precedents that traced a path from *Griswold* to
the most profound constitutional crisis of the twentieth century: *Roe v. Wade*.
Companion cases, *Roe v. Wade* and *Doe v. Bolton*[39] in 1973, completely altered the
terms of privacy and American politics. The most well-recognized court case in
Supreme Court history, *Roe v. Wade* argued that a doctor, in consultation with his
woman patient, could decide to perform an abortion in the woman's first

trimester of pregnancy (*Doe v. Bolton* protected the doctor's autonomy in the abortion procedure, forbidding hospital oversight of his decision). *Roe* and *Doe* were argued under rights to privacy and autonomy, but for the first time the citizen under scrutiny was inescapably a woman. The shift of privacy from the zone and marriage ultimately confronted a pregnant—and therefore nonuniversal—body. In so doing, an accessory was attached to the private decision making of the citizen: the doctor. Nevertheless, feminists and right-wing activists alike perceived *Roe* to grant unprecedented autonomy to the female patient.

If the privacy debate prior to feminism incessantly measured the security of boundaries between private and public life, feminism would shift to interrogating the division itself as oppressive to women. Kate Millett's 1970 *Sexual Politics* summarizes in epigrammatic fashion the utter transformation of the question of privacy wrought by feminism. Millett introduces the "theory of sexual politics" with the following example:

> Coitus can scarcely be said to take place in a vacuum; although of itself it appears a biological and physical activity, it is set so deeply within the larger context of human affairs that it serves as a charged microcosm of the variety of attitudes and values to which culture subscribes. Among other things, it may serve as a model of sexual politics on an individual or personal plane. (23)

If the sacred zone that *Griswold* created shielded precisely this act from public scrutiny, we can imagine the discomfort that feminism's reappraisal of "personal" and "political" caused. The "personal is the political" in Millet's hands not only redefines politics, it forces a reevaluation of privacy since sexual intercourse had been granted a uniquely protected status with respect to privacy. In some sense, it is difficult to remember the shock of this reevaluation, so thoroughly has feminism and, from its insights, gay/lesbian activism reoriented the debates over privacy. In fact, it is difficult to overestimate the impact of feminism on the question of privacy. There is no more potent or longer-lasting critique of public and private in American culture than that which began with the feminist movement.

As Anita Allen argues in *Uneasy Access* (1988), after *Roe* there developed a notion of "women's privacy," which was sometimes nothing more than a substitute term for abortion rights. However, Allen took this notion of "women's privacy" a step further, applying it across the board to the many and various privacy dilemmas that faced postwar America. In other words, while instigated by *Roe*, "women's privacy" was more than the sexual autonomy promised by the decision. Allen, like the privacy commentators of the 1960s, recognized the uncertainty that colored the very notion of privacy, but she escalated rather than resolved this ambiguity by fragmenting privacy further with respect to gender. Understanding the differential effects of gender on privacy—or its violation—complicated the questions of invasion and exposure that had already been painstakingly itemized. Moreover, gender multiplied privacy's dilemmas by producing a new series of questions that pertained specifically to women, abortion being only one example. This thickening of privacy's complexities suggested that new theoretical approaches to privacy would have to consider the uneven impact of privacy boundaries for women and men.

Roe was not, of course, the only event of 1973 to reignite the American controversy over privacy, though we are unaccustomed to considering these various privacy disputes in tandem. The Watergate scandal, in a most important fashion, renewed anxieties about government surveillance, eliciting two landmark legislative acts in 1974: The Privacy Act and The Freedom of Information Act. While both acts can be viewed as extensions of the privacy defense of the 1960s, this new legislation attacked government secrecy first and foremost: The Privacy Act placed stricter limits on government surveillance, and The Freedom of Information Act permitted greater civilian access to nonclassified government files. These acts followed on the heels of a report on privacy and data collection by the Department of Health, Education and Welfare. This report, released in 1973, was accorded major attention primarily because the Watergate hearings[40] had made these "times when no one wanted to appear friendly to government surveillance over private persons" (Rule, et al. 101).[41] The significant change brought about by Watergate was that privacy violation had become routine but no longer justifiable in cold war terms.[42] However, even with a new anxiety to justify surveillance—terrorism—the 1970s witnessed the emergence of a new genre: the exposure of government secrecy. Without the cold war tension to exempt these institutions from investigation, the CIA and the FBI both came under intense scrutiny from journalists and from insiders who wrote tell-all books about abuses of power in Latin America and elsewhere. Watergate and *Roe v. Wade* reoriented the privacy debate, putting the topic back onto the agenda of American popular debate. Increasingly fractured, however, we were no longer having a debate over privacy; rather, there were multiple debates in a variety of sites, and all of them began to look independent of one another.

Each decade witnessed the same the death of privacy warnings from the same sources of anxiety, while new areas of stress were folded into the pattern of metaphors, terms, and narratives established in the early 1960s. As law professor Yale Kamisar wrote in the *New York Times* in 1987, two "plagues"—AIDS and drug use—were beginning to pose novel questions of the Fourth Amendment, not so much in the area of criminal law as in the more generalized surveillance of "administrative searches." The widespread efforts to test for HIV infection and drug use were making a mockery of the Fourth Amendment's individualizing of suspicion. Moreover, the blanket suspicion that justified this testing was also in the mid-1980s propelling various state efforts to compile master lists of those infected with HIV.[43] Since regulatory schemes do not require the same standard of suspicion as do rules of evidence in criminal court, it was not the policeman in the bedroom that worried Kamisar; it was the bureaucrat, the corporate executive, and the researcher at the Center for Disease Control.

Into this climate of high anxiety surrounding privacy rights, especially for gay men, the group most associated with the AIDS epidemic in the mid-1980s, the Supreme Court handed down the last precedent-setting privacy case of the cold war: *Bowers v. Hardwick*. Even if the decision itself never mentions the word "AIDS" and only obliquely refers to a health issue in the decision's dissent, *Hardwick* threatened to merge the administrative surveillance then so worrisome to the gay community with police surveillance by upholding the criminalization of sodomy. The case brought by Michael Hardwick appealed his conviction for violating Georgia's sodomy statute, which did not single out gay men but outlawed any act of anal/genital or oral/genital contact. When a policeman with an expired warrant discovered Hardwick engaged in an act of sodomy in his own bedroom with another adult male, Justice Douglas's image of totalitarianism had been realized. Nonetheless, the Court decided that Hardwick's sexual practice was not protected by a right to privacy. The long and slow expansion of rights to privacy had come to a halt. The sexual autonomy promised by *Griswold* to married couples and by *Eisenstadt v. Baird* to unmarried individuals would not extend to homosexual men.[44]

The refusal of the Court to recognize the police state implications of *Hardwick* was especially devastating given the context of AIDS. On the one hand, *Bowers v. Hardwick* literalized the central image of *Griswold* and the privacy debates of the early 1960s: the policeman in the bedroom. But more than this explicit echo of *Griswold* in the facts of the case, the language of AIDS replicated the boundary dangers so familiar from early moments in the cold war era. AIDS was couched as a matter of invisible enemies, boundary violation, infiltration, and surveillance, of political paranoia and the enemy within.[15] As Susan Sontag has demonstrated, these metaphors described the virus as well as those who carried it. The fears of AIDS overlapped with cold war bellicosity because the disease and its victims were cast as the internal weakness that made America vulnerable to internal decay and, perhaps even worse, drained the United States of its will to combat the ideological enemy. AIDS was more than a privacy dilemma, it was cold war redux. When Tony Kushner featured Roy Cohn and a spectral Ethel Rosenberg in his epochal *Angels in America* (1992), he set his drama of AIDS and America's apocalyptic destiny in terms of its cold war past.

The multiple and paradoxical effects of AIDS on privacy heightened the tension between protecting individuals from state scrutiny and broadening the scope of self-disclosure that had defined the postwar era. One of the principal effects of AIDS was to deprivatize sex. First, AIDS in the United States was a confessional disease. To have AIDS was to be revealed as a member of an outcast group: a homosexual or, less visibly (initially), a drug addict. Second, because the disease was infectious, no sexual act could be divorced from the history of the participant's sexual experience and the network of people they slept with. Therefore sex was not between two people anymore, much less two married people. This socializing of sex worked two ways, creating a web of sexual/social relations but also producing a new proximity between heterosexuality and homosexuality, revealing the blurring of practices that hopelessly complicated a binary structure of sexual identity. The private realm was no longer clearly marked off from the social, and its inhabitants were no longer married heterosexual adults who in Harlan's vision in *Poe* could be trusted not to misuse their sexual autonomy.

Following the announcement of *Hardwick*, ACT UP, the most vocal and visible political organization of the AIDS crisis, launched its highly theatrical campaigns, goaded by the explicit exclusion of gay men from the right considered since the mid-1960s to be a crucial component of modern American citizenship.[46] With its emphasis on self-disclosure and publicity, ACT UP swung the debate over AIDS away from the consolidation of privacy rights and towards a strategy of confession and self-disclosure. "Silence = Death" ensured that the politics of privacy would be replaced by the politics of visibility, making the political response to AIDS—as many commentators have noted—primarily discursive and even confessional. Like the example of *Roe*, *Hardwick* and the shifting privacy concerns that followed it suggest that privacy rights rest on a foundation of visibility, that confession in fact underwrites privacy—especially for those with the most fragile claims on citizenship.

Just as it is impossible to understand the privacy crisis without the backdrop of the cold war, so is it also essential to recognize the host of new pressures on what were retrospectively imagined as ordinary or self-evident borders between public and private. A great number of material changes in American life beyond advances in surveillance technology—for example the new medium of television,[47] the growth of the suburbs, the popularizing of psychoanalysis, the application of behaviorism to advertising, the use of computer databases—generated concerns of their own, exacerbating the anxiety related to the national security state. The cold war seems to have coincided with—and exaggerated—a widely experienced topological crisis in which bounded spaces of all kinds seemed to exhibit a frightening permeability. All sorts of entities were imagined as bounded spaces: nations, bodies, homes, and minds.[48] The power of homology created a structural link between these quite dissimilar entities, mapping boundary dangers across different domains. The boundary dangers of one easily migrated to or transformed into the boundary dangers of the other.

Cold war containment ideology, therefore, looks like a specific, indeed peculiarly American case of a larger and more general crisis in late modern culture. Social theorists increasingly reached for the terms "public" and "private" to explain changes in postwar culture, both in Europe and in the United States.[49] Of course, this interpenetration of public and private life in American culture resonates with the dominant critiques of modernity that emerged in Europe during the latter half of the twentieth century, indeed during the period we've been reviewing. These critiques, widely influential in the United States, contributed to the visibility of privacy in the late twentieth century while also providing historical and theoretical ways of accounting for it. Frankfurt School theorists such as Hannah Arendt, Theodor Adorno, and Jürgen Habermas sought first and foremost to protect the public sphere of rational discourse, even while acknowledging that private life had been flooded by bureaucratic supervision. Their emphasis on public life forms a crucial distinction between Frankfurt School reflections on the collapse of public and private and those that derive from an Anglo-

American tradition. In the United States, this collapse was nearly always imagined as threatening the private sphere. Therefore the energies harnessed to secure this boundary were directed toward shoring up the protections for private space. In a sense, then, the dilemma of modernity defined as the collapse of public and private unites U.S. and European political thought; both present this dilemma as a question of a zone that needs protection, but they differ on which zone tenders the freedom that a civil democratic society requires.

Confessional culture is often cast as a danger to both public and private spheres. However, perhaps nowhere more than in the United States, with its faith in privacy as the location of free deliberation, has confession constituted such an important mode of political engagement and cultural expression. Michel Foucault's now axiomatic insight into the nature of confession—that it is always already coerced—refuses liberalism's fundamental privileging of the private sphere. Indeed, Foucault's denial of the liberatory potential of confession stems from his argument that the private is already infiltrated by power. That is, there is no real space of privacy, merely the illusion of privacy instituted in the formation of Enlightenment political institutions. Confessions cannot liberate a private self—indeed, they can only perpetuate the illusion that there is such a thing. Foucault's uneven reception in the United States, as David Halperin has argued in *Saint Foucault* (1995), rests on his destabilizing of this distinction, one that was so crucial to cold war ideology.

The attempts to secure a space of privacy in the face of bureaucratic meddling, police scrutiny, and media spectacle in the Uninted States seem to contravene the equally ubiquitous confessionalism of postwar U.S. culture. However, both projects represent a deep investment in the private self as the source of freedom, individuality, and authenticity. At the same time, as we shall see, confessions are not only moments of exposure. They also teach us as much about the kinds of privacy available to and withheld from a citizen/subject in late-modern Western society as do legal arguments for a new constitutional right.

Part II: Sovereign Domains

It is commonplace to think of the courts, particularly in the late twentieth century, as the most potent institutional custodian of individual autonomy. Even with appointees whose judicial philosophy is diametrically opposed to the rights-based liberalism of the Warren Court in the 1960s, battles over state and majority interference in individual decision making have remained largely the province of the courts. The privacy rulings of the Supreme Court are, therefore, an ideal place to gauge the changing dimensions and distribution of privacy in the late twentieth century, not only for the ways in which privacy has been protected but also, and as important, in the arenas in which it has seemed impossible to extend privacy to a given segment of the population or category of citizen. Lyric poetry is another site of intense preoccupation with privacy since it has been classified, most insistently in the nineteenth and twentieth centuries, as the most private form of expression, a genre of intimacy that must, of course, pass through public expression. The lyric, as many have argued, perpetually returns to questions of boundaries, intimacy, protected space, and exposure. Like the private space protected with constitutional safeguards, the lyric has been imagined as a domain of sovereignty that offers a representation of the experience of autonomy, or at least its fiction.[50]

Constitutional law and lyric poetry can be considered generic institutions of privacy.[51] Of course, law and lyric do not alone figure, negotiate, protect, or abandon privacy. The novel, for example, called the genre of "subjectivity oriented toward an audience" in Habermas's *The Structural Transformation of the Public Sphere* (1989), provides Habermas with the locus of a modern notion of privacy, a new form of both literary and political self-consciousness. However, it is particularly the "orientation toward an audience" that suggests the unique relationship of the lyric poem to a particular kind of privacy, what J. S. Mill so famously defined as the "self overheard speaking to itself" (*What Is Poetry* 12). Both constitutional law and lyric poetry assume a notion of pure autonomy or self-sovereignty that might only be experienced in private. This does not mean that purity is ever possible, as Mill himself well knew.[52] The Supreme Court, as the final arbiter of constitutional interpretation, perpetually balances autonomy and self-sovereignty against the need for social order. Likewise, as Allen Grossman has argued, lyric derives from the threat to autonomy and self-sovereignty rather than its fulfillment. Nevertheless, constitutional law and lyric poetry have negotiated privacy as it comes closest to the ideals of autonomy and self-sovereignty that Enlightenment political philosophy offered to citizens of a liberal democracy.

But what happened to these generic institutions of privacy when "overhearing" began to seem not the condition of lyric self-regard but of all speech? Inevitably perhaps, when privacy became an object of intense preoccupation in the late twentieth century, both constitutional privacy doctrine and confessional poetry emerged to become major, if controversial, developments in their respective fields. Both participated in the rigorous evaluation of privacy that began to mark American culture in political, social and aesthetic spheres at this historical moment, though in contradictory, even paradoxical ways. We have already traced in some detail the response to the sudden visibility of privacy in the law. Let us now turn to the lyric.

Since M. L. Rosenthal, in *The Modern Poets: A Critical Introduction* (1960), first named a subgenre of poetry called "confessional," critics have labored to understand the outpouring of confessional poetry that followed. Disagreeing about precisely what incited poets to scrutinize the most intimate aspects of their personal lives in their work, critics nonetheless have concurred in their assessment that confessional poetry was a "private" art. However, because a variety of meanings and values were assigned to the concept of privacy, this apparent consensus masked deeper disagreement, one that reflects the social and historical context of confessional poetry and the nearly unbroken attention to the question of autonomy in lyric poetry. Resituating confessional poetry within this context transforms a private art into a contribution to a central political debate. Anne Sexton, Sylvia Plath, Robert Lowell, and W. D. Snodgrass were not simply "private." They were preoccupied with the nature of privacy itself.

There is widespread agreement in literary histories of the late twentieth century that the major shift from modernism and revolt against the reigning critical methodology, New Criticism, was effected by the confessional movement in poetry, launched by Allen Ginsberg's "Howl" (1956) and Robert Lowell's *Life Studies* (1959). Virtually every major account of late-twentieth-century poetics suggests that these works turned poetry away from modernist impersonality and toward a poetics of autobiography and an aesthetics of authenticity.[53] This shift dates remarkably well with the general crisis in privacy from the late 1950s to the early 1970s, with the unprecedented exposure of private life in such landmark confessional works as Robert Lowell's *Life Studies* (1959); W. D. Snodgrass' *Heart's Needle* (1959); Anne Sexton's *To Bedlam and Part Way Back* (1960), *All My Pretty Ones* (1962), and *Live or Die* (1966); Sylvia Plath's *Ariel* (1965); Allen Ginsberg's *Howl* (1956) and *Kaddish* (1960); and John Berryman's *77 Dream Songs* (1964). Even in the later 1960s to early 1970s, when confessional poets were generally perceived to be moving away from strictly confessional writing, these poets published such works of self-disclosure as Lowell's *For Lizzie and Harriet*

(1973) and *The Dolphin* (1973); Sexton's *Love Poems* (1969) and *The Death Note-books* (1974); Berryman's *Love and Fame* (1972); and Plath's *Crossing the Water* (1971) and *Winter Trees* (1972), published nearly a decade after her death. Perhaps more important, confessional writing was not limited to these particular poets but became the dominant form of the lyric. Creating legions of followers and im-itators, confessional poetry transformed the lyric by revolutionizing expecta-tions of self-revelation in poetry.

In *Five Temperaments* (1977) David Kalstone defines the niche that confes-sional poetry held within the larger movement toward autobiography by claim-ing for it that which was "desperate and on the edge" (8) as subject matter: insanity, divorce, sex, and alcoholism. It is certainly true that *the* "confessional poets" were an extreme group: Sexton, Plath, and Berryman committed suicide; Lowell, Sexton, and Plath were repeatedly hospitalized for mental breakdowns; as a group they suffered from alcoholism and drug addiction. But the term "con-fessional" is not "misleading" as Kalstone worried; rather, it is an important benchmark of privacy. Because they represented the "desperate" edges of the autobiographical trend in late twentieth-century poetry, confessional poetry drew a bright line around the "too private" in a genre that seemed to have colo-nized private life as its special terrain.

As the marker of the "too private," the confessional poem demonstrated that there were recognizable social and aesthetic limits to the private self that the lyric could unveil, not only the taboo, but also the quotidian. That is, poetry could not extend the madness conventionally associated with lyric inspiration into the domain of mental illness, nor could it broaden the modernist embrace of the concrete to include the routine of domestic life. However, these distinc-tions might not have changed our sense of the generic limits of the lyric's priva-cy as profoundly had confession not functioned so asymmetrically with respect to gender and sexuality. Because privacy's deprivations belonged primarily to women and its autonomy primarily to men, because privacy offered sanctuary to heterosexuals and only secrecy to homosexuals or other sexually marginal-ized people, the crisis of privacy, the exposure and mediation of these bound-aries, fragmented the concept. Similarly, this "too private" realm showed that the so-called private or domestic sphere might not serve as a refuge from scrutiny. The confessional poem depicts a private self that is perpetually monitored by others, most often but not always family members, which redefined the private address in the poem as a fundamentally social act encumbered by what Robert

Pinsky, in *Poetry and the World* (1988), has called "the coercion of circumstance" (169). The reception history of confessional poetry continually returns to this contravention of assumptions about the privacy of lyric expression and about the autonomy this privacy was believed to confer.

The historical fluctuation of the boundaries of privacy has been central to the criticism of confessional poetry in a variety of ways. In "What Was Confessional Poetry?" (1993) Diane Middlebrook opens her essay by placing confessional poetry in a time capsule as a "cultural icon" of its time, "cold war politics and all." She says that

> within a very short time confessional poetry established itself as a poetic type that could not be dismissed or ignored. This was thoroughly middle-class art—produced by WASP writers—that violated the norms of decorum for subject matter in serious literature. . . . Answers can be sought in the relevance of the themes of confessional poetry to other areas of culture that had obvious influence on middle-class life at the time: Psychoanalysis as a mode of address to postwar existential misery, anticommunism as a pressure on American artists and intellectuals, and television as a solvent of boundaries between public and domestic life. (633)

Middlebrook sees the boundary crossing of the poetry as "iconic" for the period and places this adjacent to other forms of boundary trouble for the American white middle class.[54] Certainly, confessional poetry was nearly exclusively a white, middle-class, and even predominantly heterosexual genre, perhaps because white middle class heterosexuals enjoyed the greatest expectation of privacy, and were therefore the most likely to experience its violation.[55]

Paul Breslin's *The Psycho-Political Muse* (1987), like Charles Molesworth's *The Fierce Embrace* (1979), interprets confessional poetry as part of a general personalizing of public discourse in the cold war era. The private world of the poet, as Breslin sees it, was too easily made "representative" of broader social and political ills, much to the disservice of that larger public world. Drawing a link with New Left politics, Breslin interrogates the assumption of representativity in confessional poetry, which made the mental illness of the poet a manifestation of the insanity of the social world, R. D. Laing's influential (if not exactly medically sound) theory of schizophrenia, posited in his *The Divided Self* (1960). Breslin sees this search for the authentic private self as an echo of the general social commentary about 1950s American culture in David Reisman's *The Lonely Crowd* (1950), William Whyte's *The Organization Man* (1956), C. Wright Mills's *White Collar* (1951), and Herbert Marcuse's *One Dimensional Man* (1964), all of which decried the individual's submission to organized bureaucratic institutions, whether state or corporate. Finally, Robert von Hallberg suggests that the status of the term "privacy" among postwar intellectuals was deeply influenced by the counterexample of the Soviet Union.[56] While Soviet writers questioned the value of individualism in poetry, American poets latched onto the private self of the lyric. The preeminence of the private lyric poem suggests most pointedly that the autonomy and self-sovereignty associated with democracy were going to be figured in the lyric.[57]

The respect for the lyric's privacy in the postwar era, indeed the insistence on it, nevertheless required that this privacy be guarded from overexposure from within. Marjorie Perloff's *Radical Artifice* (1991) accounts for the shift away from confessional writing in the late 1970s by pointing to the requirement to be "candid" in American popular culture. She says:

> Consider . . . the modus operandi of a television show first aired in 1968 and still running strong: namely, the Donahue show. . . . What sort of authentic speech do we hear and see expressed on *Donahue*? . . . Topics are almost always and reassuringly "everyday" and amenable to "normal speech"—for example, premarital and extramarital sex, masturbation, impotence, incest, rape, the rights of gay fathers and mothers, artificial insemination, surrogate motherhood, in-laws, day care, two-career couples, older man-younger woman marriages and the converse, alcoholism, drug abuse, AIDS education in the public schools—the list is all but endless. (37)

Perloff's description of one of the most publicly flagellated media of the late twentieth century—the TV talk show—overlaps the topics that made confessional poetry so controversial, even "extreme": madness, illness, depression, alcoholism, etc. However, for Perloff their ubiquity in popular culture meant that there was no longer a space of privacy to be revealed by the poet. Instead, the public sphere, at least the mass mediated sphere, was saturated with the falsely private. For Perloff, unlike for David Kalstone, revelations even at the extreme do not count as revelations; they do not constitute the boundary of the too private; indeed they are not private at all. When private life became the lingua franca of American culture, the lyric could no longer explore or liberate a buried private self.

The suffusion of American popular and literary culture with self-disclosure has suggested to many public intellectuals that we no longer share any significant norms of self-restraint. The absence of self-restraint in the domain of personal revelation would therefore seem to portend the gradual impossibility of confession; everything would be exposed and therefore no meaningful transgression could take place. We would, as Perloff suggests, have no way of registering privacy. However, this destruction of confession has not happened. As confessional poetry surprisingly illustrates, because the forms in which we recognize transgression mutate, form conserves privacy. We will return to this idea presently, but first it is important to understand the stakes of this proposition.

The privacy of the lyric poem mattered because it was inseparable from the autonomy it was meant to establish (that is, the poem's transcendence of history, biology, politics, economics, and social life more generally) and the autonomy it was meant to reflect (that is, the isolated speaker deliberating with himself or herself). It is not an exaggeration to say that the autonomy of the poem has been an object of supreme importance to poetics and to genealogies of literary history in postwar literary criticism.[58] One might even argue that the autonomy *in* and *of* the poem has been the driving question of twentieth-century poetics. Nowhere is this interest in calibrating the autonomy of the lyric more apparent than in the reception history of confessional poetry and in the canon building that it shaped.

After Robert Phillips's *The Confessional Poets* (1973) and Paul Lacey's *The Inner War* (1972), works from the early 1970s that took the confessional poets as a school, literary critics such as Charles Molesworth (*The Fierce Embrace*, 1979), Charles Altieri (*Enlarging the Temple*, 1979), and James E. B. Breslin (*From Modern to Contemporary*, 1984) began to back away from the confessional label. Most literary histories focused on Lowell as the representative confessional figure, deflecting the "extreme" element of the confessional label onto Sexton, Plath, and Ginsberg. Moreover, as they took Lowell as their exemplary confessional poet, they began to drain him of his confessionalism, reorienting his work toward his historical imagination. Indeed, as the 1970s progressed, "confessional" was increasingly bracketed by scare quotes and the term "so-called." Even critics receptive to the autobiographical impulse in poetry, such as Alan Williamson or David Kalstone, felt the need to concede the danger of the term, which, as James E. B. Breslin said, had become firmly associated with solipsism, literalism, narcissism, mental illness, and shame.

However, this sense of the label's toxicity was rarely, if ever, measured against the elevation of the term in feminist criticism.[59] Because they didn't acknowledge one another, two canons of late-twentieth-century poetry and the genealogies that formed their antecedents began to run parallel. It is crucial to rejoin the two, however, because the embrace or dismissal of the term "confession" reflects an assessment of central cultural values in postwar American culture. Feminist literary critics, who took Plath and Sexton as their exemplary figures for confession, celebrated their willingness to transgress public and private distinctions. Sandra Gilbert, for example, argued that the "confessional genre . . . may be (at least for our own time) a distinctively female poetic mode."[60] Indeed, crossing the boundaries of private and public became the signature trope of the newly archived women's tradition in poetry. Suzanne Juhasz, echoing the mantra of the feminist movement, argued in *Naked and Fiery Forms* (1976): "The personal and the political unite in this commitment to the self in poetry, in the need to validate the personal and the private as legitimate topics for public speech and in the need to integrate the private and the public worlds" (5). So, too, did the editors of *No More Masks!* (1973), one of the first anthologies of women's poetry. Editors Florence Howe and Ellen Bass prefaced their collection by saying:

> The poem distinctively by a woman is not always a private one. Some poets speak mainly in public voices—Marianne Moore, for one. Other poets, like Kay Boyle, characteristically choose public subjects. . . . And while most of the poems in this volume are "private" ones, we have included as well, for diversity and in order to suggest the range of women's poems, a representative body of public poems whose themes quite naturally reflect our world: war, poverty, racism, drugs, pure air, poverty. But among young poets, for whom the life of a woman is a public matter, such distinctions between public and private fall away. For young feminists the poem that celebrates their sexuality is as political as the one that defines them as women in a hitherto male world. (3)

Two arguments about women's writing and privacy then structure these canons: one, women's poetry is already "private," attached to the negative characteristics of confession (narcissism, solipsism); and two, women's poetry ought to be more private, that is, expose the condition of women trapped in the private sphere.

Alicia Ostriker, whose *Stealing the Language* (1986) represents the last important work in this line of criticism, points toward the ways in which confession
became aligned with autonomy in feminist criticism, rather than against it, as I
will suggest in a moment. She understands the criticism of women poets
through the ages: "Above all, the poet who attempts to explore female experience is dismissed as self-absorbed, private, escapist, nonuniversal—although as
Carolyn Kizer puts it, women writers 'are the custodians of the world's best-kept
secret: / Merely the private lives of one-half of humanity' " (6). Ostriker seeks to
invert this criticism by embracing the "privacy" of women's poetry but turning
it inside out with respect to autonomy: "At the core of the women's poetry movement is the quest for autonomous self-definition" (58). This autonomy is primarily a function of confession because it refuses the self-effacement required of
women poets before her crucial starting point, 1960, which is, as we know, the
birth of confessional poetry. For Ostriker, not only must the lyric poet refuse
self-effacement but she must also effectively supplant the false "public self" of
woman with the real and authentic "private self" of the lyric poet. In this revelation, the woman poet achieves her autonomy.

The ascendancy of confession in Anglo-American feminist criticism would be
challenged in the mid-1980s by critics such as Jan Montefiore, who argued in
Feminism and Poetry (1987) against a confessional and essential woman poet, and
somewhat later, Rachel Blau Duplessis, who retained the term "confessional" in
The Pink Guitar (1990) but shifted it into a more abstract category of representations that challenge the conventional depictions of women. Finally, Kim
Whitehead in *The Feminist Poetry Movement* (1996) asserts that feminist critics
have become less enamored of the liberal feminist position that equated the private self with the autonomous self. Whitehead says:

> I side with those critics who recognize differences among women and per-
> ceive feminist forms of liberal humanism as just additional acts of erasure of
> women for whom gender could never be considered the only condition of
> oppression and ultimately an empty challenge to Western notions of subjec-
> tivity. As Norma Alarcon has said, the "most popular subject of Anglo-Ameri-
> can feminism is an autonomous, self-making, self-determining subject who
> first proceeds according to the logic of *identification* with regard to the subject
> of consciousness, a notion usually viewed as the purview of man, but claimed
> for women." (51)

Like Alarcon, critics who were increasingly wary of the confessional label in the 1970s had discarded the assumption that the revelation of the private and authentic self was automatically political for a number of related reasons. Exposure was no longer liberation because the private self no longer held an exclusive purchase on authenticity. Moreover, the representativity of the private self, always a crucial divide between men's and women's poetry, was beginning to lose its axiomatic status, as Paul Breslin contended. But finally, and most important, the liberation of the bourgeois, middle-class self from the organizing institutions of modernity was no longer considered political; it was instead a distraction from politics. Personal autonomy was no longer deemed the most significant aesthetic or political goal, a shift that feminist criticism replicated approximately a decade later.

Autonomy was not universally abandoned, however. For some poets and critics, the search for autonomy remained an animating aesthetic goal but the means toward this autonomy no longer derived from confession. Robert Pinsky maintains that poetry cannot embrace the biographical and embodied facts of one's life but, rather, must move through form away from these. If the revelation of these facts was meant to liberate the private self in the confessional poem, Pinsky will retain the sense of liberation, but make it decidedly nonconfessional, and perhaps even anticonfessional. He says:

> To be sweepingly optimistic about such questions, perhaps every historical circumstance, every limitation of politics or inherited identity, is something to push against, a possible control. Perhaps form, in its truest manifestations, must be an appetite, an appetite for being autonomous and oneself, more bold and naked than any external preconception of oneself. A poem may be the least confused, most free thing one says (or hears) because it is the most deliberately physical, and so the most naked. Form expresses the craving to be free of imposed, controlling abstractions. It is a made, bodily abstraction to challenge the abstractions of circumstance. (*Poetry and the World* 169)

Pinsky maintains the lyric as a cultural space for the autonomous and free self, but only so long as form obscures the "unfree" facts of human life. To be naked is not to reveal but to banish "the social facts about me, that I was born in 1940 to Milford and Sylvia Pinsky, in Long Branch, New Jersey, and so forth. If social facts control us, control is (it is banal to say) what appetite [for art] pushes against" (160). For Pinsky, the equation between confession and autonomy is broken from both ends: confession does not make you naked or autonomous, form does.

No two fields have more jealously guarded the autonomy of their objects than literary criticism, particularly of poetry, and legal scholarship. Moreover, this autonomy was of particular interest during the early cold war era. As Norman Rosenberg asked:

> Is it just accidental that the penchant of postwar legalists, for example—to narrow their focus to the precise meanings of legal texts and to de-emphasize questions of economic power and social context echoed the techniques coming into favor with the "new critics" in art and literature or with many of the practitioners of the new consensus history and behavioral sciences? ("Gideon's Trumpet" 121)

The autonomy of the object became a disciplinary focus during this period because of the profound questions about the intrusion of political or commercial interest into sovereign domains such as the home, but also such as the law and "high culture."[61] That is, legal decisions and lyric poems had to be conceived as formally autonomous in order to preserve the autonomy they were meant to protect and model. As the boundaries between public and private came to be viewed as ever more permeable, there were intense disciplinary investments in erecting barriers around the object.[62] Precisely for both formal and disciplinary reasons, then, we ought not to *under*estimate the structural similarities, indeed formal resemblance between law and literature, especially with regard to the lyric, and in the domain of privacy.

Part of the fiction of privacy's imminent demise resided in the fantasy of a stable and universal privacy that lay somewhere in the past. As Vance Packard writes:

> It should be remembered that the Founding Fathers of the U.S.A. were contemplating a society in which a man or woman could have a great deal of latitude about choosing his style of living. It was assumed that you were free to lead your own life—if you were not an unpunished criminal, a certified maniac, or a conscripted soldier. You could go into solitude when you felt in the mood for contemplation. You could be footloose, even though it might endanger your own life in hostile Indian territory. You could, with general

approbation, horsewhip anyone who pried unduly into your affairs simply to satisfy curiosity or to profit by feeding idle gossip. And you could live in dignity any way that you conceived the term. (*Naked Society* 207–08)

Packard's image of the founding fathers' "rights to privacy" appears quite exaggerated to us now. Nevertheless, this nostalgic image of a coherent but vanished privacy structures much of the popular reflection. In *The Privacy Invaders*, Myron Brenton comments:

Early in 1963 the *Saturday Evening Post* printed a letter from a woman, clearly an elderly lady, who said that in her day people didn't ask questions and didn't pry. She was unable to understand why things had changed. In point of fact, that fine old American expression, which was at once emphatic and had in it an element of dignity—the expression that went, "It's none of your business"—has disappeared from our collective lexicon. (20)

Brenton gestures to a new location—the previous generation—but privacy remains self-evident, if just beyond reach. Thirty-five years later the *New York Times* continues to assert the lost quality of privacy in the nearly continuous stream of articles dealing with the death of privacy in 2000. Reporter Joyce Purnik asserts: "For those who came of age when public figures had private lives, when photographers respectfully aimed their cameras away from President Roosevelt in his wheelchair, or reporters did not seek a full report on President Kennedy's illness, the change has been nothing short of astonishing" ("First, Call a Doctor"). Ironically, but characteristically, as the *Times* looks backward, it finds stable conventions of privacy, this time located at the very moment (the Kennedy administration) that Brenton and Packard were announcing to the country that privacy was dead. In every case, in comparison to the broad, authoritative, and universal privacy that has been lost, contemporary privacy seems partial, diluted, and besieged. Amnesiac and nostalgic at the same time, popular media continually mourn the death of privacy without being able to recognize the forms of privacy that continue to make the concept viable.

However, as Americans were being warned in rather strident terms about the dangers to their privacy, it was apparent in some contexts that privacy was no longer a self-evident concept. Paradoxically, as privacy became an object of knowledge, something to be studied, defined, and categorized, it constantly broke down under pressure of investigation. Greater scrutiny of privacy seemed not to settle but to defamiliarize the concept. Constitutional law and lyric poetry with their distinctive and even inflexible obligations to their own histories repeatedly demonstrate that privacy is neither as familiar, nor as perishable as popular media suggest. In other words, law and lyric equip us to pursue the ways in which an increasingly organized modern world continually *invented* notions of privacy, autonomy, and self-sovereignty that we mistook for eternal and stable components of liberal democracy.

I am referring to "stare decisis" ("Let the decision stand") in law, which names the obligation to follow precedent when deciding a case, and to the less formal but, I would argue, no less compelling duty to tradition—to poetic precedent if you will—in lyric poetry. Stare decisis creates a productive tension between stability and innovation. On one hand, there are substantial impediments to overturning precedent because to do so risks the court's integrity, authority, and legitimacy. Faith in the rule by law, rather than by judges, rests in part on the stability of precedent. On the other, because precedent is not immutable, it is also an avenue of innovation within a bounded universe of terms, which themselves change under pressure. This tension between stability and innovation is accompanied by mandatory self-consciousness about the conceptual choices and categories that the Court employs. For our purposes, examining the transformations of privacy over the latter half of the twentieth century, the Court's precedential hermeneutics offers a way to track the migrating terms of privacy over the course of forty years.[63]

Precedent and the formalism that is so often associated with it have provided a generic and historical bridge between law and literature.[64] Even though there are symmetries between legal and literary uses of precedent, nowhere are these symmetries more pronounced than with lyric poetry's unusually intense relationship to its own tradition. Of course, poets are not obliged to *follow* precedent; indeed, since the Romantic period, they are obliged to deviate from it. Poets, unlike Supreme Court justices, bear a burden of innovation—originality being the mark of greatness for a poet, which is determined by the way that a poet innovates on tradition. Nevertheless, innovation is only visible from within a recognizable tradition and with the means of invoking its relevant precedents.

Finally, confessional poetry helps us to see the degree to which privacy is a formal concept, requiring more than a particular kind of revelation to verify the transgression of privacy. For example, as Alicia Ostriker noted, Plath begins to break forms more willfully and aggressively in *Ariel*.[65] *Ariel* retains only the skeleton of the traditional meter and rhyme that was displayed more elaborately in her earlier volume, *Colossus* (1960), with its use of terza rima and rime royale, for example. Indeed both Plath and Lowell moved to a more open style as they moved toward writing autobiographical poems. What makes Lowell and Plath successful in this first confessional moment is not only the breaking of form—the relaxation of familiar stanzaic structure and rhyme scheme as well as the meter of the lines—but the fact that this break is incomplete. In nearly any *Life Studies* poem, rhyme, blunted by enjambment, and iambic meter remain available to the ear even while the poems scan with a deliberately proselike rhythm. This is to say that Plath and Lowell make the breaking of the form clear by preserving the formal enclosure in the poem. They are, therefore, caught in the act of breaking out of the form, which makes their transgression of boundaries visible and audible. Form alone cannot account for the prolonged fascination with the confessional poets, but their various experiments with it do suggest that the crossing of the public and private boundary cannot be secured in content alone. What we consider private content may appear to be wholly emptied into the public sphere, but formal innovations in confession refresh the perception of crossing that boundary.

By selecting these two discursive forms out of the tremendous range of material that registered privacy's demise in the late twentieth century, I am not suggesting that Supreme Court justices or lyric poets have fundamentally deeper insight into the dilemmas of privacy in the modern world than journalists, filmmakers, or television writers. In fact, when Justice Douglas proclaims in his 1966 dissent in *Osborn v. U.S., Lewis v. U.S., Hoffa v. U.S.* (1966),[66] that "we are rapidly entering the age of no privacy, where everyone is open to surveillance at all times; where there are no secrets from government" (341), he sounds just as apocalyptic as Vance Packard in *The Naked Society*. When Sylvia Plath muses in a poem called "Eavesdropper" on the "desert of cow people / Trundling their udders home / To the electric milker, the wifey, the big blue eye / That watches, like God, or the sky / The ciphers that watch it" (*Collected Poems* 261), her vision of routinized suburban surveillance resembles a scene from the paranoid sci-fi 1964 television program, *The Outer Limits*. Rather, I'm arguing that even when Supreme Court justices and lyric poets are no more insightful than their counterparts in the mass media, they are generically obliged to imagine privacy within a history of its forms and that these forms have been intensely preoccupied with calibrating the limits of self-sovereignty. This attention to past formations or definitions of privacy prevents either poet or jurist from imagining privacy as a static or self-evident category of experience or thought. As different as court cases and lyric poems so evidently are, their absorption in their own histories and their unique generic relationship to privacy authorize an interrogation of the concept that yields an especially complex account of its transformations in late-twentieth-century American culture.

TWO

"Thirsting for the Hierarchic Privacy of Queen Victoria's Century"

Robert Lowell and the Transformations of Privacy

> Should revelation be sealed like private letters,
> till all the beneficiaries are dead,
> and our proper names become improper Lives?
> —Robert Lowell, *The Dolphin*

An emphasis on national context has obscured the extent to which so-called American norms of privacy were forged in a more specific local context: Boston. Disregarding this regional specificity prevents us from taking stock of one of the important shifts produced by cold war anxieties about state scrutiny: the migration of privacy from a hierarchic and patriarchal privilege to a democratic and masculine right. On closer examination, it is not quite an "American" norm of privacy that was at issue when privacy suddenly became a ubiquitous topic in the early 1960s; rather, it was what many critics called "Anglo-Saxon" privacy.[1] By situating Robert Lowell's *Life Studies* within an early 1960s debate about a right to privacy in the realm of tort law, we might see that these poems anticipate, and complicate, the migration of privacy from the hierarchic to the democratic. In turn, seeing the legal analysis of privacy in terms of the cultural upheaval in norms of self-disclosure renders visible the assumptions about class, ethnicity, and gender that surfaced when privacy shifted from a social to a juridical entity.

In the early 1960s the growing awareness of pressures on individual privacy triggered a major reevaluation of "The Right to Privacy," the 1890 article written by Boston law firm partners Louis Brandeis and Samuel Warren. Though these pressures were not found primarily in the domain of torts (that is, in conflicts between an individual citizen and the media, for example), legal commentators such as Morris Ernst of the ACLU (*Privacy: The Right To Be Let Alone*, 1962), William Prosser ("Privacy," 1960), the so-called "dean" of tort law, and Edward Bloustein ("Privacy as an Aspect of Human Dignity: An Answer to Dean Prosser," 1964), a much-cited scholar on constitutional privacy rights, naturally turned to the tort origins of privacy law for the simple reason that a constitutional right to privacy did not yet exist.[2] Bloustein wrote with a hint of frustration:

> Warren and Brandeis obviously felt that the term "privacy" was in itself a completely adequate description of the interest threatened by an untrammeled press; man, they said, had a right to his privacy, a right to be let alone, and this was, for them, a sufficient description of the interest with which they were concerned. (970)

As Bloustein recognized, the informal precedent of Brandeis and Warren's article would prove a shaky foundation for a constitutional right not simply because it lacked the authority of a court decision. The problem would be twofold: not only was a constitutional right to privacy literally unprecedented, privacy itself was no longer obvious or self-evident.[3]

When Lowell published the first volume of poems to be called "confessional poetry" in 1959, the right to privacy was largely a defense against what Brandeis and Warren called "the evils of the invasion of privacy by the newspapers" (195). Lowell's willing exposure of his own family was, however, an "evil" they did not anticipate. Nevertheless, Lowell's confession of his "Mayflower" family tree rests upon Brandeis and Warren's article, which Morris Ernst called the "Plymouth Rock" of privacy law (viii). This emphasis on "Mayflower" and "Plymouth Rock" is more than a fortunate coincidence of terminology. As home to both the confessional movement in poetry and the legal right to privacy, Boston itself seems to have prompted questions about self-disclosure in a more acute and contentious way than any other American city. Brook Thomas explains in his article "The Construction of Privacy in and around *The Bostonians*" that, "constructed out of [Henry] James's milieu," the legal right to privacy has been from the start ambiguous. As part of an "elitist, bourgeois ideology," privacy has been criticized as "undemocratic" (723), while it has been defended more recently as the very essence of democracy, the sole arena in American life where individual dignity is protected. While these debates have not ended—Thomas notes that "staunch defender of the free market" Richard Posner objects to privacy rights as monopolistic (724)—the national controversy over privacy in the late twentieth century witnessed a gradual displacement of the questions of "hierarchy" as faith in privacy's democratic potential became increasingly important to cold war America. Though Boston is often a synecdoche for the nation, particularly in the fields of law and letters, this relationship of part for whole began to break down in the late 1950s. The ability to render Boston distinct from "America" is in fact a legacy of the enormous shifts in cultural, legal, and literary hierarchies that register in the debates over privacy during the cold war.[4]

Robert Lowell is a particularly good marker of this cultural shift because he was uniquely positioned to understand the migration of privacy and its relationship to politics and form. Helen Vendler takes a measure of his originality in a reading of "For the Union Dead," the poem for which Lowell is best known for reflecting on public poetry and personal memorial. Vendler imagines an envious poet asking himself: "Why didn't I think about doing a Boston poem?" and "Why didn't I think of writing a poem redefining the manliness of the hero as composed of vigilance, gentle tautness, privacy, and uprightness, instead of belligerence, vengeance, valor, and cunning?" This she says is the proof of Lowell's greatness: "Modernity and originality have to do with reconceiving the old subgenres, as well as with expanding the new subgenres" ("Reading a Poem" 130–31). Vendler's questions about poetic originality are intended to reaffirm New Critical principles of educated reading, but they also direct us back to historical questions. If we return to this moment in American cultural history, we may speculate on why Lowell's position as a gentleman of Boston, "suffocating for privacy" like the hero of his poem, might have made certain generic choices meaningful. In a sense Lowell's originality lay in his exquisite sensitivity to his own unique position. What other American poet could possibly have felt these questions about Boston and its gentlemen with anything like Lowell's insight, an insight born not only of genius and temperament but also the accident of birth? If the privacy crisis of the late twentieth century had not had its Robert Lowell, it would have had to invent him.

When he published *Life Studies* in 1959, Lowell was the most distinguished American poet of his generation. A Pulitzer Prize winner and a Library of Congress poet laureate, he commanded the respect of the country's best poets and most influential critics for the crabbed genius of his dense symbolic line. Nevertheless, by the early fifties, Lowell had become disenchanted with the tight metrical forms that had earned him his reputation, and he began to experiment with a looser, more proselike line.[5] Crucially, however, and much to the dismay of one of his most important mentors, Allen Tate,[6] he began experimenting with what was manifestly an autobiographical poem, one that chronicled the demise of the "Lowells" and his own continuing struggle with mental illness. What Lowell called his "breakthrough back into life" (*Paris Review* 346)[7] wagered his brilliant reputation by introducing transgressive autobiographical detail in lines that seemed to offer immediate access, a kind of linguistic transparency. The gamble was amply rewarded. *Life Studies* became the most admired and imitated collection of its time precisely for this breakthrough, which is now taken, with remarkably broad consensus, to mark a sea change in twentieth-century American poetics.

Poet Robert Hass has called this experiment one of the great revolutions in metrics in English-language poetry (*Twentieth-Century Pleasures* 108). I would describe this revolution as the creation of poetic intimacy. Lowell's breaking of his characteristically dense line was a gesture of invitation that transformed the reader's relationship to the poem. His innovation was to make himself—the "real Robert Lowell" as James Merrill noted—available, not as the abstract and universal poet but as a particular person in a particular place and time.[8] In essence, Lowell created a social and poetic informality in formal terms. But what makes this informality so instructive is that it takes place with the ghost of formality— the iambic meter, the tight rhyme scheme—right behind it. The formal ghost whispers from the background of Lowell's new informal address.

We seriously misconstrue the cultural logic of *Life Studies* if we separate Lowell's "breakthrough" poetics from his social experiment, that is, if we imagine his departures from poetic and social decorum to be unrelated. The social stakes of Lowell's transformation were important to his audience and obsessively interesting to him. Lowell's Boston Brahmin pedigree, a genealogy that critics rarely failed to mention in reviews of his work, had made him something of a celebrity before he earned his fame as a poet. The Lowells, who by popular maxim spoke only to the Cabots (who spoke only to God), were one of Boston's first families and included a Harvard president, poets famous (James Russell Lowell) and infamous (Amy Lowell), and innumerable minor luminaries in the country's early history. Moreover, Lowell's maternal ancestors, the Winslow/Starks also of Boston, were equally "historic" (perhaps more so, as *Life Studies* suggests), though not as instantly recognizable as his father's.

Lowell himself ironically noted the cachet of the name in "I Take Thee, Bob," one of the autobiographical sketches that formed the basis of *Life Studies*. In one draft he remarks that "Mother fell in love with Father's name and his deep blue, collarless ensign's uniform," and in another he has her reassuring her best friend (contemplating marriage to the dull Alfred Putnam Lowell) that "a Lowell with a perfectly good Harvard Law School degree was nothing to be sneezed at in Boston."[9] Even if the Lowell prestige had dimmed by his mother's generation— for both Bob and Alfred "Lowell" is buttressed by supplementary credentials, naval rank or law degree—the name alone guaranteed a place in Boston society. However, while Lowell's sense of his family's place in history and their impending displacement from it everywhere mark the autobiographical prose (it is indeed one of the preoccupations of the draft memoir), *Life Studies* takes great pains to rob his name of its luster. And it is the final dishonoring of the famous "House of Lowell" that contributed to the remarkable influence of *Life Studies*.

Critics have lamented the brutal exposure of the Lowell family without examining how these particular revelations structured Lowell's emerging poetics. Lowell's stylistic breakthrough cannot be disentangled from his self-conscious violations of the WASP regard for personal privacy. "Skunk Hour," the most acclaimed poem of the collection as well as the one Lowell completed first and considered the "anchor" of the sequence, displays his careful reckoning of social status and the privacy it conferred.[10] In a symposium on "Skunk Hour," Lowell divided it into two halves: the first four stanzas he describes as "dawdling," "casual," "chancy," "drifting" and a "random" portrait, which suggests that he imagined himself not as selective of but simply open to the context in which he wrote, absorbing the drift of his times (*Collected Prose* 226). The second four stanzas in contrast "come alive" in the "dark night" of the poem by focusing on the wandering mentally ill poet, the individual whose experience becomes central to the poem as a whole (226). In this respect Lowell's account of the poem's structure seems to bear out the critical conventional wisdom that in his poetry the private is a metaphor for the public, different in scale but not in kind. This is the sense of Lowell as representative sufferer that confessional poetry has depended upon to lift it from "mere" autobiography to some precarious social, political, or aesthetic relevance.

In imagining Lowell's personal trauma as a metaphor for social decline, "private" and "public" have long occupied a central vector of interest in Lowell's poetry and in confessional poetry more generally. But "Skunk Hour" addresses the shifting notions of public and private much more directly than we have imagined. Pressing his division of this poem further, we discover a parallel split, one that demonstrates how self-consciously Lowell was reflecting on these issues while composing *Life Studies*. "Skunk Hour" also cleaves in two between the "hierarchic privacy" of the "Nautilus Island's hermit heiress" and the voyeurism of the mentally ill poet/speaker in the "dark night." Dedicating a poem that literally hinges on privacy to Elizabeth Bishop,[11] a poet known for her personal reserve, signaled his attention to privacy as he published the volume that would launch the confessional movement in poetry.[12]

"Skunk Hour" is an epochal poem poised at a generational and temporal shift. The opening two stanzas of the poem register uneasiness with the upheavals in contemporary life occasioned by the loss of a certain kind of privacy. Nautilus Island at first appears to have escaped modernity:

> Nautilus Island's hermit
> heiress still lives through winter in her Spartan cottage;
> her sheep still graze above the sea.
> Her son's a bishop. Her farmer
> is first selectman in our village;
> she's in her dotage. (*Life Studies* 89)

The first stanza—with its repetition of "still," its simple declarative sentences, stative verb "is," and series of static equations between person and station—presents us with a tenacious, though weary, pastoralism. However, with the complex sentence of the second stanza, Lowell immediately insinuates that this pastoralism represents a resistance to the complications of historical change:

> Thirsting for
> the hierarchic privacy
> of Queen Victoria's century,
> she buys up all
> the eyesores facing her shore,
> and lets them fall. (*Life Studies* 89)

What separates tradition and modernity (from which the "hermit heiress" recoils) is simply this: the erosion of "hierarchic privacy." The modifier "hierarchic," which calls to mind its opposite—a nonhierarchical or even democratic privacy—fractures what might be imagined as a timeless or universal concept. We no longer have a private/public divide, but multiple divides between privac*ies* and their respective opposites. Moreover, by associating this particular kind of privacy with "Queen Victoria's century," Lowell locates the concept in history. We are prepared in an oblique way for a distinctly contemporary rendering of privacy to emerge.

By flagging the demise of a historically specific culture of privacy in "Skunk Hour" and in *Life Studies* more generally, we find Lowell in the midst of privacy debates just beginning to emerge in American legal scholarship and mass media. Like many of the popular accounts of the demise of privacy, Myron Brenton's best-selling *The Privacy Invaders* reads almost as a gloss on "Skunk Hour": "We are, most of us, not inclined to be hermits. We don't want to build so high a wall of privacy around ourselves as to be shut off from others. And there is no turning back the clock—which with every tick denudes us further still" (13). The ubiquity of privacy invasions and enticements to confess, which form the cold war context of Brenton's comments, effected a profound transformation in popular discussions of privacy that find a kind of metaphoric encapsulation in "Skunk Hour." One of the complications of cold war debates on privacy was the tension between the hierarchies of privacy that remained from the late-nineteenth-century origins of privacy law and two forces in postwar American culture: the omnipresent intrusion of the organized society/security state[13] and the dramatic relaxation in cultural prohibitions against self-disclosure that was just beginning to reach beyond popular magazines such as *True Confessions* and *Confidential* into the realms of "high art." A number of questions began to organize the center of the privacy debate: How exactly can citizens generally *reclaim* a "right" to privacy when such private space had historically belonged to the privileged classes? Who will defend the right to withhold information when people willingly divulge personal data to pollsters, to researchers in medical experiments, to newspaper and television reporters? Moreover, if indeed the right to privacy is a product of "Queen Victoria's century," can it be transported without modification to a new generational, political, and social context?

William Prosser's taxonomy of the right to privacy pokes fun at the hierarchic privacy that Lowell ambivalently mourns in *Life Studies*. Prosser begins his review of tort privacy law with a mocking portrait of the social setting behind the 1890 publication of "The Right to Privacy." That this story has proved to be a myth does not weaken its importance to cold war conceptions of privacy. Rather, Prosser's creation of it, and its widespread acceptance, testify to the esteem in which he was held in the legal community and, more significant for this moment of rethinking privacy, the sympathetic outrage that accompanied his story of intrusion. This was not just any violation that Prosser imagined but an intrusion on a wedding ceremony.[14]

> In the year 1890 Mrs. Samuel D. Warren, a young matron of Boston, which is a large city in Massachusetts, held at her home a series of social entertainments on an elaborate scale. She was the daughter of Senator Bayard of Delaware, and her husband was a wealthy young paper manufacturer, who only the year before had given up the practice of law to devote himself to an inherited business. Socially Mrs. Warren was among the elite; and the newspapers of Boston, and in particular the *Saturday Evening Gazette*, which specialized in "blue blood" items, covered her parties in highly personal and embarrassing detail. It was the era of "yellow journalism," when the press had begun to resort to excesses in the way of prying that have become more or less commonplace today; and Boston was, perhaps, of all of the cities in the country, the one in which a lady and a gentleman kept their names and their personal affairs out of the papers. The matter came to a head when the newspapers had a field day on the occasion of the wedding of a daughter, and Mr. Warren became annoyed. It was an annoyance for which the press, the advertisers and the entertainment industry of America were to pay dearly over the next seventy years. (383)

Prosser's ironic understatement throughout the introduction reduces the outrage that marks the origin of tort privacy to the petulance of an oversensitive Boston "blue-blood." The intrusions into the Warren's social privacy are clearly not, for Prosser, the end of the world as we know it, as Brandeis and Warren seemed to believe. When they began their article trumpeting, "Political, social, and economic changes entail the recognition of new rights" (193), Brandeis and Warren felt themselves to be meeting modernity head-on with an expanded legal notion of the human person. Prosser, however, reads their urgency as a personal, not legal, sense of injury—"hurt feelings"—cultivated in a particular social class in a particular place: Boston, which he defines as remote and provincial by ostensibly having to locate it for his readers as a "large city in Massachusetts." With its quaint and distinctly regional social customs ("of all of the cities in the country . . . ladies and gentlemen kept their names and their personal affairs out of the papers"), Boston, he suggests, has imposed its exaggerated fear of social vulnerability onto the nation. In Prosser's view, the Boston elite had made law out of social custom, created legal penalties to assuage personal affront and, in so doing, infringed on two revered freedoms—the freedom of the press and the freedom of the market—by imposing restraints on newspapers, advertising, and industry.

In sum, Prosser seems to have objected to the right to privacy because he perceived it to be at its root hierarchical. Casting himself as the voice of common sense and perhaps the common man, he remarks throughout the article on "blue blood" sensitivity, in one place specifically invoking those family names that symbolize the social context that he's mocked. He writes of the injury that the right to privacy protects:

> It is the plaintiff's name as a symbol of his identity that is involved here, and not his name as a mere name. There is, as a good many thousand John Smiths can bear witness, no such thing as an exclusive right to the use of any name. Unless there is some tortious use made of it, any one can be given or assume any name he likes. (403)

Then he quips:

> The Kabotznicks may call themselves Cabots, and the Lovelskis become Lowells, and the ancient proper Bostonian houses can do nothing but grieve. (403)

Prosser's gibe indicates that there is something obviously antidemocratic about the Cabots' and Lowells' investment in their names, and as he demonstrates, the right to privacy chiefly involves proper names and the injury to reputation. Moreover, these jokes accompany his general distrust of the right to privacy, which he dismantles in the process of describing. Finding this right to be nothing more than four separate, familiar injuries such as libel and trespass, Prosser argues that there may be no such thing as a general right to privacy, no matter how much the Warrens, or the Cabots and the Lowells, may wish there to be.

Not all legal commentators have shared Prosser's suspicion of the hierarchies of privacy. Though writing some thirty years later, William Strong, a copyright attorney who contributed to the privacy debate surrounding Diane Middle-brook's biography of another confessional poet, Anne Sexton,[15] bemoans the erosion of what we might now see as "hierarchic privacy" when tracing a generational decline in respect for privacy:

> Brandeis and Warren would have been shocked [by the prying of the biographer] as would probably anyone of their generation. Remember Henry Stimson, who as Secretary of War refused to read certain intelligence reports because "Gentlemen do not read other gentlemen's mail." ("The Grave's a Fine and Private Place" 6)

Strong mourns a time when the boundaries of decency were maintained by *self*-control, not adjudicated in lawsuits, that is, when privacy was maintained socially rather than juridically. However, the nostalgia Strong expresses manifests itself equally powerfully in Brandeis and Warren's article; in striving to prevent *further* erosion of privacy, they sought to impose in the form of legal principles the internal discipline that forbids the display of private life. In other words, this self-regulation was already on the verge of extinction, preserved only among gentlemen, which means that the fantasy of a stable and coherent privacy was lost even to the generation that Lowell assumes best represents the old hierarchies of privacy: Queen Victoria's. Like Lowell, Brandeis and Warren also discovered privacy as something already "lost." In tracking this generational decline in restraint, however, we can see how limited this cultural reserve was imagined to be. Gentlemen, it would seem, observe the privacy of other gentlemen—not necessarily anyone else's—which makes it an exercise in judgment that cements class fraternity, possibly (depending on how far we take Stimson's personal code of conduct) at the expense of national security.

Part of what made Lowell's opening of the Social Register to ridicule so compelling was the transgression of the allegiances of class. While reviewers of *Life Studies* cringed at this breach of class solidarity, Lowell's violation departs significantly from Brandeis and Warren's imagined horrors in two different ways. First, Lowell was exposing himself and his family to the public. This choice to elect exposure, rather than have it forced upon him, was unimaginable to Brandeis and Warren. In "Skunk Hour," the "hermit heiress," who "buys up all / the eyesores facing her shore, / and lets them fall," empties out her view to remove herself from sight. The "eyesores facing her shore," the evidence of decay that she sees as well as the eyes facing her, also constitute the uncomfortable gaze of the masses peering into her private space. However, Lowell was not enticed by this sort of exposure. As he remarked in a letter to his cousin Harriet Winslow: "I shudder to think of the water works lady reading *Life Studies*, and still more of next year when it will be paper-bound and on sale in the drugstores. A Russian poet I met boasted of his sales a minimum of fifty thousand. I've decided that only a few should be allowed to read poetry."[16] Clearly Lowell's self-revelation was underwritten by the elite status of poetry, which was to guarantee him an audience of gentleman readers, not working-class women.

More than betraying his own family and social circle by providing humiliating personal recollections, *Life Studies* shifts the terms of privacy by taking up the voyeuristic gaze. Driving his "Tudor Ford," which makes him, ironically of course, an aristocrat and so positioned like the "hermit heiress," Lowell searches out the private life of the townspeople of Nautilus Island in a reversal of gazes that was also unthinkable to Brandeis and Warren, for whom intrusion ran in only one direction—up—from the masses to the elite. However, something interesting happens when the voyeuristic gaze gets turned upon the ordinary inhabitants of the town. Nothing about what Lowell views is significant, only the fact of voyeurism itself. Marked by its banality—the refrain of a generic pop song, "Love, oh careless love," drifts in the background as the voyeur makes his rounds—voyeurism becomes unhooked from the object of the gaze and the gaze itself becomes the object of interest, not the glimpses of wealth, privilege, or social prestige that it might reveal. Without hierarchy, which Lowell destroys in his confessions, the interest of voyeurism becomes simply, or not so simply, the relationship between viewer and viewed. This interest in the gaze itself is one of the supreme markers of the cold war era.

From the first elegy in *Life Studies*, Lowell had figured himself as a voyeur: "unseen but all-seeing, [he] was Agrippina / in the Golden House of Nero" ("My Last Afternoon with Uncle Devereux Winslow" 59).[17] Moreover, the speaker's voyeurism in the second half of "Skunk Hour" was clearly Lowell's central problem in revision.[18] Drafts of the poem show three important changes in Lowell's thinking about the voyeur: the explicitness of voyeurism, the mobility of the speaker, and the relationship of voyeurism to poetry. "I am the visionary, the voyeur . . . / Unable to move . . . ," one version of stanza five reads, "I am the visionary, the *voyeur*— . . ." another. Lowell gradually softened the explicitness of the speaker's voyeurism, moving to "half-voyeur / I cannot move . . ." in yet another draft of the poem, finally eliminating it in the final version of the poem.[19] The published version of the fifth stanza, which reads

One dark night,
my Tudor Ford climbed the hill's skull;
I watched for love-cars. Lights turned down
they lay together, hull to hull,
where the graveyard shelves on the town. . . .
My mind's not right. (*Life Studies* 90)

makes voyeurism both searching and mobile while rendering its relation to vision more ambiguous. What seems to be crucial in these drafts, nonetheless, is that poetic intuition requires the breach of public/private boundaries—vision being the profit of voyeurism—which means that retreating to a notion of privacy based in the hierarchies of private property can only recapture Victorian notions of propriety at the expense of poetry itself.

A second revision, which follows in tandem the reshaping of voyeurism in the poem, sheds light on how Lowell modernizes the dilemmas of privacy when the return to "hierarchic privacy" has been renounced. After tinkering with its shape, Lowell abandons the line "Everyone in town is in bed / with everyone else" for the voyeuristic vision of "love-cars" in the graveyard bordering the town.[20] If in the drafts the paralysis of the voyeur coincides with this image of ubiquitous sexual transgression, we can see that the major shift in his revision is between modes of surveillance, between the small-town network of informal observation and the voyeuristic gaze of an increasingly anonymous social organization. No one, much less the paralyzed voyeur, could see the entire town engaged in illicit activity, nor would the speaker stand in privileged relationship to this information. "Everyone . . . in bed / with everyone else" is simply gossip, shared secrets, which suggests the mode of surveillance befitting the "hermit heiress's" traditional community. Furthermore, "everyone" with "everyone else" comprises a closed circle made up of known individuals; in contrast, the "love-cars," rather than lovers, lack a human face, and so remain anonymous, metaphorically at the border of the town, neither of nor outside the community. The voyeur is thus able to penetrate privacy without compromising his, or their, anonymity.

These revisions address the paradox Lowell created for himself in pluralizing privacy: the condition on which he rests his vision—voyeurism—requires privacy to be conserved even while it is being violated. Therefore, in some fashion, the poem will have to construct privacy at the same time that it destroys it. Lowell accomplishes this double move by imagining privacy as contextual or situational rather than spatial. "Love-cars," which "[lie] together, hull to hull," represent sexuality that is not safely sheltered at home ("everyone . . . in bed") but mobile and public, if still secret; cars, plural, have migrated to the graveyard for sex, making it a distinctly 1950s public, private act. Lowell creates this space as private by making the graveyard a public and erotic space, slyly inverting Andrew Marvell's famous warning in "To His Coy Mistress": "The grave's a fine and private place, / but none I think do there embrace." In a contextual rather than spatial model of privacy, all space, like the graveyard that becomes a sexual playground at night, may be either public or private. Its status as one or the other is not the simple—yet reliable—definition of the space; rather, privacy derives from a social agreement: the lovers in the love-cars implicitly confer privacy on one another in order to maintain their own. In contrast to spatial privacy, like the "hermit heiress's," which can as private property be restricted by ownership, this social but nonhierarchical privacy is universally accessible just as it is demonstrably vulnerable to those who will not obey its etiquette.

In these shifts in voyeur and the object of his gaze, Lowell treads upon the complication that rendered tort privacy so increasingly difficult to adjudicate: what does it mean to violate privacy when the social hierarchies that prevent intimate life from being exposed dissolve? That is, when self-disclosure joins the withdrawal into private spaces as accommodations to an intrusive modern world, the boundaries of privacy become increasingly indistinct. At the end of his deconstruction of the right to privacy, Prosser nods toward the changing limits of self-disclosure with a rhetorical question: he asks "whether, for example, a lady who insists upon sun-bathing in the nude in her own back yard should really have a cause of action for her humiliation when the neighbors examine her with appreciation and binoculars" (422). Though the private body has only inched beyond the doorframe of the home into the back yard, for Prosser what Brandeis and Warren called the "obvious bounds of propriety and decency" (196) and the "boundaries of propriety natural to every man" (202, n.1) clearly no longer carry much force. Neither the "lady," nor the gentleman voyeur can begin to recognize what was for the men of "Queen Victoria's century" self-evident.

Even though Brandeis and Warren had employed a series of common law precedents to formulate a right to privacy, the real boundary lay in the natural discretion of the gentleman. Without this self-restraint, the boundary of privacy is completely unreadable and, therefore, to Prosser, legally unenforceable. The changing limits of self-disclosure thus returned the problem of privacy to the realm of social custom and removed it, in Prosser's account, from the arena of law. However, as we see in "Skunk Hour," the realm of social custom was a dangerous place to locate limits of privacy since gentlemen themselves no longer upheld the privacy that was theirs to safeguard. Privacy after 1960 would enter a period of extended volatility for precisely this reason: this fantasy of self-evident privacy disappeared with every attempt to define it more precisely and narrowly. The social and legal coherence of privacy was indirectly proportional.

The "gentlemen's agreement" that sustained hierarchic privacy was further complicated by the political transformations wrought by the cold war.[21] By 1964 cold war anxieties about the invasiveness of the security state and the organized society had supplanted the fear of mass media intrusion at the core of the debate surrounding the legal protection of privacy. In recognition of these dangers, Edward Bloustein in the *New York University Law Review* attempted to rescue the right to privacy from the fragmentation, and hence evisceration, of Prosser's 1960 analysis.[22] Citing works by Vance Packard, Myron Brenton, and Hannah Arendt among others, Bloustein concluded that only a general theory of privacy, by confronting both tort and constitutional violations, could meet the challenges of the cold war. In order to create this general right out of the "haystack in a hurricane" of privacy law,[23] Bloustein departed from convention and sought to merge the tort and constitutional traditions. In the process he emptied out the right to privacy of another hierarchy in order to create a more universally available, which is to say democratic, right by shifting away from a patriarchal to a masculine notion of privacy.

Bloustein returns to Brandeis and Warren and reanimates their primary transgression—that to "inviolate personality," which he calls "human dignity." However, in order to establish a special urgency to protect human dignity, Bloustein repeatedly casts intrusion as a threat to masculinity. Two examples will suffice:

I take the principle of "inviolate personality" to posit the individual's independence, dignity, and integrity; it defines man's essence as a unique and self-determining being. It is because our Western ethico-religious tradition posits such dignity and independence of will in the individual that the common law secures to a man "literary and artistic property"—the right to determine "to what extent his thoughts, sentiments, emotions shall be communicated to others." The literary and artistic property cases led Warren and Brandeis to the concept of privacy because, for them, it would have been inconsistent with a belief in man's individual dignity and worth to refuse him the right to determine whether his artistic and literary efforts should be published to the world. *He would be less of a man, less of a master over his own destiny, were he without this right.* (971; emphasis mine)

Beginning with an ostensibly ungendered liberal humanism, Bloustein intensifies the dangers of intrusion in the last sentence: "He would be less of a man, less of a master of his own destiny, were he without this right." Somewhat later in the same article, he returns to this theme in his inventory of cold war fears about privacy: "A man whose home may be entered at the will of another, whose conversations may be overheard at the will of another, whose marital and familial intimacies may be overseen at the will of another, *is less of a man, has less human dignity, on that count*" (973; emphasis mine). The rhetorical intensification of the first passage—the threat to manhood—has now swapped places with "human dignity" as the core violation; here human dignity flows from intact manhood, which itself proceeds from strict control over self-disclosure. Brenton makes a similar type of claim: "[Anglo-Saxon man] knew that nothing was more devitalizing and degrading to *his stature as a man* than to live with the constant fear that somebody might be looking over his shoulder or barging into his quarters" (226; emphasis mine). Attempting to rescue the right to privacy from Prosser's critique of its implicit class privilege, Bloustein democratizes privacy by masculinizing it. This rhetorical sleight of hand suggests that the cold war, with its attendant security anxieties, insinuated itself into everyday life as the threat of emasculation.

These appeals to manhood are not simply the "generic he." The phrases quoted above are rhetorical flourishes, akin to exclamation points, and seem to change only the tone not the argument of the sentence. These phrases were not intended to exclude women from the protections of privacy. In fact, Bloustein's key point of reference is a case from the nineteenth century, *DeMay v. Roberts* (1881), in which a stranger intruded on a woman in labor; he declares it an example of the kind of violation that would become commonplace without a universal and constitutionally recognized right to privacy.[24] But the masculinizing of privacy is no less potent for being unintentional. Precisely because security anxieties endangered the citizen's "stature as a man," masculinity was smuggled into conceptions of privacy in the universalizing gesture. The path to a more democratic and universally accessible right to privacy went through masculine autonomy.

When Bloustein tried to reimagine Brandeis and Warren's patriarchal right as one grounded in masculinity, he implicitly deflated the hierarchy they took for granted. Bloustein's interest in "the individual's independence, dignity, and integrity . . . man's essence as a unique and self-determining being" suggests a privacy grounded in the autonomy of the individual not in the prestige of a family name. While Brandeis and Warren would have had no objection to this individual dignity, there is a crucial difference in their sense of the individual's privacy, which is that patriarchal privacy encompassed more than the patriarch's individual self-representation.

They justified the abstract injury to reputation by showing how over time the common law had seen the conception of "human" evolve from the corporeal to the incorporeal, expanding from the body of a man to *include* the bodies in his domestic circle. Brandeis and Warren argued that "Man's family relations became a part of the legal conception of his life, and the alienation of a wife's affections was held remediable" (194). They explained in a footnote:

> then the feelings of the parent, the dishonor to himself and his family, were accepted as the most important element of damage [of seduction] . . . The allowance of these damages would seem to be a recognition that the invasion upon the honor of the family is an injury to the parent's person, for ordinarily mere injury to parental feelings is not an element of damage, e.g., the suffering of the parent in the case of physical injury to the child. (194, n.5)

Brandeis and Warren's example demonstrates that the expansion of the legal conception of man to consolidate "reputation" or "name" as part of selfhood simultaneously incorporates the domestic circle, including the wife, into his person. As Brook Thomas argues in "The Construction of Privacy in and around *The Bostonians*":

> Because the domestic circle has such an important social role, it was established by a contract much more public in nature than the business contract.

This public contract created a sacred sphere that should not be violated by public or private parties. Private as that sphere might seem, however, it was not a sphere in which husband and wife could legally assert "the right to be let alone" against one another. On the contrary, the marriage contract created one legal body out of two. (729)

Thomas reveals that the exceptional privacy of the domestic sphere, held together by its uniquely public contract, contains at its heart an exceptional *lack* of privacy: husband and wife could not legally assert their "right to be let alone" from one another.

However, the potential conflict of competing privacies—husband's and wife's—was resolved by incorporating the wife's privacy into the husband's. Under this rubric, Brandeis and Warren can be understood to have defended patriarchal rather than individual privacy because no one else in the family circle could have made a legitimate claim to this right. That is, if "seduction" (of a daughter) or "alienation of a wife's affection" represents an injury to the father, there is no similar right to protection from the patriarch or right of autonomy within his domain.[25] Moreover, when this patriarchal privacy breaks down, one thing that will be liberated from it is the wife's separate autonomy. A new privacy will be created when the older self-evident privacy breaks up, and this we will find in *Griswold v. Connecticut*, a relational right of married couples, which by acknowledging the couple began to undermine the patriarch's exclusive authority over privacy. I will return to this with Lowell's *The Dolphin*.

Patriarchal control over the domestic sphere collides, however, with the very definition of privacy Brandeis and Warren imagined. Bloustein characterizes the legal foundation of privacy as "the right to determine whether [one's] artistic and literary efforts should be published to the world" (971), which, taken with his emphasis on individual autonomy, suggests a paradox at work in the evolution of legal privacy: the right to privacy contains within it the right to publicity.[26] As Bloustein repeatedly notes, Brandeis and Warren conceived the right to privacy not "to prevent inaccurate portrayal of private life, but to prevent its being depicted at all" (as quoted in Bloustein 968). Theirs was an absolute notion of privacy that understood the revelation of private life to be inherently humiliating. And yet, as Bloustein, Brandeis, and Warren seem to agree, the right to determine self-publication defines the "inviolate personality." Without the "natural" reticence ascribed to the gentleman, the right to privacy can swing in the opposite direction and become the right to assert one's autonomy from the patriarchal father who guards the family name, to become an autonomous individual, an "inviolate personality." *Life Studies* directly confronts this conflict between the autonomy of the individual and patriarchal control over family name, marking the strange slippage of privacy into publicity, which is the direct result of imagining the modern self to be composed not only of flesh and blood but also of text and image.

The patriarch's centrality to the origins of legal privacy corresponds to the position of the father in the definition of confessional poetry. If the ultimate violation of privacy as the law conceives it is the exposure of the father, M. L. Rosenthal's review of *Life Studies*, which names "confessional poetry" and Lowell a confessional poet, forges the link between confessional poetry and the violation of the father. Rosenthal says:

> About half the book, the prose section called "91 Revere Street," is essentially *a public discrediting of his father's manliness* and character, as well as of the family and social milieu of his childhood. . . . The father, naval officer *manqué* and then businessman and speculator *manqué*, becomes a humiliating symbol of the failure of a class and of a kind of personality. Lowell's contempt for him is at last mitigated by adult compassion, though I wonder if a man can allow himself this kind of ghoulish operation on his father without doing his own spirit incalculable damage. (*The Modern Poets* 109; emphasis mine)

Similarly, Robert Phillips in *The Confessional Poets* jokes:

> One could be facetious and say that *a Father Complex and the willingness to write openly about it is a necessary criterion for becoming a confessional poet*— since the reader will encounter here such poets as Sylvia Plath, John Berryman, Theodore Roethke, and Robert Lowell, all of whom appear obsessed by father love/hatred or by the necessity of father atonement, as is Stanley Kunitz. (xii; emphasis mine)

Phillips rightly points to the preponderance of anxious and hostile poems about fathers in the confessional corpus, but given the relationship of patriarchal fathers to cultural constructions of privacy, it's worth considering how we might invert the relationship between the confession and the "father complex." Instead of imaging the father complex as the psychological prerequisite of confessional writing, we might also understand confession as a social act that engenders a complex about fathers. The confessional poet's bid for autonomy beyond the family's (father's) domain necessarily conflicts with the patriarch's exclusive right of self-representation. This anxiety about the hostility to fathers then reveals the special relationship that the patriarch enjoyed with respect to privacy. Though confessional poetry contains equally damning portraits of mothers, there is no parallel crisis over privacy because the mother's right to it is less secure. Alan Williamson's observation that "patriarchally minded critics have found the portrait [of Lowell's father] cruel, even indecent" (*Pity the Monsters* 72) reminds us that the cruelty to others in the memoir—to Lowell's mother or wife for instance—barely registered. The outrage that greeted Lowell's exposure of his father manifests the cultural investment in patriarchal privacy that was, as Lowell himself made clear in *Life Studies*, in the process of shifting.

Lowell's elegies track a generational decline in patriarchal power that parallels the patriarch's dwindling control over familial privacy. In "During Fever," the final elegy of the collection, Grandfather Winslow, the patriarchal father, and Robert T. S. Lowell, the "unmasterful" father, are juxtaposed: the patriarch is the invader of other people's privacy while the weakened father is subject to the conspiratorial whispers of his wife and son. The final stanza explores the hierarchic privacy of the patriarchal home:

> Born ten years and yet an aeon
> too early for the twenties,
> Mother, you smile
> as if you saw your Father
> inches away yet hidden, as when he groused behind a screen
> over a National Geographic Magazine,
> whenever young men came to court you
> back in those settled years of World War One.
> Terrible that old life of decency
> without unseemly intimacy
> or quarrels, when the unemancipated woman
> still had her Freudian Papa and maids!

Here the patriarch, the guardian of courtship, is "hidden" in plain sight. However, his is not the "unseen but all seeing" voyeurism of Lowell in "Last

Afternoon with Uncle Devereux Winslow," the first family poem, nor the visionary voyeurism of "Skunk Hour," the final poem of the autobiographical sequence, but, rather, a voyeurism that is fully, if coyly, acknowledged. His right to
view the scene is unquestioned, part of his authority and even his charm. In contrast, Lowell's father is also a guardian, but he performs his duties like a servant
rather than a master. "Often with unadulterated joy, / Mother, we bent by the fire
/ rehashing father's character— / when he thought we were asleep, / he'd tiptoe
down the stairs / and chain the door." Lowell's father, instead of monitoring
other people's privacy, is himself the subject of inspection and exposure. Defined
by his lack of privacy rather than by his control over private spaces, Lowell's
father is opened up for examination by those over whom he should have domin-
ion. The patriarch's exclusive right to self-representation is doubly violated, first
in the intimate conversation between mother and son, again in the poem that
reports it. Finally, unable to care for his daughter, Lowell stripped himself of
even the pretense of patriarchal mastery or meek guardianship. Confessing inep-
titude, father and daughter speak in one voice: " 'Sorry' she mumbles like her
dim-bulb father, 'sorry.' "

The diminished control over privacy relates directly to the confessional project. Paradoxically, patriarchal surveillance proceeds "without unseemly intimacy." Because the father regulates the home, intimacy arises in a quasi-public fashion, its very "seemliness" testimony to the hidden, but acknowledged, spectator.
Private spaces are always already public spaces for everyone within the patriarch's domain—everyone, that is, except the patriarch. Moreover, the quasi-public structure of privacy holds intimacy in check, permitting the mother's
"Freudian" attachment to her father by forbidding displays of "unseemliness,"
which suggests that the patriarch's control of privacy fosters a "terrible" emotional latitude by holding in check the expression of feeling. The confessional
poet, in contrast, in giving expression to unseemly emotions might be understood to have moderated such fierce attachment. The publicity given to private
emotion both manifests a diminished allegiance to family and further erodes
such commitment.

The demise of the patriarch precedes, then, perhaps even engenders, the confessional impulse. Throughout *Life Studies*, Lowell's father disappoints because
he falls short as a model of patriarchal authority. Portraying himself as a wor-
shipper of authority and in love with all things military—as a boy in "91 Revere
Street" he put himself to sleep by memorizing the names of French generals—
Lowell admits that his contempt for his father derives from his failure to live up

to his naval uniform. This failure of patriarchal fatherhood permits the central violation of privacy in *Life Studies*: Lowell can expose him because his father has forfeited his exemption from exposure. Like his father, Lowell is "forlornly fatherless" but consequently freed from the prohibitions against self-disclosure that might injure the father and his reputation. "Sailing Home from Rapallo" completes the erasure of his father: "In the grandiloquent lettering on Mother's coffin, / *Lowell* had been misspelled *LOVEL*." Not only does this misspelling remove the mother's identification with the Lowells in the family graveyard (her family's graveyard) but one cannot help but hear the word "level" and "love" in the misspelled "Lovel." In fact, as Lowell's autobiographical prose mentions, the misspelling was merely a lost "l"—"Lowel"—which Lowell further edits to "Lovel." In choosing to "level" father's name, even while also loving him, Lowell renders explicit the leveling that the autobiography accomplishes: the erasure of his father's name. He frees himself to make his self-disclosures by suggesting that the proper name is already so defaced that he cannot be understood to injure it.

Having displayed the descent from patriarchal to unmasterful fatherhood, the confessions of *Life Studies* wrestle with the problem of stripping away the mask of the patriarch without endangering masculinity altogether. When W. D. Snodgrass wrote *Heart's Needle* about the pain of his divorce and consequent estrangement from his daughter, the favorable reviews mingled with ridicule; Snodgrass was a "sentimental" poet. Lowell, who was much influenced by *Heart's Needle* in writing *Life Studies*, defended Snodgrass against this accusation (in poetry most often linked to the "poetess") not by denying this sentimentality but by embracing it. *Life Studies*, along with *Heart's Needle*, embraces the private man in a way that patriarchal notions of privacy simply do not allow. In other words, merely by representing the private man in the domestic realm, Lowell (and Snodgrass) was undermining patriarchal manhood. In some sense, representing the demise of patriarchal authority constitutes one of *Life Studies*'s most important confessions. But at the same time, it engenders one of Lowell's deepest conflicts. Left without a patriarchal model, Lowell spends much of *Life Studies* searching for an inhabitable masculinity.[27]

Bloustein's emphasis on manhood and privacy suggests a rather strange context for the burst of confessional writing by men. Yet *Life Studies* suggests why maintaining the masculine individual in private might not be what the Supreme Court imagined in *Griswold* as a solution to the oppressive surveillance associated with the cold war. *Life Studies*'s exposure of the unmasterful father undermines the promise that Bloustein, Brenton, and the Supreme Court found in the protection of the "zone of privacy." Cold war rhetoric, even while it produced a vigorous defense of this "zone," maintained a sharp gendering of private and public space. This gendering, as *Life Studies* shows, meant that there was no space to be a man. Lowell writes of the menace of feminine usurpation of the private sphere in the autobiographical prose that forms the basis of *Life Studies*:

> Mother had no business coming into the upstairs den "undressed." She wore pale pink slippers, a pale pink night-gown, a pale pink woolen throw-over and a pale pink lace night-cap. . . . I knew that pink was a sissy color, and probably invented by a sissy, whom my Grandmother Winslow, Gaga, called Louis Quinze. I felt like pushing in all directions with my arms, and making pink stay put in Mother's bedroom. And here was Mother cruising throughout the house, and spilling all out over everything, like some Chinese dragon jack-in-the-box with a too powerful spring. I felt meshed and menaced. One way to get around Mother was to think of the man's colors, blue and tan. Father's chair was leather and oak. . . . I was a tower of muscle rushing into air and water. Then I did my best to look straight ahead and into Mother without seeing her.[28]

In a more literal but no more sinister way than in "91 Revere Street," Mother's "pink" has begun to migrate into spaces where it does not properly belong. Instead of being contained in the bedroom, femininity has come to occupy the house as a whole. There is no defense against its pervasive encroachment other than to pretend it isn't there—to "look straight ahead and into Mother without seeing her"—in other words, to retreat to the only space left to preserve masculinity: the space of imagination, where Lowell will become purely phallic, the "tower of muscle rushing into air and water."

Especially in the fifties, this feminization of the home was perceived to threaten homosexuality in young boys—the "sissy color" pink that Lowell physically wards off with his arms—and more generally to render young men unfit for masculine pursuits such as war. The fact that masculinity has been displaced in the home creates a specifically cold war dilemma: the necessary retreat from public into private to shelter manhood from the emasculation of the state becomes a withdrawal *into* femininity. Lowell's father lives precisely between these two uninhabitable spheres. The final revelation of "91 Revere Street" is

Commander Billy Harkness's joke that he knows why Bobby is an only child: Commander Lowell does not sleep at home. As retribution for Mrs. Lowell's purchase of a grand home for the family outside of the naval base, the naval commander required that his first officer, Robert T. S. Lowell, spend each night on the base. Lowell's father epitomizes the man with *no* space, no retreat from the state, the naval yard, or the femininity that pervades the home. He shuttles between the two realms, his space of masculine withdrawal shrunk to the blue and tan chair in his den, which mother's pink threatens to overwhelm. The question for Lowell's father, as it was more generally for the "organization man," is where can he be a man. The promised retreat of privacy to which Brenton, Bloustein, and the Supreme Court held fast was for Lowell precisely the place where masculinity was most compromised.

Robert Lowell's two most famous and controversial volumes of confessional work, *Life Studies* and *The Dolphin*, punctuate the privacy crisis. In 1973, Lowell published his last confessional work, *The Dolphin*, a sonnet sequence that narrated his divorce from Elizabeth Hardwick and remarriage to Lady Carolyn Blackwood. The volume was to be far more controversial than *Life Studies* because Lowell created poems out of Hardwick's private letters. As Lowell was preparing this manuscript for publication, Elizabeth Bishop wrote him an anguished letter explaining her objections to the manuscript:

> Lizzie is not dead, etc.—but there is a "mixture of fact & fiction," and you have *changed* her letters. . . . IF you were given permission—IF you hadn't changed them . . . etc. *But art isn't worth that much.* I keep remembering Hopkins' marvelous letter to Bridges about the idea of a "gentleman" being the highest thing ever conceived—higher than a "Christian" even, certainly a poet. It is not being "gentle" to use personal, tragic, anguished letters that way—it's cruel.[29]

Lowell, himself, recognized that the "terrible thing" in *The Dolphin* was not the confusion of "fact and fiction" or the changing of the letters "but the wife pleading with her husband to return—this backed by 'documents.' "[30] And though he did revise in response to Bishop's criticism, he refrained from eliminating Hardwick's "documented" presence.

Lowell's use of Hardwick's letters can be viewed as the final chapter in his very astute, if also rather excruciating experiment with the dynamics of privacy.

During the writing of *The Dolphin*, Lowell was especially conscious of letters and their various privacy dilemmas. His correspondence with Hardwick makes reference to two arenas in which he confronted the problem of private letters. First, he registered his discomfort at Hardwick's exposure of him: "Such boiling messages, all as public as possible on cables and uninclosed postcards. It's chafing to have the wicked, doddering, genial old All Souls' porter take down your stinging cables," he complained.[31] He also vacillated over how to dispose of his own letters when both Harvard and SUNY Stonybrook vied to acquire his archive. Lowell frequently expressed dismay at the idea of having his letters open to the public, especially to critics, an anxiety that appears time and again in *The Dolphin*, perhaps most obviously in these lines from "Doubt: I. Draw": "Should revelation be sealed like private letters, / till all the beneficiaries are dead, / and our proper names become improper Lives?" Lowell did not want his letters open to the public in his lifetime; the same courtesy was not afforded to Hardwick.

Given Lowell's anxieties about epistolary privacy, his publication of Hardwick's letters appears even more cruel. But measuring Lowell's cruelty is not my point. Perhaps no one protested his cruelty more passionately than Adrienne Rich did in her review of *The Dolphin*. Other critics have understood his use of Hardwick's letters as the mark of a voracious, even cannibalistic ego.[32] David Gewanter, on the other hand, has suggested that *The Dolphin*, which he describes as a "collaboration, a postmodern poetry of multiple voices and authors," represented a major advance in poetics that Lowell was simply unwilling to abandon ("Child of Collaboration" 178). I agree that Lowell did advance poetics in this "collaboration," but not in the way that Gewanter imagines. Instead, Lowell's use of Hardwick's letters offers a major insight into the forms of privacy.

In the "original" manuscript, Gewanter claims,[33] the clarity of Hardwick's voice gave her a kind of "autonomy" and "integrity" that diminished her violation. This relationship of the marital "we" and the autonomy of its individual parts was very much Lowell's concern, just as it was very much the center of legal privacy debates during this agitated period.[34] Lowell plays with this confusion in the poems that begin to disentangle him from Hardwick. "Letter"— obviously drawn from Hardwick's correspondence—from the series "Hospital II," illustrates how Lowell uses the voice of the "other" to break apart the marital "we" and expose it as an "I." "We wanted to be buried together in Maine . . . / You didn't, 'impractical, cold, out of touch.' " The ellipsis at the end of the first line conveys Lowell's nostalgic remembrance of the married "we," which is interrupted by the "You" of the next line. The quotation marks (around "impractical,

cold, out of touch") then visually divide the other from the poet, creating a separate space for her voice within the poet's narrative, thereby accentuating the
cleaving of the marital "we" by giving autonomy to "you." Implicitly, too, this
"we" is being revised to expose its fiction of unity—for if "you" did not want
what "we" did, clearly the "we" was a misnamed "I." Moreover, the chief instrument of this differentiation is voice. Hardwick's voice begins to emerge in coun-
terpoint to Lowell's.

Privacy and its relation to individual autonomy were two of the most compelling and contentious issues of the early 1970s. Gewanter's insights into the
problem of Hardwick's autonomy in the uneven collaboration of *The Dolphin*
ought to be examined more carefully in light of these debates. Returning to the
premise of my reading of *Life Studies*, I would like to suggest that *The Dolphin*
takes its form, particularly in the use of Hardwick's letters, by working within
the shifting terrain of privacy.

The year 1973 was a major turning point in the cold war debate over privacy.
The Watergate investigation, which dominated the headlines, spelled the ironic
end to one incarnation of the cold war security state by generating a mandate for
new openness in government. New legislation was drawn up to open the
dossiers that had been accumulating since the early cold war era. While this
openness has always been more fantasy than reality, the debate over privacy and
secrecy swung decisively toward dismantling the privileges of the state to inquire
into the lives of its citizens. However, the most significant argument about privacy in 1973 was the Supreme Court's *Roe v. Wade* decision. This decision marked
the culmination of the most vigorous period of the feminist movement.
Elizabeth Hardwick located the pressures that were transforming American culture in the early 1970s in her essay "Domestic Manners," where she concludes
that "the arrival of women's ambition, transforming as it does private life, inner
feeling, and public life is not at all simple but instead resembles the subtle shift-
ings of human thought and life brought about by enormously challenging ideas
such as evolution and Freudianism" (*Bartleby* 96). In placing feminism at the
crux of her question: "How are we living today?" Hardwick points to the
reordering of public and private life wrought by the women's movement, which
was increasingly important to American culture when Lowell was writing *The
Dolphin*. To see Lowell's major project of the early 1970s—that of reordering his
own work to distinguish between the private/domestic/erotic spheres and the
public/historic/political spheres—in terms of the women's movement alerts us

to the many ways in which Lowell engages with feminists in *The Dolphin* over the nature of privacy.

Lowell's writing of *The Dolphin* took place in a context in which he was acutely conscious of measuring the relationship between private and public, both in his personal life and in the culture more generally. During the period in which he composed and revised *The Dolphin*, Lowell reworked the hundreds of poems he had already published twice as *Notebook 1967–68* (1969) and *Notebook* (1970) into two new volumes: *History* (1973) and *For Lizzie and Harriet* (1973), the latter a collection dedicated to Hardwick and their daughter.[35] These revisions of *Notebooks* are a key to the innovation in form in *The Dolphin*, which is the use of the letters. The three volumes of 1973 can be read as an effort on Lowell's part to *resituate* his own voice within the categories of public and private by reclaiming the publicness of his own voice.

Notebook's blank verse sonnets allowed Lowell the openness to contend with "History" as a quotidian phenomenon. His compositional practice, what Paul Mariani has described as Lowell's increasing interest in process (351–52), allowed his mind to roam, alternately attending to the riots following Dr. Martin Luther King's assassination, reflecting on his daughter or his marriage, imagining his rivalry with literary contemporaries, or brooding on the legacies of Sir Thomas More, Martin Heidegger, or Eugene McCarthy. The openness of the blank verse sonnet remained compelling to him in his revisions, but the blend of personal, social, historical, domestic, and political figures and events no longer seemed appropriate or coherent to him by the early 1970s. In other words, the fluidity of public and private that marked the *Notebooks* in the 1960s seemed in need of restructuring after the fact. Lowell's reputation seesaws between the two poles of this rewriting: for some he is fundamentally a historical poet, for others essentially a confessional poet. It seems crucial, given the dilemmas of privacy that surrounded Lowell, to hold these two configurations of his career in tension, to resist any attempt to resolve them in favor of one or the other classification.

To be clear: Lowell did not expunge the personal from *History* in the revision; his personal experiences in or reflections on the events of his time are central to the poems. And critics have found this integration of the personal and historical to be one of Lowell's great achievements in the volume. At the same time, however, most critics agreed that carving out the poems that make up *For Lizzie and Harriet* represented a *clarification* of both sets of poems. This is to say that the elimination of the domestic—Lowell called these the "family poems"—from

History made eminent sense to both Lowell and his readers. Nevertheless, the "family poems" are not, strictly speaking, about family. As Gabriel Pearson has observed, there is only one sonnet in all of *For Lizzie and Harriet* that includes the three members of the family (*"For Lizzie and Harriet*: Robert Lowell's Domestic Apocalypse" 197). There is a long sequence called "Mexico" that narrates Lowell's affair with a much younger woman. This could hardly be said to "make sense" as a domestic poem or to have allowed his wife and daughter much pleasure in the dedication of the volume. So it is more accurate to say when we speak of Lowell's revised volumes that they reorganized specific aspects of private life and declared by arrangement that the erotic and the domestic had no place in "History." In sum, the revisions of *Notebook* into *History* and *For Lizzie and Harriet* permitted Lowell to calibrate his private and public voices quite precisely. And it is in the process of this calibration that Lowell composed *The Dolphin*.

Lowell's writing in *The Dolphin* reflects the quandary about autonomy and marriage that we find in the landmark privacy decisions. In the brief period from *Griswold v. Connecticut* in 1965 to *Roe v. Wade* in 1973, the right to privacy was located within the home and *between* husband and wife. The logic of pairing *The Dolphin* with these Supreme Court decisions goes beyond mere historical parallel. These decisions and this sequence of poems reflected on the problems of defining privacy as both a relational right *and* a foundation of individual autonomy. At the same time that the right to privacy withdrew the marital couple from the public sphere, it made privacy and moral autonomy dependent on the relationship between the couple. Justice Douglas formulates the constitutional right to privacy as follows:

> The present case, then, concerns a *relationship* lying within the zone of privacy created by several fundamental constitutional guarantees. . . . Would we allow the police to search the sacred precincts of marital bedrooms for telltale signs of the use of contraceptives? The very idea is repulsive to the notions of *privacy surrounding the marriage relationship*. . . . Marriage is a coming together for better or for worse, hopefully enduring, and intimate to the degree of being sacred. (485)

By saying that marriage is "intimate to the degree of being sacred," Douglas implied that the sanctity of marriage lay in direct proportion to its withdrawal from the public realm. The word "sacred" that reverberates throughout the decision withdraws marriage from scrutiny as an institution. The power of this ideal of marriage, as Lauren Berlant has argued, lies in its *not* being expressed, quantified, qualified, or described in public ("Live Sex Acts" 1995). The paradox here is that marriage—though silent—grounds individual moral autonomy, which is guaranteed by the heterosexual marriage contract.

In his concurrence in *Griswold*, Harlan, too, staked out privacy as a right of married couples, referring the Court to his dissent in *Poe v. Ullman* where he argued:

> I believe that a statute making it a criminal offense for *married couples* [emphasis in the original] to use contraceptives is an intolerable and unjustifiable invasion of privacy in the conduct of the most intimate concerns of an *individual's* personal life. (539; emphasis mine)

Though in this sentence Harlan sees the Connecticut statute as an "intolerable" invasion of privacy in an "individual's personal life," he is not making privacy a right of individuals; instead he is assuming that all individuals will marry. He summarizes his position as follows:

> In sum, even though the State has determined that the use of contraceptives is as iniquitous as any act of extra-marital sexual immorality, the intrusion of the whole machinery of the criminal law into the very heart of marital privacy, requiring husband and wife to render account before a criminal tribunal of their uses of that intimacy, is surely a very different thing indeed from punishing those who establish intimacies which the law has always forbidden and which can have no claim to social protection. (553)

By transferring the issue of the morality of the Connecticut statute itself to the constitutionality of its enforcement, Harlan granted tremendous moral autonomy to the married *couple*. Arguing that "the secular state is not an examiner of consciences: it must operate in the realm of behavior, of overt actions, and where it does so operate, not only the underlying, moral purpose of its operations, but also the *choice of means* becomes relevant to any Constitutional judgment on what is done" (547), Harlan differentiates between married couples and non-married adults. The state is not an examiner of married persons' consciences, according to his formulation, but a perfectly justified examiner of the unmarried adult. Admitting that birth control is "iniquitous," he nevertheless exempts married couples from the enforcement of a moral law because "the intimacy of husband and wife is necessarily an essential and accepted feature of the institution of marriage, an institution which the State not only must allow, but which always and in every age it has fostered and protected" (553). In order to rationalize the exceptional privacy of the marital couple, Harlan makes state regulation of marital sexuality appear an aberration from the protection it has received "always and in every age." Like Douglas, Harlan appeals to a timeless conception of marriage that stands outside of the law. However, unlike Douglas, Harlan stresses that *only* marriage sanctions adult moral autonomy; the state will enforce morality in cases involving adults who are not married. Moral autonomy can only be achieved by entering into heterosexual marriage; without this relationship, the citizen remains a ward of the state.

The structuring of a right within marriage and the nuclear family—the family that can be housed in the "zone" of privacy created in *Griswold* with its protection in mind—turns out to have been short-lived. The "marital privacy" in *Poe v. Ullman* and *Griswold v. Connecticut* marked a departure from Brandeis and Warren's concept, which situated privacy in the domestic circle but nevertheless defined it as a proprietary interest in the family name. The couple form of *Griswold* marked an initial departure from the patriarchal privacy of Brandeis and Warren since granting the couple's autonomy implicitly removed the patriarch's absolute authority over the "zone of the home." That is, the patriarch was no longer the only individual with privacy rights within the private space. By 1972 the birth control challenges out of which the Court "found" the constitutional right to privacy forced recognition of competing privacies: husband's and wife's. Reasoning in *Eisenstadt v. Baird* (1972) that the marital couple was not "an independent entity with a heart and mind of its own but an association of two individuals each with separate intellectual and emotional makeup" (452), the Court refocused on the individual members of the "association" called marriage. What individualized the right to privacy, then, was the discovery of the wife's autonomy from her husband. And when women gained a right to privacy independent from their husbands' in *Roe v. Wade*, the notion of familial privacy was completely undone.[36]

Confessional poetry presents family membership from the perspective of individuals with conflicting needs of privacy and self-disclosure. Unlike the individual right to privacy in which withdrawal from scrutiny produces autonomy, the conflict between different family members' privacies places withdrawal and autonomy at odds, revealing a number of paradoxes in a relationship-based notion of privacy. In conceiving himself as a member of a family, Lowell realized that withdrawal would not create autonomy because withdrawal collapses all privacies into one. Emphasizing one's family membership—seeing oneself in relation to another—paradoxically entails subjecting that relationship to scrutiny; permitting the "other" his/her privacy subordinates both individuals to the family unit. Putting the privacy interests of different family members in conflict explodes the unit, releasing the writer from the group identity of the proper name, but at the cost of violating an intimate's control over self-disclosure.

If Hardwick achieves her autonomy from the marital "we" in Lowell's coarticulation of her voice, exactly what kind of voice does she have? Lowell negotiated the conflicting demands of privacy in marriage and divorce by partitioning the domains of their voices. From his early appropriation of her voice, situated in the bedroom in *Life Studies*, to the later inclusion of her letters, Hardwick had become for Lowell the voice of privacy itself.[37] Through the sonnets composed of Lizzie's words, Lowell was able to explore the domestic circle not simply by writing of it but by letting it appear to write itself, simulating the "real" presence of intimate others, separate yet integral voices in his autobiography. Because Lowell quite literally allows the reader to eavesdrop on a private conversation, the reader of the poetry seems to glimpse a purely private person, unguarded and unmasked.

Hardwick's own words are far more exposing than any of Lowell's could be because the poetic shaping, though present in the fourteen-line stanzas, does not eliminate the "documenting" of Hardwick's presence. Critics have defended the use of the letters by saying that Hardwick is a literary creation and that her exposure is mitigated by the transformation of her letters into blank verse sonnets. That is, we can easily see Lowell's artifice because Hardwick could hardly have written letters in iambic pentameter. This argument unravels, however, when we examine the revisions that Lowell made to the poems.[38] For example, most likely to temper the fury of the first "letter poem"—"Voices" from "Hospital II"—Lowell changed the following line: "your clowning makes us want to vomit— you bore / bore, bore the friends who want to save your image" to "your clowning makes visitors want to call a taxi, / you tease the patients as if they were your friends."[39] Hardwick's original version, or at the very least less doctored version, is iambic. Apparently, judging from the progress of the drafts, in rewriting the letter poem Lowell fractures the iambs of the earliest version, which makes it sound *less* like a poem. Lowell's revision makes Lizzie's letter sound more like a letter and less like a poem, which is to say to make it more, rather than less, revealing of her.

Using the letter as confession, precisely because it is *not* lyric in origin, allows the reader to hear the real Hardwick, and the desperation of Hardwick's pleading confirms that impression. This creation of the real Hardwick reanimated the confessional poem, which depends upon the reader's sense of what David Gewanter calls a "crushing" disclosure. Content alone does not produce the crushing disclosure. In fact, there are no "crushing disclosures" (197). Lowell constantly refers to the banality of the subject matter, what he calls at one point the "common novel plot." Given the ordinariness of the content, Lowell can no longer depend on revelation to secure the impression of "the *real* Robert Lowell," which is a vital component of his first confessional poetry in *Life Studies*. Nevertheless, he understands that a confessional poem depends upon a kind of violation, a crossing of the line, which is why the letters are so crucial to the confessionalism of *The Dolphin*.

Lowell now transgresses privacy by *triangulating* it—setting the speaker and listener of private utterance before a witness, or a witnessing public. The confessional poem, precisely because it is highly aware of audience, does not convey the sense of intimacy that the letter does. Lowell etches clear boundaries between public and private in *The Dolphin* by making confession depend on the context of reading rather than the nature of content. This is the truly brilliant, and chilling, insight of *The Dolphin*. As private life has come to occupy the center of public discourse, all private revelations flirt with banality. Maintaining the shock of revelation becomes increasingly difficult, but not impossible. There is no consensus about what belongs in which sphere, so to secure the violation, the transgression of revelation, there must be a visible act of witnessing. Hardwick confesses her anguish to Lowell, and we watch. This triangulation is remarkably similar to the innovations in the talk-show format today. It is no longer sufficient to simply tell your shocking story because there are no shocking stories. You must tell your story to an intimate in front of an audience. The witness's shock becomes the audience's gauge of transgression. As in Lowell's *Dolphin*, there is nothing that is by definition private; there is only the context in which we can imagine a secret being told. Even though the content of privacy has been emptied out, this does not mean that privacy has disappeared, only that the ways in which we recognize it have been transformed.

Had Lowell offered Hardwick a truly collaborative opportunity, meaning had she had some choice about whether or not to publish her letters as poems, he might have accomplished the revolutionary work Gewanter imagines: two voices narrating one autobiography. At the same time, permitting her an intentional collaboration, a response that would have acknowledged an audience other than Lowell (which she would almost certainly have refused), Lowell would have lost the wages of his innovation: his control over the boundaries of public and private. His project represents the possibility of dual collaboration in autobiography as a strategy for writing the self in relation. But Lowell used the absolute "privateness" of Hardwick's coerced collaboration to secure the publicness of his own voice.

In many ways *The Dolphin* is the essential companion to *Life Studies* if we want to understand what happened to privacy during this period of intense reflection. The year 1973 marks the end of the cold war's first great obsession with privacy. From *Life Studies*'s mirroring the demise of aristocratic privacy, to *The Dolphin*'s revitalizing confession through the triangulation of exposure, we find that Lowell is caught in a web—or net, to use a prominent *Dolphin* metaphor—of his own making. Lowell seems to have thought that he could give his privacy away without actually losing it. Or to put it another way, he imagined that he could give away his privacy without losing the publicness of his voice. *The Dolphin* shows both the violence that accompanies an attempt to reacquire the order of the two realms and the person on whom that violence falls.

THREE

Penetrating Privacy

Confessional Poetry, *Griswold v. Connecticut*,

and Containment Ideology

> The notion that confessional poetry is solipsistic is so ingrained that
> the phrase "confessional solipsism" is like the phrase
> "communist aggression": you never see the first word without the second.
> —James E. B. Breslin, *From Modern to Contemporary*

Robert Lowell's *Life Studies* can be read as an anatomy or, rather, an autopsy, of the "hierarchies of privacy" that began to break down at the end of the 1950s. *Life Studies*, which Lowell situated on the cusp between generations, ushered in a new dialogue about privacy by signaling the inadequacy of traditional social and literary forms to new social conditions. One of the ways that critics have figured this transformation of forms of self-disclosure in the lyric is through the metaphor of the house. Richard Wilbur, whose work often stands in literary histories as the foil to confessional poetry, preferred to think of lyric poems as windows that offered a "partial vision of the world." Wilbur argued that when a poet misunderstood the architecture of the lyric poem, that is, mistook the window for a door, "the artist no longer perceives a wall between him and world; the world becomes an extension of himself and is deprived of its reality. . . . This is bad aesthetics . . . and incidentally, bad morals" (as quoted by Mark Doty in "The 'Forbidden Planet' " 136). Mark Doty takes this metaphor one step further to suggest the innovation of confessional poetry: "a generation of poets would then find it necessary not only to open the windows but to break them, to widen them into doors, and the result would be a revisioning of the entire house" (137).

Enlarging the points of entry into the house meant opening the lyric form to provide greater access to intimate material, a more intense, familiar, and as Allen Grossman suggests in *The Sighted Singer* (1992), familial idiom for American poetry (33). The home is considerably more than a structure or a piece of property; it is instead a central political and formal metaphor of what it means to be private, the most common metaphor of privacy in the cold war.

Of course, Lowell's relationship to this metaphor is necessarily different from the confessional poets who followed his lead in amplifying the intense intimacy of the postwar lyric. That is, when the poets Sylvia Plath and Anne Sexton took up Lowell's confessional project, the confession itself was bound to change. Sexton and Plath did not share Lowell's special relationship to the codes of self-disclosure associated with upper-class gentlemen. Their interest in privacy was not as an individual negotiating the difficult inheritance of a proper name but as one of a type, a category of person for whom the home signified the space of identity. Sexton and Plath were supremely interested in houses because they were, as Sexton quips in "Housewife," married to them. Replacing Lowell's aristocratic notion of the "House of Lowell"—the property that is family name—is a middle-class, suburban vision (Lowell reminds us that "in 1924 people still lived in cities," which suggests that by 1959 they did not) of the private home and the nuclear family. When we turn to Plath and Sexton, we are plopped down into the very flux of middle-class life, out of which new norms of privacy were being calculated and appraised.

Sexton and Plath are more useful in taking stock of this shift precisely because the changing notions of privacy diminished the importance of both property and privacy's anchor in *upper*-class distinction.[1] As we have seen, the privacy debate of the early 1960s registered the suffusion of everyday life with surveillance. Supreme Court justices and confessional poets, sociologists and journalists seemed equally apprehensive about the threat of this penetration, its ability to transform the boundaries of public and private life as well as the meaning of self-disclosure and reticence. At the same time and in direct proportion to this growing awareness of surveillance, a right to privacy was vehemently affirmed as necessary to combat the technological and organizational intrusions of modern life. As I have shown, by tracing the intersections of Lowell's *Life Studies* and William Prosser's study of the tort privacy, the controversy remained between citizens and how intimately they might view or disclose themselves to one another. As the decade progressed, however, the anxieties about privacy swung dramatically toward limiting surveillance, in particular police and administrative surveillance, rather than media scrutiny. Confessional poetry and constitutional law provide access to a particular shift in American notions of privacy from a nineteenth-century gentlemen's right toward a middle-class and increasingly feminized notion of personal privacy and rights to self-disclosure.

Perhaps no one has explained the cold war investment in the home better than Elaine Tyler May, who was among the first scholars to extend the containment metaphor to American domestic life and its rigid gender arrangements. In *Homeward Bound* (1988), May has argued that cold war insecurity in the domain of foreign policy shaped the patterns of marriage and childbearing that were so peculiar to the 1950s. Because of the vulnerability that Americans felt in response to the atom bomb and the fears of communist infiltration, the home became a symbolic bunker into which the individual and the family retreated to secure a measure of control over their lives. As May explains, the home became increasingly figured as *the* locus of freedom, *the* privileged American space to defend from the fallout of potentially catastrophic international conflict. May takes as her paradigmatic example the 1959 "kitchen debates" between Nixon and Khruschev in which the world leaders squared off on the relative merits of washing machines and domestic appliances. The United States would win the cold war, it was argued, because it produced the most satisfying home life. Paradoxically, however, as the home moved into a central position in American political rhetoric, it achieved a vital political and symbolic significance insofar as it was imagined to exist entirely outside the realm of politics.[2]

This is the cold war paradox of privacy out of which the confessional poets and the Supreme Court confronted changing norms of self-disclosure and shifting limits of state intervention in private life. *Griswold v. Connecticut*, the 1965 case that first guaranteed a constitutional right to privacy in the "zone" of the home, takes its shape from this paradox. We should see *Griswold* as grounded in antitotalitarianism, an investment in normative domesticity, and in the period's emblematic confusion of the two. Similarly, the confessional poetry of women such as Anne Sexton, Sylvia Plath, and Adrienne Rich can also be viewed in tension with antitotalitarianism and the domestic ideology of the containment project. We have more readily understood the late 1950s confessionalism of writers such as Allen Ginsberg ("Howl") and Norman Mailer (*Advertisements for Myself*) as part of their resistance to conformity, routinely marked as the harbinger of domestic totalitarianism. And even though—perhaps because—the trespass of private and public boundaries has been the signature trope of women's writing (as defined in the canon of women's literature assembled in the 1970s and 1980s), we have been almost completely unable to grant Plath and Sexton a similar historical vantage point. However, their treatment of the cold war's most symbolically charged private space, the home, consistently identifies the incoherent aesthetics and ideological investments in privacy of the period. Sexton, Plath, and Rich undermined the assumptions about the privacy of the home, its sanctuary from surveillance, and its nourishment of individual autonomy—that is, the foundations of the cold war discourse on privacy. Since the home of containment ideology was principally a metaphor and a contradiction, a figure for conformity as well as for libertarian individuality, exposing the metaphor of the ideal home as the fantasy that it was meant undermining a cherished ideological bulwark against totalitarianism.[3]

Defining the private home as the crucible of democratic citizenship—the symbol and locus of the liberty offered to the citizen of a pluralistic democracy—seemed simultaneously to deny it a place in public discourse as anything but an ideal. Likewise, elevating domesticity to a sacred and quintessentially American virtue silenced the experience of women, the citizens who were to occupy this realm as their exclusive domain. In this context, women confessional poets wrote at the crossroads of the politicization, silencing, and surveillance of domestic life. As they well understood, in order to enter the public sphere women writers had to violate privacy and confront the myths of the private home as a source of liberty and even, ironically, of privacy itself. Writing from within the home about the home, these poets not only changed literary decorum, they also transformed a central political metaphor, legitimizing the discussion of what went on inside the home and making that discussion a reasonable concern of public discourse. In keeping with the 1960s' radical questioning of American at-home authority and ideology, women poets such as Plath, Rich, and Sexton provided evidence that the threat was no longer just "out there," it was also "in here," and its very containment was making the home unfit for its political purpose. Confessional poetry's contribution to public discourse was dismantling domestic ideology through the act of exposure itself, through the self-disclosure of that which should have been the subject of surveillance.

In his dissent from *Osborn v. U.S., Lewis v. U.S.,* and *Hoffa v. U.S.* (1966), Justice William O. Douglas, author of the constitutional right to privacy named in *Griswold v. Connecticut,* provided a succinct and dramatic retrospective of the assaults on privacy that had provoked widespread concern during the first half of the 1960s. This trio of cases, all of which revolved around the limits of law enforcement to monitor suspects,[4] provided Douglas with an occasion to enumerate the dangers of a surveillance society. Never one to pass up an opportunity for rhetorical drama, he declared:

> We are rapidly entering the age of no privacy, where everyone is open to surveillance at all times; where there are no secrets from government. The aggressive breaches of privacy by the Government increase by geometric proportions. (323)

He then sketched a harrowing portrait of the "age of no privacy" by citing examples culled from the Senate Committee on the Judiciary's 1965 hearings on "Invasions of Privacy":

> Secret observation booths in government offices and closed television circuits in industry, extending even to rest rooms, are common. Offices, conference rooms, hotel rooms, and even bedrooms . . . are "bugged" for the convenience of government. Peepholes in men's rooms are there to catch homosexuals. . . . Personality tests seek to ferret out a man's innermost thoughts on family life, religion, racial attitudes, national origin, politics, atheism, ideology, sex, and the like. Federal agents are often "wired." . . . They have broken and entered homes to obtain evidence. Polygraph tests of government employees and of employees in industry are rampant. The dossiers on all citizens mount in number and increase in size. Now they are being put on computers so that by pressing one button all the miserable, the sick, the suspect, the unpopular, the offbeat people of the Nation can be instantly identified. These examples and many others demonstrate an alarming trend whereby the privacy and dignity of our citizens is being whittled away by sometimes imperceptible steps. Taken individually, each step may be of little consequence. But when viewed as a whole, there begins to emerge a society quite unlike any we have seen— a society in which government may intrude into the secret regions of a man's life at will. (323–24)

While I have not fully transcribed Douglas's record of invasions, I quote him at some length because his dissent, as wide-reaching as it is well-documented, reproduces the most striking rhetorical feature of the popular literature on the death of privacy that sold millions of copies during the first years of the decade: their exhaustive catalogues.[5] Battered by example after example of the intrusiveness of modern life—Douglas indicts primarily government (local law enforcement, the FBI, federal bureaucracies) but also big business, educational institutions, and new technology (computers)—the reader quickly surmises that there is no space to retreat from the inquisitive eye of the state and the market. In the context of this encyclopedia of surveillance, the right to privacy, which one judge had dubbed a "sizable hunk of liberty" (*On Lee v. U.S.* 315) seemed to have shrunk to the merest sliver.

The interpretation that Douglas placed on the government's dossier system, which could identify "all the miserable, the sick, the suspect, the unpopular, the offbeat people of the Nation," indicates that rather more than crime control was perceived as motivating this immense project of governmental surveillance. Justice Douglas, more than any of his colleagues on the Warren Court, was articulating a broad right to privacy under the logic and persuasive force of antitotalitarianism. Beginning in 1958 with his lectures to Franklin and Marshall Law School, Douglas had been working out the rationale and even the language that would form the basis of the right to privacy in *Griswold* in 1965. In this address, Douglas characterizes privacy as the "right to keep the officers of the law out of one's bedroom" (*The Right of the People* 149), a formulation that would be less surprising had any of the birth control cases in which the right to privacy was developed reached the Supreme Court when Douglas imagined it in 1958. So when Douglas asks in *Griswold*: "Would we allow the police to search the sacred precincts of marital bedrooms for telltale signs of the use of contraceptives?" (485), he echoes his earlier imagined invasion from *Poe v. Ullman*, a precursor case to *Griswold* from 1960: "If we imagine a regime of full enforcement of the law in the manner of an Anthony Comstock, we would reach the point where search warrants issued and officers appeared in bedrooms to find out what went on" (651).

It is not simply that Douglas is advancing the logic of antitotalitarianism but that this image of policemen in bedrooms moves from dissent to majority, as the overwrought fantasy of 1958 became increasingly plausible. Slowly the Court was convinced that this invasion was indeed a legitimate and urgent threat to American democracy. More than the legal histories of the American right to privacy have recognized, the Court perceived the Connecticut statute legitimating the surveillance of the bedroom to be more threatening in the context of a heightened awareness of the invasions of privacy.

We can see the strange fork in privacy law in Norman Redlich's "Are There 'Certain Rights . . . Retained By the People'?" published in the *New York University Law Review* in 1962. This article, which was to prove enormously important to the defendants in *Griswold*, predicted the development of a "new right" essential to 1960s America: the right to privacy. Redlich argues that this right was *not* emerging in cases of police surveillance but instead in the cases brought in Connecticut over the state's prohibition on the use of birth control. Echoing (perhaps unintentionally) Brandeis and Warren's 1890 call for "new rights" to meet the exigencies of modern society, Redlich asserts outright that the existing Bill of Rights was no longer adequate to protecting human dignity and liberty. We were reaching, yet again, a new threshold in privacy, a renewed sense that the instruments and organization of modern life posed problems that were unprecedented and required a blueprint for new standards of privacy.

What happens to the right to privacy, however, when we situate *Griswold* in the extreme anxiety about massive organized surveillance that marked the early 1960s? The awareness of the manifold invasions on privacy, which I have outlined at some length in chapter 1, represents, on one hand, the undoing of the cold war's ideology of containment. Very simply, the Court balked at the state's growing police power and began to subject it to a heightened level of scrutiny. On the other hand, it is vital to recognize that the ideology of containment was also reinforced by the *Griswold* decision. In other words, the constitutional right to privacy represents a paradox: it both refused the logic of containment, which justified the intrusion into private life to protect that same privacy, and extended its logic by resting the right to privacy on the exceptional idealization of the home. This chapter will track these two different problems: the growing recognition of surveillance of private life and the central importance of normative domesticity in securing relief from surveillance. The echoing and crossing between the poets' and the court's meditations on the changing nature of privacy reveal the complex and paradoxical nature of containment as a political substructure of American notions of privacy.

Sylvia Plath, a poet who is rarely considered political, registers the pervasiveness of surveillance in ordinary life and links it to a transformation of confession. The following poems written in 1962, for example, "The Other," "Words Heard, by Accident, over the Phone," "The Detective," "The Courage of Shutting-Up," "A Secret," "The Jailer," "Purdah," and "Eavesdropper," some of which were marked for inclusion in the *Ariel* collection, illustrate Plath's extraordinary sensitivity to surveillance and the assault on privacy.[6] In these works, metaphors of policing, interrogation, and spying permeate her poems, transforming the home into a crime scene, and so a subject of surveillance. Plath's poem, "The Other," reveals the overdetermination of guilt that results from surveillance:

> The police love you, you confess everything.
> Bright hair, shoe black, old plastic,
>
> Is my life so intriguing?
> Is it for this you widen your eye-rings? (*Collected Poems* 201)

There may be no crime to confess to ("Is it for this you widen your eye-rings?"), but it does not matter; everything—"bright hair, shoe black, old plastic"—constitutes evidence of a crime, everything contributes to the confession. When surveillance is never identified, the observer always controls the questions. The watched have no idea to what they might be confessing because they have no idea of what they are suspected. Plath shows how omnipresent surveillance takes interpretation further out of the hands of the observed when she quickly shifts position from criminal to investigator, from confessor to interpreter. As if making an arrest, she begins her interrogation:

> Open your handbag. What is that bad smell?
> It is your knitting, busily
>
> Hooking itself to itself,
> It is your sticky candies. (201)

From the evidence she collects, again, "sticky candies" are as innocuous as "old plastic," Plath supplies her own answers, offering the interpretation that should be supplied by the silent defendant. Because both the questions and the answers are supplied to the confessor, the interpretation of the watchers is all that matters. Everything becomes a confessional object or statement because possessions begin to speak for their owners. Therefore, you can be confessing even while attempting to maintain your silence.

Plath's analysis bears an uncanny similarity to that which the Court used to explain the relationship between an invasion of privacy and a coercion of confession. Two cases that were decided on the same day in 1960—*Mapp v. Ohio* and *Poe v. Ullman*—suggest the lines of force that came together in *Griswold*. *Poe* we will return to a bit later. *Mapp* is a case in which policemen carried out an extensive and undefined search of a woman's home that went far beyond the express scope of the warrant. Clearly searching for anything incriminating, the police eventually found pornography and arrested the defendant on obscenity charges. In deciding that the police had overstepped the limits of their authority to penetrate the private space of a home, the Supreme Court extended to the states the "exclusionary rule," which dictates that evidence obtained by the police in violation of the Fourth Amendment would be inadmissible in court. In 1914, in *Weeks v. U.S.*,[7] the Court had declared that federal courts would have to abide by this rule. In *Mapp*, the Court overruled itself, that is violated stare decisis (the orderly following of precedent), by overturning *Wolf v. Colorado*, in which the Court had refused to extend the exclusionary rule to the states in 1949. The Court decided, as we shall see, that the violation of the Fourth Amendment in *Mapp* constituted a violation of privacy by coercing confession.

What we see in juxtaposing *Mapp* and Plath's poetry is how widely the invasion of privacy was taken to constitute a coercion of confession. In *Mapp* the Court gave a stout defense of privacy as a "basic constitutional right" (which it was not):

> Indeed, we are aware of no restraint, similar to that rejected today, conditioning the enforcement of any other basic constitutional right. The right to privacy, no less important than any other right carefully and particularly reserved to the people, would stand in marked contrast to all other rights declared as "basic to a free society" (*Wolf v. Colorado*). This court has not hesitated to enforce as strictly against the States as it does against the Federal Government the rights of free speech and of a free press, the rights to notice and to a fair, public trial, including, as it does, the right not to be convicted by use of a coerced confession, however logically relevant it be, and without regard to its reliability. . . . And nothing could be more certain than that when a coerced

confession is involved, "the relevant rules of evidence" are overridden without regard to the "incidence of such conduct by the police," slight or infrequent. Why should not the same rule apply to what is tantamount to coerced testimony by way of unconstitutional seizure of goods, papers, effects, documents, etc.? (656)

Why did the court change its mind eleven years after *Wolf*? Justice Hugo Black, whose interpretation of the constitution often led to the restriction of judicial review, concurred in *Mapp* because "reflection on the problem . . . in light of the cases coming before the Court since *Wolf*, has led me to conclude that when the Fourth Amendment's ban against unreasonable searches and seizures is considered together with the Fifth Amendment's ban against compelled self-incrimination, a constitutional basis emerges which not only justifies but actually requires the exclusionary rule" (662). The flood of privacy violations, in other words, protested in the courts, had eroded the Court's reluctance to extend the rule in *Wolf*. The manifest increase in abuses by law enforcement, some of which were associated with cases of compelled confession during the HUAC hearings, had necessitated a reconsideration of an important court doctrine.[8] Black, shocked by the pumping of a suspect's stomach in *Rochin v. California* (1952)[9], had concluded that modern police tactics had come too close to "the rack and the screw."

In Plath's "Eavesdropper" official surveillance becomes increasingly detached from a central source and parceled out to proxies. A primary feature of surveillance, she suggests, is its contagion and its ability to generate itself in a vacuum. Absence itself, as we know from the FBI search for subversives, does not end surveillance but justifies its intensification.[10] In this poem in which neighbors spy on one another, the confessional poem becomes a hall of mirrors in which the watcher and the watched cannot be distinguished from each other:

Do not think I don't notice your curtain—
Midnight, four o'clock,
Lit (you are reading),
Tarting with the drafts that pass,
Little whore tongue,
Chenille beckoner,
Beckoning my words in—

The zoo yowl, the mad soft
Mirror talk you love to catch me at.

How you jumped when I jumped on *you*!
Arms folded, ear cocked,
Toad-yellow under the drop
That would not, would not drop
In a desert of cow people
Trundling their udders home
To the electric milker, the wifey, the big blue eye
That watches, like God, or the sky
The ciphers that watch it. (*Collected Poems* 260–61)

As she watches "you" reading, the reader watches her in the "mad soft / mirror talk you love to catch me at." Not only is Plath caught looking at herself, this "mirror talk" is what she reads—the words of her confessional poems. "How you jumped when I jumped on *you*!" reverses the watcher and the watched again. Plath watches her rival, her "sister-bitch," watch herself in her [Plath's] writing, creating an endless series of reflections in which each regards the self watching the other. This mirrored watching allows each to keep the other and the self in view, all the while policing the self while appearing to police the other. Moreover, this mutual regard, this double scrutiny, takes place beneath another all watching force: "the big blue eye / that watches, like God, or the sky / the ciphers that watch it." Beyond their personal surveillance, a larger investigation is taking place, one that, "like God or the sky," is simply inescapable. And yet, once again, the doubling redoubles as the watcher—blue eye, God, or sky— watches the "ciphers" watch it. By using the word "cipher"—which can encode meaning or indicate its absence—Plath suggests both the riddles of their behavior and its meaninglessness. This endless watching ultimately becomes exposed as a futile and paralyzing process for it only reveals more surveillance.

Though it vaguely connects to some all-watching god, some larger eye that watches, the surveillance Plath dissects is not always directed from one authoritative gaze (the police) but is often atomized, diffuse, generalized, and informal. Tracking the mobility of the surveying gaze suggests one of the important features of the cold war debate over privacy: its perpetual relocation. The cold war gave a particular trajectory to anxieties about privacy—that is, the eradication of privacy would lead to totalitarian domination—but it did not alone create the new ambiguities in the concept. Instead, it intensified these ambiguities. The pervasive sense of surveillance produced by the fear of communism—and, ironically, the fear of anticommunism—reverberated in the mass-production of privacy in the postwar suburban expansion. The suburban home was supposed to offer the opportunity to live out the democratic dream of privacy in postwar America. And yet, at the same time, true to the paradox of postwar privacy, suburban homes in the earliest and most influential accounts of suburban life were associated with a profound *deprivation* of privacy as well.[11]

I take William Whyte's *Organization Man* (1956) and Betty Friedan's *Feminine Mystique* (1963) as my examples because their analyses of middle-class life have become the conventional wisdom of the period.[12] Perhaps no two writers' accounts of suburban life were more widely read or more influential for later scholars than these two. In one sense, with respect to privacy, Whyte and Friedan have very similar perceptions. Whyte describes in some detail the changing culture of privacy in Park Forest, Illinois:

> On the matter of privacy, suburbanites have mixed feelings. Fact one, of course, is that there isn't much privacy. In most small towns there is at least enough living room to soften the shock of intimate contact, and, besides, there is usually some redoubt to which the individual can withdraw. In Park Forest not even the apartment is a redoubt; people don't bother to knock and they come and go furiously. The lack of privacy, furthermore, is retroactive. "They ask you all sorts of questions about what you *were* doing," one resident puts it. "Who was it that stopped in last night? Who were those people from Chicago last week? You're never alone, even when you think you are."

> Less is sacred. "It's wonderful," says one young wife. "You find yourself discussing all your personal problems with your neighbors—things that back in South Dakota we would have kept to ourselves." As time goes on, this capacity for self-revelation grows; and on the most intimate details of family life, court people become amazingly frank with one another. No one, they point out, ever need face a problem alone.

> In the battle against loneliness even the architecture becomes functional. Just as doors inside houses—which are sometimes said to have marked the birth

of the middle class—are disappearing, so are the barriers against neighbors. The picture in the picture window, for example, is what is going on *inside*— or, what is going on inside other people's picture windows . . .

Even the most outgoing, of course, confess that the pace of court life occasionally wears them down, and once in a while they reach such a point of rebellion they don't answer the phone. Such a purely negative response, however, is not enough. To gain privacy, one has to *do* something. One court resident, for example, moves his chair to the front rather than the court side of his apartment to show he doesn't want to be disturbed . . .

But there is an important corollary of such efforts at privacy—*people feel a little guilty about making them*. Except very occasionally, to shut oneself off from others like this is regarded as either a childish prank or, more likely, an indication of some inner neurosis . . .

Privacy has become clandestine. Not in solitary and selfish contemplation but in doing things with other people does one fulfill oneself. (*Organization Man,* 389–90)

Whyte's insights here are quite remarkable. The deprivation of privacy rapidly erodes conventional markers of public and private, quickly transforming standards of self-disclosure. And as these standards change, the choice to remain private becomes increasingly suspect. Privacy is "clandestine." Self-disclosure is, therefore, perpetually coerced because it has become the default mode of social interaction. Withdrawing oneself into a private space, removing oneself from social congress, has become an antisocial act that provokes suspicion. Privacy is not, therefore, the site from which one enters public life but a space that must be actively and surreptitiously procured.

While Whyte treats all suburbanites as equally subject to the loss of privacy in the suburbs, Friedan understands that these physical and communal structures have a particularly profound impact on women who spend the majority of their time in them. For Friedan, a diffuse sense of surveillance was built into the structure of the new suburban homes themselves through the design of "open space," which did away with doors and windows, maximizing the sense of space but minimizing the opportunity for privacy. Friedan diagnosed the results of

such a loss of privacy when she associated the open plan in contemporary houses with the problem of the "feminine mystique." As she said in 1963, the open
plan forced woman "to live the feminine mystique. . . . There are no true walls
or doors . . . she need never feel alone for a minute, need never be by herself. She
can forget her own identity in these noisy open-plan houses" (246).

In other words, the suburban home, while marketed as a source of privacy
and upheld in cold war political rhetoric as the acme of American democratic
self-governance, was in fact defined by surveillance, especially though not exclusively for women. For Anne Sexton, like most women of her generation, the
home was not a private place at all. However, because it offered little opportunity for adult communication, for public or political discourse, it was not really
public in any significant way just as it was not private in any meaningful way.
We can see this paradox of mass-produced privacy in Sexton's "Self in 1958," a
poem written in 1958 and revised in 1965:

What is reality?
I am a plaster doll; I pose
with eyes that cut open without landfall or nightfall
upon some shellacked and grinning person,
eyes that open, blue, steel, and close.
Am I approximately an I. Magnin transplant?
I have hair, black angel,
black-angel-stuffing to comb,
nylon legs, luminous arms
and some advertised clothes.

I live in a doll's house
with four chairs,
a counterfeit table, a flat roof
and a big front door.
Many have come to such a small crossroad.
There is an iron bed,
(Life enlarges, life takes aim)
a cardboard floor,
windows that flash open on someone's city,
and little more.

Someone plays with me,
plants me in the all-electric kitchen,
Is this what Mrs. Rombauer said?
Someone pretends with me—
I am walled in solid by their noise—
or puts me upon their straight bed.
They think I am me!
Their warmth? Their warmth is not a friend!
They pry my mouth for their cups of gin
and their stale bread.

What is reality
to this synthetic doll
who should smile, who should shift gears,
should spring the doors open in a wholesome disorder,
and have no evidence of ruin or fears?
But I would cry,
rooted to the wall that
was once my mother,
if I could remember how
and if I had the tears. (*Complete Poems* 155–56)

The second stanza of the poem describes the suburban structure that underlies so much of Sexton's work: "I live in a doll's house / with four chairs, / a counterfeit table, a flat roof / and a big front door. / Many have come to such a small crossroad." For Sexton, it was the inevitable predicament of this doll in the doll's house to live a paradox—to dwell entirely within the walls of the home, which, though completely divorced from the public, is neither private nor individual. Although no reference to a "doll's house" can fail to recall Ibsen's Nora and her dramatic exit, in Sexton's poem the speaker seems immobilized, caught in the crosshairs of an oppression ("life takes aim") so generalized as to defy naming. The feeling of being a watched target extends beyond the threshold of her home so that, unlike Nora, she cannot simply close the door behind her to escape. If "*life* takes aim," there is no outside to escape to nor inside to hide within; there is only an overpowering sense that every action is monitored and that a wrong move will be violently suppressed. From her position trapped in her doll's house, "windows . . . flash open on someone's city / and little more," offering no more than a glimpse of "someone's city"—a public world so far removed from her own life that she cannot even name it. Even so, this unknown city is the only view from her window.

This correlation between the physical architecture of the house—its absence of personal privacy—and the psychic structure of women—their loss of personal identity—governs confessional poetry as well. The loss of personal identity, which derived from a loss of privacy, gave birth to an autobiographical mode of writing that appeared to construct the personality of the poet obsessively while eschewing any notion of privacy. Compounding the lack of privacy within, the scrutiny of the home from without further dissolved the binary between public and private, obscuring the line between voluntary self-disclosure and forced confession. The open door of Sexton's last stanza symbolizes the suburban mandate to be open, which is the most effective surveillance of the home because the housewife who made an exhibition of her openness policed herself. What is demanded by Sexton's unnamed observer is clear: "What is reality / to this synthetic doll / who should smile, who should shift gears, / should spring the doors open in a wholesome disorder / and have no evidence of ruin or fears?" Sexton implies that "they" demand a fiction of openness, which exposes a pretense of health; she is permitted some "disorder" only so long as it is "wholesome." Most important, the openness conveys that there is nothing to hide, which is all the more oppressive for it necessitates a willingness to be observed. In these terms confessional poetry would seem to be the open door, and as such, a submission to surveillance through self-exposure.

Nevertheless, Sexton turns this openness inside out and instead uses it as her most effective disguise. On the one hand, her "disorders" are never "wholesome" and so she defies the unstated agreement to reveal only that which is not secret. On the other, the fiction of openness is always misread as the transparent fact of openness. The confession that appears to "tell all" hides all the more effectively for telling only some, and so renders a paradoxical privacy. As a result Sexton can appear to comply with the imperative to be open—all the while subverting it—by taking advantage of one of confessional poetry's defining tropes: the fiction of sincerity. Sexton's ironically triumphant exclamation, "They think I am me!" attests to the success of this impersonation, which is nothing more than playing herself seamlessly. Instead of claiming another role, Sexton consistently acknowledges that she herself is the role, and that therefore she has no authentic self to reveal. However, while she clearly deceives "them," the fiction of sincerity begins to erode her sense of reality. When she asks, "What is reality to this synthetic doll . . . ?" she suggests that the complete erasure of privacy does away with truth as a component of confession; the confessor not only does not tell the truth, she can no longer distinguish what that truth might be.

The poem, "Live," in which Sexton responds directly to criticism of her confessional work, addresses the limitations of the fiction of sincerity. The second stanza reads:

Even so,
I kept right on going on,
a sort of human statement,
lugging myself as if
I were a sawed-off body
in the trunk, the steamer trunk.
This became a perjury of the soul.
It became an outright lie
and even though I dressed the body
it was still naked, still killed.
It was caught
in the first place at birth,
like a fish.
But I played it, dressed it up,
dressed it up like somebody's doll.
Is life something you play?
And all the time wanting to get rid of it?
And further, everyone yelling at you
to shut up. And no wonder!
People don't like to be told
that you're sick
and then be forced
to watch
you
come
down with the hammer. (*The Complete Poems* 167–68; emphasis mine)

For Sexton, nakedness is also a disguise, one among the many that she employed to create the "perjury of the soul" that is her confession. Yet, her lament that "even though [she] dressed the body / it was still naked, still killed," attests to the power of the confessional label that makes every costume appear "naked"— that is, transparent, literal, real—and so "killed," that is, metaphorically dead and dead to metaphor. Regardless of the fact that she describes her work as a "perjury" and an "outright lie," the consistent reading of her work as pure confession denied it a metaphorical status, which is to say the status of poetry. Rather than giving in to "everyone yelling at you to / shut up" in the belief that they are reading a confession rather than a poem, Sexton attempts to shift her "human statement" from confession, implying guilt, to testimony implying witness.

This idea of witness is carried through to Sexton's explanation that "People don't like to be told / that you're sick / and then be forced / to watch / you / come / down with the hammer." The warning that she's sick and the idea that her watchers are forced, however, complicate this watching. In what way does Sexton "force" "them" to watch? Who or what compels them to watch her "come down with the hammer?" This belief that watching is not a choice but a requirement forces us to understand the confessionalism of Sexton's work as a response to a sense of widespread and unavoidable surveillance. In the case of the open door of the suburban home—as with the self-revelation of the confessional poem—the watching will happen. "They," it appears, must watch.[13]

Placing Sexton's and Plath's work in the context of the Supreme Court's anxieties about privacy and the Court's concerns in relation to the poets' illustrates the ways in which the coercion of confession produced new forms of self-disclosure *and* new forms of privacy. That Plath and, for example, Justice Tom Clarke should elaborate similar insights into the problem of the coerced confession suggests that coping with the invasion of privacy occupied a wide swath of American public discourse, to quite different effect. If this reading confirms the Foucauldian hypothesis—that confession is always already coerced—it is also true that Foucault's insights are predicted in the privacy debates of the early 1960s, when cold war anxieties most obviously shaped the transformation of the borders of private and public life.

The surveillance everywhere marking American culture produced a novel approach to privacy rights, one that, while hardly unprecedented in American life, shifted the weight of privacy onto the metaphorical "sacredness" of domesticity from the tangible, though limited literalness of property. James Boyd White has explained that surveillance itself, especially in the form of wiretapping or electronic eavesdropping, had the effect of abstracting privacy rights from property.[14]

> At one time, property law was conceived of as drawing a bright line around the individual, defining in relatively clear and certain terms a zone of autonomy and privacy. In this view, as we know from *Olmstead*, there was no search if there was no trespass, and the Fourth Amendment normally did not apply to such things as wiretapping and eavesdropping. But this position had its protective side too, for under it no search whatever was permitted except for items in which the state or another had a superior property interest, such as stolen goods or contraband. . . . Understandably enough, the Court has found the "property" view insufficiently protective of individual privacy, especially in an era of sophisticated electronic devices, and at the same time excessively restrictive of legitimate state interests in searching for and seizing evidence. (*Justice as Translation*, 179–80)

Paradoxically, when privacy was secured in the zone of the home, it became less, not more, dependent on property. Privacy was becoming more abstract and, crucially, more dependent on the "sanctity of life" within the home than on the physical, literal property of the home. Moreover, if we return to the highly unstable notion of privacy in the early 1960s, we can see that in tandem with surveillance, the special symbolic importance of the home braced this abstraction, making it appear solid, compelling, and natural.

Meyer v. Nebraska (1923)[15] defined liberty as "freedom from bodily restraint . . . the right of the individual to contract, to engage in any of the common occupations of life, to acquire useful knowledge, to marry, establish a home and bring up children, to worship God according to the dictates of his own conscience, and generally to enjoy those privileges long recognized by common law as essential to the orderly pursuit of happiness by free men" (399). When the Court reached back to *Meyer* to find precedent for its constitutional right to privacy in *Griswold v. Connecticut*, it magnified the home as the central component of liberty by lifting only the right to "marry, establish a home and bring up children." In his dissent, Justice Black cautioned the Court about the historical obsolescence of *Meyer*, pointing out that in this list of protected liberties, "the right to contract" had been at the center of a dispute in one of the Court's most controversial decisions and was no longer viewed as a fundamental right. Numerous other cases of excessive police invasion of the home were being argued alongside this case. However, these cases, which dealt with warrants (*Mapp v. Ohio*) and wiretapping (such as *Silverman v. U.S.*[16] [1961] and others) did not produce a widely recognized constitutional right to privacy, even though they provided the logic and the precedents that compose the foundation of *Griswold*.[17]

We often forget that the sanctity of marital sexual conduct was far from an accepted feature of privacy rights in the early 1960s. Though the rapidly changing sexual mores of the twentieth century might predict that marital intimacy was not a very radical concept, the *Griswold* legal team had not only to define but also painstakingly defend it. The ninety-six-page brief submitted by the defendants took enormous care to establish with copious scientific documentation buttressed by the support of respected clergymen of different faiths that the sexual intimacy of married couples was: (a) valuable (it preserved marriage); (b) healthful (it contributed to the mental fitness of both partners); and (c) that to do without it constituted a grave deprivation of liberty (a lifetime of celibacy, which the state conceded as a possible outcome of upholding the Connecticut statute, had to be argued as a danger to the health and welfare of married individuals and to the institution of marriage itself).[18] This is to say that there was nothing self-evident, natural, or given about the intimacy of the married couple, despite the *decision's* claims to the contrary.

Griswold hinged on the Court's sympathy for the married couple, who, it should be remembered, were not implicated in the arrest (a clinic provider and doctor were arrested). Connecticut's prosecutors summarily dismissed claims for a general right to sexual intimacy. State attorney Joe Clarke stated in oral argument, "that single people should be allowed to use a contraceptive device is so contra to American experience, thought, and family law that it does not merit further discussion" (Garrow, *Liberty and Sexuality* 243)[19] and the Court, in obvious agreement, pressed him no further. Everywhere this "new" right to privacy was defended—and the briefs and arguments acknowledged it to be new—we find the words "sanctity" and "marital intimacy." The legal argument as well as the media discussion surrounding the case stressed the marital "core" of privacy. For example, *Griswold* attorney and Yale Law professor Fowler Harper argued in a *CBS Reports* interview: "One of the most intimate and sacred relations of life is the relation of a man and his wife in the privacy of their home. And when the long arm of the law reaches into the bedroom and prohibits a man and his wife doing what they want to do, and what medical advice suggests that they do, it seems to me that this is a merciless invasion of the freedom and liberty of the citizens of this country" (*Liberty and Sexuality* 214). Combining the threat of a totalitarian police state with the "sacred relation of a man and his wife" proved a widely popular argument, one that echoed throughout the country in newspaper editorial pages.

Nevertheless, in the *Griswold* decision the zone of the home was consistently figured as an a priori privacy that was to be *re*claimed by imposing legal barriers to surveillance. In his rousing conclusion, Douglas himself placed the right of privacy anterior to constitutional protections, arguing:

> We deal with a right of privacy older than the Bill of Rights—older than our political parties, older than our school system. Marriage is a coming together for better or for worse, hopefully enduring, and intimate to the degree of being sacred. It is an association that promotes a way of life, not causes; a harmony in living, not political faiths; a bilateral loyalty, not commercial or social projects. Yet it is an association for as noble a purpose as any involved in our prior decisions. (486)

Likewise, the zone of privacy—the home—that Justice Harlan described in *Poe v. Ullman* in 1960 moves from the tangible realm of property rights to the abstractions of sacred domesticity:

> If the physical curtilage of the home is protected, it is surely as a result of solicitude to protect the privacies of the life within. Certainly the safeguarding of the home does not follow merely from the sanctity of property rights. The home derives its pre-eminence as the seat of family life. And the integrity of that life is something so fundamental that it has been found to draw to its protection the principles of more than one explicitly granted constitutional right. (551)

Both these arguments rest not just on the physical zone but also on a metaphor that gathers ideological gravity from the layers of abstraction that both idealize and mystify it. The language that Douglas and Harlan use points to the fundamentally metaphorical character of the home as a space imbued with the sacredness of an idealized domesticity. "Sanctity," "seat of family life," and "sacred," all indicate that the ideal privacy being lost in the view of the Court is an abstract domesticity, not merely a space marked out as a preserve of democratic autonomy, as we might imagine from the antitotalitarian rhetoric that also shapes *Griswold*.

If the Court was increasingly dependent on the metaphorical potency of the home as a space of sacred domestic liberty, confessional poetry earned its reputation by profaning these metaphors. Like the Court, Sexton figures the home as a "zone of privacy" in a poem called "Man and Wife: To Speke of Wo that Is in Marriage."[20] However, instead of the marital bedroom—Douglas calls it in *Poe* the "innermost sanctum of the home" (521)—Sexton figures the zone of privacy as a bathroom, which conserves the notion of privacy but does not admit the mythologizing "sacredness" of the Court and domestic ideology more generally. The intimacy of sacred and profane remains hidden in plain sight in the Court's rhetoric, which Sexton's poem highlights for us. Her "two-seater outhouse" coarsens the "seat of family life."

> Now they are together
> like strangers in a two-seater outhouse,
> eating and squatting together.
> They have teeth and knees
> but they do not speak.
> A soldier is forced to stay with a soldier
> because they share the same dirt
> and the same blows. (*The Complete Poems* 117)

Sexton's "two-seater outhouse" captures the paradox of marital privacy: the couple shares privacy from the outside world, but they are neither private from one another, nor intimate, still "strangers" because they "do not speak." Like two soldiers "forced to stay . . . because they share the same dirt / and the same blows," the married couple remains together because of their secret violence. Under Sexton's terms, the home is private because it is violent, profane, and shameful, not because it is intimate, erotic, or familial. This is, of course, confessional poetry's characteristic move: privacy is deprivation rather than repose; it is self-sacrifice rather than autonomy. This is the dark side of private life that—as feminists have long argued—privacy law shielded in protecting the home from legal scrutiny.[21]

Moreover, the privacy that the outhouse affords is viewed as less protective than it is suffocating for its inhabitants.[22] If the zone of privacy is defined by the "ineffable," Sexton maintains the silence but revises it as "unspeakable." At first Sexton admits: "we have nothing to say"; at the end, the couple are "two asthmatics / whose breath sobs in and out," two invalids who do not have "a language" but a "kind of breathing," what we might characterize in cold war parlance as a kind of "conspiracy." They do not talk but "gasp in unison behind our window pane," two people whose privacy renders them mute. In their silence each is isolated from the other and the outside world; privacy is unspeakable because it has no language. This inability to speak the private is not its sacred purity, its self-evident and natural value; rather, it is its emptiness and airlessness.

In "Housewife" Sexton fuses "house" and "wife" in order to split the effects on men and women of a too intimate identification between women and the metaphorical home. In the poem the transformation of the woman into the house makes the intrusion into the house or body a similar violation while at the same time, the collapse equates the disclosure of the private home with the exposure of the body.

> Some women marry houses.
> It's another kind of skin; it has a heart,
> a mouth, a liver and bowel movements.
> The walls are permanent and pink.
> See how she sits on her knees all day,
> faithfully washing herself down.
> Men enter by force, drawn back like Jonah
> into their fleshy mothers.
> A woman *is* her mother.
> That's the main thing. (*The Complete Poems* 77)

The merging of the woman with the house also recasts the man's relationship to the zone of privacy. Unlike Douglas's or Harlan's vision of the man as sovereign of the private sphere, Sexton's line "Men enter by force, drawn back like Jonah" suggests that men have a very temporary (as opposed to "permanent") presence in the house and that their position in this space is unnatural. Their entry "by force" evokes a rape and the analogy to Jonah, the disobedient prophet who was expelled from the whale three days after his ingestion, reminds us of men's flight from the home rather than their coexistence in it. The unnaturalness of their position inside the home becomes clearer when we find that they are drawn into their "fleshy mothers." For a man, to be inside the house is therefore to be inside the mother, which provides two equally unpleasant alternatives: he becomes either a perpetual fetus or an incestuous rapist. With this invocation of the mother, the structure of the house completely disintegrates—public and private, inside and outside intertwine; generational divisions disappear ("a woman *is* her mother"); and history draws to a halt. Instead, there is an endless cycle of transgression that perpetually returns to the beginning: the mother. From this perspective the home becomes a nursery peopled not by adult citizens but by mothers and their children.

The poem works by literalizing the word "housewife," defining it first as the wife of a house—"some women marry houses"—and then as the wife who is a house. Just as the poem begins by describing "some women" and concludes by defining all women ("A woman *is* her mother"), so too does the woman who marries a house inevitably become that house. Initially the woman remains separate from the structure: "It's another kind of skin; it has a heart, / a mouth, a liver and bowel movements"—indicating that while the house is a body, it is not clearly human nor specifically female. However, with the line "the walls are permanent and pink," the house is no longer "it," comfortably separate from the woman, and so the distinction between the woman and the house begins to break down. By the time we "[s]ee how she sits on her knees all day / faithfully washing herself down," the woman has completely merged with the house and, as a result, we are privy to her most intimate moments—we see her bathing—and so the distinction between the public and private, the threshold to the home, no longer exists external to the woman. Instead, she has internalized it and so the only private space left to her is that which is within the body. All spaces external to the body have become public spaces. All speech has become confessional because it must necessarily transgress the public/private divide.

When the woman becomes the house and internalizes the public/private boundary, she is both exposed *and* silenced. What's more, her transformation marks the moment of the reader's and speaker's *dis*identification with her as the subject of the poem. For the first time, the speaker addresses the reader with an imperative—"see"—shifting the relationship to the woman from one of possible identification to one of observation. We are explicitly instructed to become voyeurs, and as a result the poem takes place at a remove from the woman. Because reader and poet speak about—but no longer with or to—her becoming the house has excluded her from the public discourse the poem engages. As Sexton shows, this disconnection of the woman from public discourse was one of the results of marking the threshold of the home as the border between public and private and then idealizing privacy. While men risked committing violence by crossing into the private sphere, they could move and speak freely beyond the threshold of the house. Furthermore, the internalization of the threshold meant any entry by a woman onto the public stage would be perceived as a kind of exposure. In terms of Richard Wilbur's demand that the distinction between the inside and the outside of the house be observed in art, Sexton's "housewife" cannot but transgress in both aesthetic and moral terms.

This intimate connection between spaces, bodies, and speech is also played out in the Court's contraceptive decisions, which will intensify to the point of breaking in *Roe*, as we will see in the next chapter. That contraception should be the arena in which the Court defined the right to privacy tells us, surprisingly, about the homology between the *male* body and the space of the house. For Sexton, her gender is not threatened by her exposure; exposure is a condition of her gender. In *Poe* we find quite the opposite. Douglas's footnote to his imagined enforcement of the law—policemen in bedrooms—relates Connecticut's contraception statute to another invasive law. He notes:

> Those warrants [to search the bedroom of the suspected birth control user] would, I think, go beyond anything so far known in our law. The law has long known the writ of *de ventre inspiciendo* authorizing matrons to inspect the body of a woman to determine if she is pregnant. This writ was issued to determine before a hanging whether a convicted female was pregnant or to ascertain whether rightful succession of property was to be defeated by assertion of a suppositious heir. (651)

Douglas's reading of the invasiveness of the Connecticut statute bears investigation. In his interpretation the "writ of *de ventre inspiciendo* authorizing matrons to inspect the body of a woman to determine if she is pregnant" is less invasive than a warrant to enter a bedroom. By his standards the intrusion into the bedroom "goes beyond anything so far known in our law." Yet it is difficult to equate the inspection of a woman's body in order to verify pregnancy with the invasion of a bedroom, much less to perceive the bedroom's trespass as the more aggressive intrusion. What we can determine from Douglas's use of this analogy, however, is that the bedroom acts like a kind of body for the man, almost like Sexton's "permanent and pink" walls. The house, then, or at least the bedroom, which is the synecdoche for the private home in the Court's decision, can be penetrated in the same way that the woman's body is violated by the police. To allow the police to penetrate the bedroom is to allow them to figuratively penetrate the man's body. That the woman's body can be literally invaded, in fact that the policing of her body makes up a long tradition in "our law," demonstrates that women's privacy is not of central concern in birth control cases such as *Poe v. Ullman* and *Griswold v. Connecticut*; rather, it is the father's privacy that is being defended. The surveillance of the woman's body for the purposes of patriarchy—to determine inheritance—is a legal legacy that reemerges in *Roe v. Wade* in the person of the doctor who has replaced the matron.

We can see that the privacy safeguarded as a newfound constitutional right is the privacy of patriarchal moral autonomy, which is challenged by the paternalism of the state. The public intervention in the home represented by the state prohibition against contraception infringed upon patriarchal authority and masculine sexual autonomy. The blurring of the boundaries of public and private represented for the Court an improper contamination of the private sphere with public concerns, as if those concerns manifest themselves only in the physical intrusion of the home. The Court therefore reasserts patriarchal privilege when it redraws the boundaries between public and private. In contrast, Sexton's poems about the home denied the possibility of an a priori privacy and repositioned the home as a social, rather than private, territory, one that was political because implicated in public concerns but private only insofar as it was isolated from public forums. Defined by its lack of privacy, the home of the confessional poets is neither properly public nor safely private. This confusion of married couples with sanctity and of male bodies with private spaces suggests why the Court's attempt to curtail police power in a modern surveillance society proved to be surprisingly inflexible. There seemed to be nothing to prevent the "sizable hunk of liberty" wrested back from an overintrusive state from being extended as a basic right of citizenship. And indeed, many liberal thinkers have sought to extend privacy as a way of remedying inequality. However, while Americans increasingly sought rights to privacy and began to assume their right to it regardless of their gender, marital status, or sexual practice, the invisible preconditions of moral autonomy prevented the concept from extending very far beyond its original location.

Sexton's "For John Who Begs Me Not to Enquire Further" and Harlan's dissent in *Poe v. Ullman* form a dialogue about the relationship between private spaces to public discourse, between exposure and silences. *Poe v. Ullman*, a forerunner to *Griswold v. Connecticut*, was a case brought by a married couple, a married woman, and their doctor, which asked the court to grant declaratory relief from the Connecticut statute prohibiting the use of birth control. *Poe's* plaintiffs were women who feared physical trauma or death from pregnancy, had already miscarried numerous times, or could anticipate carrying a severely deformed fetus that had little chance of surviving the pregnancy and less of remaining alive after birth. Though *Poe* was held by the majority on the court to be nonjusticible (meaning that the Court could not rule on it) because they perceived no imminent threat of arrest, Justice Harlan's dissent became a crucial building block in the formation of constitutionally protected privacy. Sexton's poem and Harlan's dissent conceive the relationship between public and private quite differently, which manifests the way that the intense scrutiny of privacy was beginning to undermine the self-evidence of the concept. Harlan's vision of privacy aspires to a complete silencing of private life and retains the strict binary opposition between public and private that cold war ideology held in place. Sexton, in contrast, maps out the territory *between* the public and the private, acknowledging both the danger and the impossibility of maintaining a rigid division between the two.

Twenty-five years after *Griswold v. Connecticut*, Catherine Roraback, one of the attorneys who had argued in state court on behalf of Estelle Griswold and Planned Parenthood, reflected on the evolution of the privacy defense. *Griswold*, we should remember, declared that Connecticut could not bar the *use* of birth control because it would intrude the state into the "zone of privacy" that is the home, or more accurately, the bedroom of a married couple. Roraback recalls:

> When these suits were begun in May of 1958, there was, as well as I can remember, no discussion of rights of privacy. Considerations of a privacy nature were of course inherent in the litigation but they were seldom articulated as such. For instance, in the suits brought on behalf of individual patients, fictitious names were used. The Supreme Court of Errors of Connecticut in sanctioning this procedure recognized that "Because of the

intimate and distressing details alleged in these complaints, it is understandable that the parties who are allegedly medical patients would wish to be anonymous." ("*Griswold v. Connecticut*: A Brief Case History" 399)

As Roraback remembers, when the attorneys began formulating their strategy in the first challenges to the birth control statute in the late 1950s, the privacy defense was legally unthinkable. There was no history of decisions protecting a right to privacy, nor was a right to privacy enumerated in the Bill of Rights. Privacy, as she remembers, was less an issue of how far the state could intrude upon the decision making of a sovereign and autonomous individual than it was a test of the boundaries of self-disclosure. The ability and willingness of these women to testify despite their shame and embarrassment provides a benchmark of the openness with which people discussed childbearing, marriage, and sexual intimacy. When Roraback imagined the dilemmas of privacy that would have to be overcome in building a case for Planned Parenthood, she first recognized the social barriers to self-disclosure that women served by the clinic[23] would have to surmount.[24]

Justice Harlan's dissent in *Poe v. Ullman* addresses the suitability of private life, particularly sexuality, for public discourse. Harlan finds the statute unconstitutional not because it criminalizes recreational (as opposed to procreational) sex but because it would require criminal prosecution, which would, more ominously, necessitate testimony about private matters. His dissent reads:

> Precisely what is involved here is this: the State is asserting the right to enforce its moral judgment by intruding upon the most intimate details of the marital relation with the full power of criminal law. Potentially, this could allow the deployment of all the incidental machinery of the criminal law, arrests, searches and seizures; inevitably, it must mean at the very least the lodging of criminal charges, a public trial, and testimony as to the *corpus delicti. Nor could any imaginable elaboration of presumptions, testimonial privileges, or other safeguards alleviate the necessity for testimony as to the mode and manner of the married couples' sexual relations, or at least the opportunity for the accused to make denial of the charges.* (498; emphasis mine)

It is frequently instructive to read the way that justices shift from the issue at hand to a more troubling issue at the margins of the case they are adjudicating.

Like Douglas, who imagined the policeman's invasion of the marital bedroom, Justice Harlan also imagined what *might happen* but what, in fact, did *not* happen in *Poe v. Ullman*: married couples testifying about their "use" of sexual privacy. For Harlan the mere possibility of this testimony justified striking the Connecticut statute. Yet the reason that this statute stayed on the books from 1879 to 1965 was that such testimony was *never* compelled; the law, not enforced in the home, functioned to prohibit the distribution of contraceptives by birth control clinics. Furthermore, married couples rarely testified on their own behalf or attached their names to briefs, hence the use of pseudonyms—Poe, Doe, and Roe—in all the landmark birth control cases. In fact the only names associated with birth control and abortion cases are those of clinic operators and doctors, providers rather than users of birth control. Harlan is concerned that the machinery of the court will intrude into the sacred domain of the married couple's bedroom. One can almost hear this machinery as the "rack and the screw" that figures as the most ominous metaphor of privacy violation (in *Rochin* and in *Olmstead*).

Justice Harlan does not deny that the state traditionally regulated the morality of its citizens; he claims that such is the business of all civilized societies. Nor does he worry whether regulating family size is a rational implementation of state power. Instead, Harlan finds that forcing testimony about private conduct, even if the testimony consisted of no more than a denial of the criminalized behavior, would constitute an unjustifiable exercise of state power even though regulating the private behavior would not. The violation is intolerable to him for he sees the physical home, sanctified as the "seat of family life," as fundamentally outside the realm of public discourse, and he cannot envision any kind of procedural safeguard that would prevent its disclosure. What Harlan, and later Justice Douglas, conclude is that the ineffable importance and "sacred" nature of private life necessitate silence about it. On the one hand, private matters derive their sacredness from being so intimate that they are withdrawn completely from public view. On the other, withdrawing from public view is what makes private life so sacred. In any case, the mutual reinforcement of sacredness and privacy necessitates that private life remain unvoiced or else risk pollution. The irony, of course, is that only when women such as *Poe*'s defendants began to volunteer their testimony in court could the right to privacy be secured.

The court argued that private life, not public discourse, would be compromised by the testimony of private life in a public forum such as the court. Critics of confessional poetry on the other hand, such as Sexton's first mentor and teacher, John Holmes, believed that public discourse would suffer from its contamination with the trivialities or tragedies of private life. Although the lyric poem was traditionally the province of the private self, confessional poetry made clear that there were unwritten rules about this privacy, that there were clearly things "too private" to be spoken even in a lyric poem. In response to his warning not to publish her first collection of poems, *To Bedlam and Part Way Back* (1960), Anne Sexton wrote a personal letter defending the publication of her confessional work and enclosed the poem that was her poetic manifesto and, ultimately, her critique of privacy: "For John Who Begs Me Not to Enquire Further."

Not that it was beautiful,
but that, in the end, there was
a certain sense of order there;
something worth learning
in that narrow diary of my mind,
in the commonplaces of the asylum
where the cracked mirror
or my own selfish death
outstared me.
And if I tried
to give you something else,
something outside of myself,
you would not know
that the worst of anyone
can be, finally,
an accident of hope.
I tapped my own head;
it was glass, an inverted bowl.
It is a small thing
to rage in your own bowl.
At first it was private.
Then it was more than myself;
it was you, or your house
or your kitchen.

And if you turn away
because there is no lesson here
I will hold my awkward bowl,
with all its cracked stars shining
like a complicated lie,
and fasten a new skin around it
as if I were dressing an orange
or a strange sun.
Not that it was beautiful,
but that I found some order there.
There ought to be something special
for someone
in this kind of hope.
This is something I would never find
in a lovelier place, my dear,
although your fear is anyone's fear,
like an invisible veil between us all . . .
and sometimes in private,
my kitchen, your kitchen,
my face, your face. (*The Complete Poems* 34–35)

In addition to its private circulation, Sexton also published the poem in her first collection and so it became a public affirmation of her decision to break down the barriers between public and private. Many feminist critics have read "For John" as Sexton's clearest expression of her motivations for writing poetry that dealt openly and even flamboyantly with subjects that cross over from the auto-biographical into the secret and shameful, subjects such as suicide, madness, adultery, menstruation, abortion, incest, and domestic violence. Yet we can see, given the reservations articulated by John Holmes, that Sexton was responding to a question of what both poetry and public discourse could represent and, more important, what its representation risked.

In "For John" Sexton mocks the narcissism of her confessions as "the narrow diary of [her] mind," "the cracked mirror," and "[her] own selfish death," bitterly but ironically exclaiming, "It is a small thing / to rage in your own bowl." Yet this "rage" is not a "small thing," the bowl is, and the bowl, often read as a fishbowl, is perhaps the most widely circulated metaphor of exposure in the period. As we can see from the next lines, her revelations do not remain private, and hence they are no longer insignificant personal matters but, rather, as Alicia Ostriker claims in *Seduction and Theory*, "transpersonal" (157). In the first crossing from one private domain to another—"Then it was more than myself; / it was you, or your house / or your kitchen"—the rage that would be small in one's own bowl repeatedly assaults the private space of the reader/John Holmes, insisting through repetition on identification—"you . . . your . . . your." This identification with the reader returns in the final lines of the poem, no longer echoing, searching for a response, but instead rendering a precise symmetry that admits no evasion: "my kitchen, your kitchen, / my face, your face." Not only does Sexton construct an analogy between face and kitchen, an unexpected alignment that links the private zone of the kitchen (not the bedroom—so it is not erotic but domestic) with the private *and* public self of the face, she suggests that the reader cannot disavow this identification. Though it happens "in private," the lessons of the confession inevitably find their way behind the "invisible veil between us all," which is the barrier imposed by the reader's fear of identification. It is not, after all, the irrelevance of her work that motivated John Holmes to attempt to silence Sexton but, rather, his identification with her that unnerved him. Sexton intimates that the motive for shrouding private life under a "veil" is the resistance to identifying with writers who make us anxious, particularly women writers, with whom she suggests male readers would identify if they permitted themselves to do so. So when she discarded her veil, refusing to disguise herself by adopting more appropriately "public" subjects and forms, she forced an intimacy and identification that changed the face of contemporary poetry.

We can see that Sexton's justification depends on speaking the private, but not simply *in* private. Private matters, according to this poem, do not need a public forum because they move inexorably from home to home through the power of identification. And yet the circumstances of publication—she addresses her reader in the public domain of a collection as well as in the private sphere of a letter—remind us that Sexton does in fact need a public forum, in this case a publisher willing to promote her work, and that it is the impending publication of her work that finally moves John Holmes to express his distaste and discomfort. At issue for Sexton, and for many of her readers, both sympathetic and suspicious, is the appropriateness of her subject—private life—for public discourse.

The title "For John Who Begs Me Not to Enquire Further" echoes Sophocles' *Oedipus*. Sexton suggests this reference in the epigraph she chose, drawing from a letter Goethe wrote to Schopenhauer, that made reference to Jocasta's warning to Oedipus "not to enquire further." As Alicia Ostriker points out, this reference to Oedipus positions Sexton in the traditionally male role of truth-seeker and public figure while placing Holmes in Jocasta's conventionally timid female role (*Seduction and Theory* 156). Furthermore, Diane Middlebrook explains Holmes's timidity as his own guilt over his wife's suicide, a guilt Sexton unconsciously exploited in her response to his complaints that her poetry gave nothing to the reader (*Anne Sexton* 98–100). But, though each critic notes Sexton's role as Oedipus and each remarks on the quest for a "transpersonal" aesthetic, neither considers the political implications of this choice of frame for her poem. Oedipus is not merely a "transpersonal" character; he is a political figure. What's more, *Oedipus the King* is a drama that revolves around the relationship of private sin to political health. It is the city's suffering, after all, that prompts Oedipus to search out and divulge his private transgressions. This complicated link between political health and private morality had long been a staple of cold war ideology as Elaine Tyler May has shown. Central to confessional poetry is the idea that personal psychological breakdown is both a metaphor and an instance of social disintegration. Sexton's allusion indicates some awareness on her part of the political implications of her personal revelations and that her manifesto, at least as part of her collection, does not depend on a "merely" personal motivation for writing. In sync with the domestic ideology of the 1950s and 1960s, Sexton affirms the symmetry between private and political health, all the while suggesting that only the exposure of private illness can cure the body politic.

The Supreme Court was hardly alone in imagining the home as the last preserve of liberty and autonomy in what was perceived as an increasingly organized, surveyed, and possibly totalitarian modern world. However, it might be instructive to remember how ardently and with what remarkably similar language this connection was maintained with regard to American literature at the time. Richard Poirier's *A World Elsewhere* (1966), a landmark work in the consolidation of American studies, claims that "*Walden* is only one of the examples of something like an obsession in American literature with plans and efforts to build houses, to appropriate space to one's desires perhaps to inaugurate therein a dynasty that shapes time to the dimensions of personal and family history" (17). Linking America's writers to its most original theorists of space, Louis Sullivan and Frank Lloyd Wright, in this project of imperial selfhood, Poirier continues:

The building of a house is an extension and an expansion of the self, an act by which the self possesses environment otherwise possessed by nature. By an act of building, so the theorists I've mentioned would have it, it is possible to join forces with the powers of nature itself, to make its style your style. But this conjunction is possible only if the imagination and space are freed from the possessive power of all that is not nature: from systems of any kind that derive from society and history, from, often as not, "Europe." (18)

Because society and history are by his observation almost always associated with Europe, America itself becomes a figure and a fantasy of private space and the radical self-determination, self-sovereignty, and autonomy it promises. Therefore, Poirier's is a double removal of literature from the public sphere: the American writer expends his (and it is nearly always "his") talent preparing a space for self-realization in a house that is a private space within a nation that is also a private space. This equivalence of spaces, one might even say homology, suggests why domestic containment in American rhetoric substitutes the home and the nation so effortlessly.

Poirier's anatomy of this American fantasy rests upon the modernist faith in the autonomy of culture, and as Donald Pease describes it, a distinctively cold war intensification of this separation between the cultural and political public spheres ("National Identities" 10). And yet, Poirier's emphasis on the house as the central metaphor *in* and *of* American literature, not only the obsessive building by literary heroes and heroines but the defining preoccupation of American writers—their "aesthetic theory of literary independence and originality" (20)—takes the separation of culture from the public sphere one step further. Poirier privatizes *American* literature, not all art and culture. This central trope of American letters barricades literature from the public realm, relocating it in the domain that was heralded as the safest, most secure zone of privacy and the symbol of American democratic liberty. Not surprisingly, the privatization of literature displays the same paradoxes that other cold war conceptions of privacy generated. The privatizing of literature paradoxically initiates "a struggle to create through language an environment in which the inner consciousness of the hero-poet can freely express itself, an environment in which he can sound publicly what he privately is" (35). Ultimately, however, "[sounding] publicly what [one] privately is" falls victim to "the impossibility of living through the 'eye' . . . the impossibility of totally divorcing the self from time, biology, economics, and the words by which the free, visionary environment of the 'eye' is translated into the social entity: the 'I,' living in relation to near things" (49). This failure derives not from an imperfect or opaque self-revelation but from the impossibility of pure self-sovereignty. Yet, even while recognizing the impossibility of this radical autonomy, we are nonetheless left with a theory of American poetics in which the greatest works of art *aspire* to both a complete withdrawal from the public realm and a complete transparency of self-revelation.

To understand how deeply the projects of lyric and political autonomy are linked, I'd like to turn to a most unlikely source, John Crowe Ransom, the New Critic who is best known for articulating a rationale for cloistering literature, and in particular lyric poetry, from "the world elsewhere." Tobin Siebers reminds us, in *Cold War Criticism and the Politics of Skepticism* (1993), that when Ransom met a crucial impasse in his poetics, he turned to "a political way of thinking" (as quoted in Siebers 30) to explain the defining feature of literature, which for him is the lyric poem. Siebers recalls Ransom's striking assertion that "A poem is, so to speak, a democratic state, whereas a prose discourse—mathematical, scientific, ethical, or practical and vernacular—is a totalitarian state" (as quoted in Siebers 30). Ransom refines his literary analysis by explaining the difference between the two states:

> The intention of a democratic state is to perform the work of state as effectively as it can perform it, subject to one reservation of conscience: that it will not despoil its members, the citizens, of the free exercise of their own private and independent characters. But the totalitarian state is interested solely in being effective, and regards the citizens as no citizens at all; that is, regards them as functional members whose existence is defined by their allotted contributions to its ends; it has no use for their private characters, and therefore no provision for them." (as quoted in Siebers 31).

The elaborateness of this metaphor for a much simpler point—that the fundamental distinction between prose and poetry is the extent to which either can be paraphrased without loss—suggests Ransom's investment in "political ways of thinking." As Siebers suggests, "The New Critics quickly established a canon of poetry to found the new republic in which a purer democracy would defeat totalitarianism and bring an end to the cold war" (31). The lyric poem could stand in for democracy itself insofar as it, too, created a space for the individual, private character of the citizen.

I'd like to extend Siebers's insight by noting that the lyric poem is fundamental to the democratic state because—in Ransom's *next* crucial metaphor—the lyric poem is best thought of as a house. Reaching another impasse in theorizing the "concrete universal," which gives to poetry its ability to mediate between the particular and the general, Ransom argued that

> The poem was not a mere moment in time, nor a mere point in space. It was sizeable, like a house. Apparently it had a 'plan,' or a central frame of logic, but it had also a huge wealth of local detail. . . . But it was the political way of thinking which gave me the first analogy which seemed valid. The poem was like a democratic state, in act, and observed both macroscopically and microscopically. The house occurred also, and provided what seems to be a more negotiable trope under which to construe a poem . . . the intent of the good critic becomes therefore to examine and define the poem with respect to its structure and texture. ("Criticism as Pure Speculation" 110–11)

I do not mean to suggest that Ransom believed that all three—lyric poem, house, and democratic state—were interchangeable; rather, that they were structurally symmetrical: each figured *and* made possible the preservation of sovereign individuality.

One final example of a lyric refashioning of the house will help to explain how women poets inserted themselves into this conversation about the autonomy, privacy, and liberty of poems and homes and the democratic states that permitted them to flourish. When Adrienne Rich takes up the metaphor of the home, she does so in terms similar to the Supreme Court's and the most influential literary critics' of the time, but with a difference. In "September 21," part of her first semi-autobiographical work, *Snapshots of a Daughter-in-Law 1954–1962* (1967), the house serves not as refuge from scrutiny but a deliberate embrace of it. Houses "tenderly appraise you, / hold you in the watchfulness of mothers," which offers a kind of surveillance "you" seek because it affirms your existence and relieves you of the terror of anonymity. In this sense, Rich's poem answers Hannah Arendt's profound question at the end of *The Origins of Totalitarianism*: what secret desires did totalitarianism satisfy? Arendt argued that totalitarianism offered relief from the agonizing loneliness, isolation, and anonymity that modern "mass" man suffered. Rich's poem suggests that domestic containment and its ideology of home might fill a similar emptiness.

Wear the weight of equinoctial evening,
light like melons bruised on all the porches.
Feel the houses tenderly appraise you,
hold you in the watchfulness of mothers.

Once the nighttime was a milky river
washing past the swimmers in the sunset,
rinsing over sleepers of the morning.
Soon the night will be an eyeless quarry

where the shrunken daylight and its rebels,
loosened, dive like stones in perfect silence,
names and voices drown without reflection.

Then the houses draw you. Then they have you. (*Snapshots of a Daughter-in-Law*; emphasis mine)

What begins as benign, even fond attention becomes threatening by the end of the poem. The poem divides in half, like the "equinoctial evening," but there is a profound difference between the two halves. At first, nighttime, a "milky river / washing . . . rinsing over sleepers," evokes a self nursed and bathed by the river, which recalls the tender watchfulness of the mother. The second half, however, transforms the night from a maternal caress to absolute abandonment and self-obliteration. The "eyeless quarry," in which "names and voices drown without reflection," threatens "you" with complete anonymity. The quarry cannot produce a self, an "I" with a voice, without an "eye," something to reflect you back to yourself. Without anyone to secure your existence by providing your reflection, you disappear into the black hole of the night, which because of Rich's Miltonic echoes (the daylight and its rebels who dive in perfect silence), suggests that to be unseen and unheard is to be in hell. We might even hear the echo of confessional poetry's grand entrance: Lowell's *Life Studies*, and in particular the poem, "Skunk Hour," which characterizes his madness in Miltonic terms: "I myself am Hell; / nobody's here—." The key to Rich's revision of the home as locus of autonomous individuality is the menace of the last line: "then the houses draw you. Then they have you." The home is not a retreat, a space of repose that fosters the realization of self, but a surrender, a withdrawal from the loneliness of autonomy. Fearing the self-obliteration of the night, "you" return to the mother, who reaffirms your existence with her infinite watchfulness. In the tone of the poem, this can hardly be thought comforting. If the equinoctial evening marks the entrance into adulthood, this forward movement is checked by the with*drawal* into the house, which is also a return to the mother. Like Sexton, Rich redefines the home, the location of autonomy, adulthood, and citizenship, as the womb. The home as mother nurtures the individual, but renders him or her incapable of venturing beyond her watchful embrace.

This "revisioning" of the house, to borrow Mark Doty's term, in which he undoubtedly evokes Rich, is not simply a refashioning of lyric poetry if we follow the chain of metaphors that Poirier and Ransom set forth in their discussion of poetics and American literature. If we return to Poirier's and Ransom's terms, refashioning the house, building a new architecture of privacy and the private self, reorienting the relationship of the home-dweller and the public world, is nothing less than revisioning American literature and the democratic state. Therefore, when confessional poetry started to admit history, biology, and society into the sacred confines of the poem and releasing the details of private life to the scrutiny of an anonymous reading public, it was suddenly unclear whether it was poetry at all. The confessional poets made a *double* transgression of the space of autonomy, violating simultaneously the rules of poetic formalism and the rules of privacy, which, it appears, were the *same* rules.

FOUR

Confessions Between a Woman and Her Doctor

Roe v. Wade and the Gender of Privacy

Today the Supreme Court made abortion legal.
Bless them.
Bless all women
Who want to remake their own likeness
but not every day. . . .
—Anne Sexton, "Is It True?"

Write poetries. Writing writings,
write readings, write drafts.
Write several selves to dissolve
the bounded idea of the self.
—Rachel Blau Duplessis,
"Otherhow" in *Pink Guitar*

The pregnant woman cannot be isolated in her privacy.
—Justice Harry Blackmun, *Roe v. Wade*

Toward the end of the 1960s the Supreme Court rapidly expanded the newfound constitutional right to privacy announced in *Griswold v. Connecticut* beyond the privileged space of the marital bedroom to the world outside the home. Responding to legislative intrusiveness and abuses of state surveillance in public spaces, the Supreme Court, through such post-*Griswold* cases as *Terry v. Ohio*, *Katz v. U.S.*, *Loving v. Virginia*, and *Eisenstadt v. Baird*, transformed the right to privacy into one that adhered to the individual and was thus mobile and dependent on context.[1] By locating privacy with the body of the citizen rather than in a protected zone, the Court had created a legal doctrine that was concerned less with the ability of the individual to withdraw from public scrutiny than with the right to self-determination and autonomy.[2] The final extension of this self-sovereignty to the individual citizen was *Roe v. Wade*, the case that found within privacy doctrine a form of autonomy that made abortion properly the domain of the woman and her doctor rather than of hospital review boards and state legislatures. My concern in this chapter is to pursue the transformation of privacy when it is relocated not in the "zone of the home" as it was defined in *Griswold v. Connecticut* but in the "zone" of the body as defined in *Roe v. Wade*. And if, as I have argued in the preceding chapter, the home was implicitly a male body in *Griswold* and *Poe*, *Roe*'s crucial precedents, what happens when that body becomes irreducibly female?

The extension of the notion of privacy toward individual autonomy culminated in the paradox of *Roe v. Wade*, a decision that marked the Court's greatest expansion of the right and first retraction of it. No longer an issue of the limits of an individual's private sphere of action, the public debate over privacy began to center on what and when a woman was permitted to choose and, less obviously, what a woman was compelled to say in order to enact that choice. That is, as legal doctrines moved away from an abstract notion of the democratic citizen to focus on gendered bodies, the cold war privacy debate was fundamentally altered. Where before the individual had existed in isolation—alone, autonomous, with rights adhering to his essentially masculine, although presumptively ungendered body—when privacy became an issue of specifically women's autonomy, a second individual, whom Anne Sexton calls in "The Operation" "the almost mighty doctor," became instrumental to female privacy. With *Roe*, the legal debate over privacy shifted into the arena of abortion rights and as a result of this shift, the right to privacy, conceived in symbolic opposition to Soviet totalitarianism, became a "woman's issue."

The Court's adjudication of abortion under the rubric of privacy has posed significant problems for feminists. As Reva Siegel demonstrates, privacy arguments tend to "occur in a framework that is individualist, anti-statist, and focused on the physiology of reproduction—that is, on matters of sex, not gender" ("Abortion" 43); instead, she proposes grounding the abortion right in equal protection law in order to account for "the social organization of reproductive relations" (43). Siegel argues that one of the major limitations of the privacy arguments that follow directly from *Roe* is the medical framework that focuses on women's bodies rather than on women's roles. Even the woman's abortion decision, she notes, is defined within this framework: "*Roe* recognizes that a woman has a privacy right to make decisions about abortion, and describes this right in medical terms: it is a right to be exercised under the guidance of a physician" (53). Siegel moves on to consider the trimester compromise of the decision, which made abortions legally permissible in the first three months of pregnancy, but I would like to pause here over the "guidance of a physician" in order to examine what this formulation of privacy says about both women's bodies and women's roles and the ways that these roles determine how we conceptualize this body. By introducing the doctor as the necessary partner in this so-called private decision, the Court transformed the right to privacy, often called "the right to silence," into one that entails confession, persuasion, and testimony. This reconstruction of the notion of autonomy when it regulated women suggests that the relationship between withdrawal into the private sphere and autonomy cannot be assumed. Moreover, insofar as bodies, especially women's bodies, are figured in spatial terms, the inherited language of privacy as a protected zone may be the very language that feminists need to interrogate and transform.

The representation of the female body matters to conceptions of privacy for the simple reason that it has historically figured the impossibility of privacy. Women and especially mothers in cold war culture often functioned as metaphors of a highly unstable border between public and private, a possibly treacherous incapacity to defend the boundaries of home and nation. As Michael Rogin has argued, across such diverse registers as film, pulp fiction, even social criticism such as Philip Wylie's *Generation of Vipers*, women and mothers are linked to "boundary invasion, body destruction, and apocalypse" (*Ronald Reagan* 245). The male body, in contrast, figured contained, private, well-regulated and bounded space. The film *Dr. Strangelove*, perhaps most famously, satirized the anxieties around the hypervulnerable (because hypercontained) male body in Air Force General Jack D. Ripper's paranoid fantasy about fluoridation, which he discovered to be a communist plot during "the act of love." Ripper's panic over the secret violation of his bodily integrity, having driven him to instigate a nuclear war, tracks with remarkably little exaggeration the inflamed rhetoric in debates over fluoridation that circulated in the American press during the 1950s.[3] By withholding his "essence" from women, Ripper expresses the paradoxical nature of female boundary trouble: not only are their borders without sturdy defenses but their vulnerability translates into his.[4]

When the cold war entered a containment crisis, it did not invent but fed upon a long line of containment dangers that took gendered forms, some of which are fundamental to the history of lyric poetry. Anne Carson's *Men in the Off Hours* (2000) locates Sappho's odes in the elaborate system of metaphors, customs, and laws by which ancient Greek society administered female behavior and female bodies to ward off the dangers of a woman's permeable boundaries and the threats she posed to other bounded spaces. As Carson explains, for a society devoted to a notion of boundedness as a political, cultural, aesthetic and moral concept,

> the pregnability of female boundaries presents [male culture with] a problem that has more than two sides. Woman is subject not only to incursion from without but to leakage from within and, for this reason, her very presence may pose a threat to the integrity of the house of which she is a part and the city that encompasses it. (142)

Exploring the matrix of images, laws, customs, and rituals that protected Greek society from the pollution of the unbounded female body, Carson demonstrates how this threat worked its way up the order of abstraction from the body to the home to the nation, from personal attire, to social custom, to civil law.

The female body, however, represents more than an unstable boundary between public and private; it figures exposure itself. Sappho's most famous lyric, Fragment 31 or the Second Ode, begins in the Greek wedding ceremony at its symbolically most powerful moment: the unveiling. At this unveiling, in which the woman is momentarily free of the ritual clothing and human chaperoning that are meant to provide the boundaries she does not herself possess, the woman is most dangerous, but also only then available to the new husband, who will properly civilize her in marriage. Carson suggests that Sappho uses this moment of ritual exposure, both necessary and perilous, to reveal her own hidden feelings for the woman facing her husband for the first time. There is then a double exposure, of the bride and of Sappho's feelings for the bride. As Carson puts it, Sappho "explode[s] the distinction between the outside and the inside of her self" (152), which is in one sense ironic: "Sappho has constructed her poem as a play upon the ritual formalities of the unveiling ceremony in order to situate her own emotions, which are intensely personal and properly hidden emotions, at the single most extraordinary moment of exposure in female life and so to bend its ritual meaning onto herself with an irony of reference as sharp as a ray of light" (152). I would like to think about Sappho's double exposure as a model of lyric that is precisely not the unique moment of transparency for a presumptively private self but one episode in an ongoing process of managing the exposure that is a prior condition of female privacy. I wish to use this explosion of the distinction between inside and outside to conceive what privacy might mean if it were not located in a contained and bounded space, however fragile, but reimagined with respect to a body defined by its exposure.

The doctor/patient relationship at the center of *Roe* read through the representation of this same relationship in confessional poetry muddies the apparent distinction between public and private. In the decade prior to *Roe*, Anne Sexton and Sylvia Plath had already imagined the necessarily confessional relationship of women to their doctors. What these women demonstrated was that their ability to be private lay not in their bodies, which could not be withdrawn from the scrutiny of the doctor, but in their language, which could alternately mask and make known. A reading of *Roe* against the poetry of Plath and Sexton impresses upon us that the privacy of the doctor's office is rhetorical: it depends on the woman's facility with language, on her ability to argue convincingly for the autonomy only the doctor can grant her. The gendering of privacy, not manifest in the Court's language until *Roe*, was in the decade preceding it examined by these poets in a variety of ways. The effect of reading confessional poetry that features women and their doctors in conjunction with *Roe* is to reconfigure privacy *for women* as an act of confession. For women, unlike for men, displaying one's scars, revealing one's insides to someone else, offering oneself up to interpretation—precisely what confessional poetry does—became the preconditions for the privacy offered by *Roe*.

The multiple intersections in the metaphorical language of these two distinct traditions of privacy, one in the law and the other in the lyric poem, help us to understand the complicated relationship between bodily privacy, sexual difference, and public discourse. The Romantic and post-Romantic lyric, the aesthetic evocation of the purely private individual, the poet "overheard" "speaking to himself," a definition that J. S. Mill devised with Wordsworth in mind, clearly encounters a major problem of address when we consider so-called private acts of self-revelation that are not voluntary but coerced.[5] In considering the doctor's relationship to the confessional poem, we should remember that the doctor was not simply "overhearing" and, therefore, the situation of the lyric was not innocent. In continually addressing their relationship to this listener, women confessional poets reimagined the private voice of lyric in dramatic and defensive terms. Their confessional poetry offered possibilities for the private individual in a society that increasingly invaded its citizens: a confession that through its own multiplication offered the privacy not available in silence.

The doctor, especially the psychoanalyst, has appeared to many critics to have provoked confessional poetry.[6] More than the psychoanalytic frame, however, we should take note of the number of times Sexton, Lowell, Snodgrass, Plath, and other poets associated with confessional poetry, such as Allen Ginsberg and Maxine Kumin, made use of a medical context to reveal the deep and pervasive intrusion of medical science into the "private" space of the body.[7] Though generally recognized for throwing off the masks of poetic convention, confessional poets were not content with merely stripping and exposing the body. Instead, in a series of what I call "operation" poems, confessional poets opened the body up to expose its inside, troubling the notion of a private internal bodily space.[8] By questioning the metaphors of surface and depth, inside and outside, that structured the privacy of traditional poetic and legal discourse, confessional poets interrogated the link between bodily privacy, sexual difference, and language that would later find expression in the legal construction of individual privacy.[9]

The "operation" poems constitute confessional poetry's most revealing confrontation: the individual's loss of bodily privacy.[10] Exposing the inside of the body in surgery (or of the unconscious in psychoanalysis) can be understood as confessional poetry's deliberate exploration of the conditions of this loss and its relationship to what appears to be a voluntary self-disclosure. To read these "operation" poems as metaphors of confession locates the poet as patient and equates both the operation and the scar with the poem. At the same time, this reading unites the doctor and reader as both viewer and interpreter of the operation/scar/poem and the poet/patient. The poet as patient is opened up, literalizing the metaphorical action of confessional poetry, while ceding interpretive power to the doctor/reader, offering up the "facts" to be interpreted by a presumably more objective and knowledgeable outsider. The metaphorical operation, like the poem itself, takes us through the steps of display, exposure, invasion, and closure in the examination, preparation, surgery, and recovery from surgery. While surgery literalizes the metaphorical opening of the confessional poem, the surgeon/doctor literalizes the intrusion of the powerful listener. Yet the figure of the surgeon is a metaphor not simply for the psychoanalyst; the surgeon becomes the metaphoric listener integral to the private moment. As women confessional poets show through their exposure of the doctor's power, their privacy was not spatial, but linguistic, which meant that privacy could not reside "within" one person but only "between" two.[11]

These poems that delved *into* the body, like Sylvia Plath's 1962 poem "The Courage of Shutting-Up," placed confession within the context of external pressures on individual privacy by featuring policemen, judges, priests, psychoanalysts, and most important, surgeons.

> The courage of the shut mouth, in spite of artillery!
> The line pink and quiet, a worm, basking.
> There are black disks behind it, the disks of outrage,
> And the outrage of a sky, the lined brain of it.
> The disks revolve, they ask to be heard—
>
> Loaded, as they are, with accounts of bastardies.
> Bastardies, usages, desertions and doubleness,
> The needle journeying in its groove,
> Silver beast between two dark canyons,
> A great surgeon, now a tatooist,
>
> Tatooing over and over the same blue grievances
> The snakes, the babies, the tits
> On mermaids and two-legged dreamgirls.
> The surgeon is quiet, he does not speak.
>
> He has seen too much death, his hands are full of it. (*Collected Poems* 209–10)

Though neither the aggrieved speaker nor the surgeon "talks" (that is squeals), the surgeon, who is the "needle" playing the "black discs . . . of outrage," is simultaneously a tatooist, transcribing these records from behind her closed lips onto the surface of her body. Through the surgeon/tatooist's art, the body rather than the surgeon or the poet will speak. The speaker of the poem, therefore, need never voice her confession; she need only be read. The body will speak for her, but the surgeon/tatooist rather than the poet will have taken pen/needle in hand to paint her "blue grievances" for the reading public's consumption. The surgeon does not so much coerce her confession—he is not, after all, "the artillery"—but he does write it out "over and over," making it visible despite her resistance. The poem confesses to the scene of confession, revealing that the relationship of surgeon and patient destroys the privacy of the body by collapsing the "zone" into a surface—the inside is written on the outside and so the outside and inside are one. Plath's questioning of the possibility of resistance, the "courage of shutting-up," depicts the "artillery" as less compelling than the doctor; the collapse of surface and depth wrought by the surgeon makes confession inevitable.

This problem of resisting confession is depicted metaphorically in two poems called "The Operation," one by Anne Sexton in *All My Pretty Ones* and one by W. D. Snodgrass in *Heart's Needle*. A comparison of these two, read in the context of the Court's evolving conceptions of individual privacy, explains how these poems that stage the transgression of the body's privacy determine our conception of confession. Diane Middlebrook argues that the exposure of the female body defined Sexton as both a woman poet and a confessional poet: "by 1962 Sexton had begun to experience the interesting social role of contemporary American woman poet as an identity with a life of its own, being shaped for her by the reception of her work . . . it was her direct treatment of the female body in such poems as "The Operation" that attracted the interest of reviewers" (*Anne Sexton* 172). That the public display of bodily experience, one of confessional poetry's generic violations, is almost exclusively associated with women poets is in part explained through its novelty in the early sixties.[12] Critics were very simply riveted by Sexton's treatment of her own body. However, that this particular poem should so firmly link confessional writing to the exposure of the female body is significant in light of the poem that preceded hers and to which she was undoubtedly responding: Snodgrass's "The Operation," which was deemed neither revolutionary nor upsetting but "rather lovely" by critic M. L. Rosenthal (*The New Poets* 80). As his poem demonstrates, male confessional poets were not perceived to expose their bodies because they were able to conserve bodily privacy while creating the illusion of its loss.

Snodgrass's "The Operation" ostensibly presents an image of the extreme violation of his body; however, a close reading of the poem illustrates that the transgression of male privacy is, in fact, unrepresentable. This problem of representing male privacy occurs not because invasions cannot or do not happen but, rather, because once they have, the subject of the violation is no longer an adult male. The violated or penetrated man is represented through the figure of a woman or a girl.[13] Snodgrass's first stanza in "The Operation" illustrates that exposure first degenders then transgenders the speaker:

From stainless steel basins of water
They brought warm cloths and they washed me,
From spun aluminum bowls, cold Zephiran sponges, fuming;
Gripped in the dead yellow glove, a bright straight razor
Inched on my stomach, down my groin,
Paring the brown hair off. They left me
White as a child, not frightened. I was not
Ashamed. They clothed me, then,
In the thin, loose, light, white garments,
The delicate sandals of poor Pierrot,
A schoolgirl first offering her sacrament. (*Selected Poems* 13)

The mood of the first lines of the stanza, prior to the shaving of the body hair, is comforting, even reverent. However, in contrast to this preparation, "paring the brown hair off" suggests castration when the "bright straight razor / inched on [his] stomach, down [his] groin." Though the razor stops short of literalizing this castration, the threat is implied and the speaker is metaphorically castrated. The process of exposing his body makes him first "like a child," then a "delicate" Pierrot, feminized but like the clown, a liminal figure neither male nor female, and finally, a female child "offering her first sacrament"—confession—completing his gender transformation and linking the exposure of the operation to the exposure of the confessional. The speaker is most assertively masculine and heterosexual immediately after the surgery. "Into flowers into women / I have come . . ." begins the stanza following the operation. Any suggestion of castration is immediately banished by the sexual potency established in the first lines of the third stanza. This return of sexual potency coincides with the recovery of the speaker's privacy.

Exposure, and therefore confession, feminize, but it is the violation of bodily privacy, not the confession alone, that calls gender into question. Allen Ginsberg's poem "To Aunt Rose" presents a remarkably similar metaphor of exposure. The second stanza of his gently teasing elegy reads:

—your long sad face
   your tears of sexual frustration
      (what smothered sobs and bony hips
under the pillows of Osborne Terrace)
—the time I stood on the toilet seat naked
   and you powdered my thighs with Calomine
      against the poison ivy—my tender
         and shamed first black curled hairs
what were you thinking in secret heart then
      knowing me a man already—
and I an ignorant girl of family silence on the thin pedestal
      of my legs in the bathroom—Museum of Newark. (*Kaddish* 46)

Here, not unlike in "Kaddish" with its portrayal of his mother, Naomi's, pathetic attempt to seduce the young Allen, the aunt's sexual desperation places his just barely emerging adolescent manhood under an uncomfortable scrutiny. The shaming of his manhood on the "thin pedestal of [his] legs," which makes his genitalia artwork on display, neuters him though it does not castrate him. While these family jewels are exhibited in the "Museum of Newark," however, they simultaneously disappear into his now feminized body. On the one hand, while we see Ginsberg's exaggerated sense of his own masculine attraction (that the aunt, no matter how sexually frustrated, harbors a fascination with her poison-ivy covered nephew's burgeoning virility stretches the imagination), the display of his family jewels shames him into losing not just his incipient sexual potency but his masculinity altogether. Like Snodgrass's, without the violent image of castration, Ginsberg's moment of exposure transforms him into a little girl.

To return to Snodgrass's poem, the distinguishing mark of the operation, besides the shifting gender of the exposed poet, is the absence of the doctor in the poem. This second stanza, scene of the surgery, never mentions a doctor.

I was drifting, inexorably, on toward sleep.
In skullcaps, masked, in blue-green gowns, attendants
Towed my cart, afloat in its white cloths,
The body with its tributary poisons borne
Down corridors of the diseased, thronging:

The scrofulous faces, contagious grim boys,
The huddled families, weeping, a staring woman
Arched to her gnarled stick,—a child was somewhere
Screaming, screaming—then, blind silence, the elevator rising
To the arena, humming, vast with lights; blank hero,
Shackled and spellbound, to enact my deed. (*Collected Poems* 14)

"[M]asked . . . attendants" whisk the poet to the "arena" of surgery where *he*, rather than the doctor, becomes the "blank hero, shackled and spellbound," ready "to enact [his] deed." Once in the "arena," a place for spectacle that implicitly acknowledges audience, rather than submit to the scrutiny and penetration of surgery, the patient becomes the performer, the "blank hero" of the poem and of the operation. Moreover, despite his nearly complete helplessness—he is "shackled and spellbound"—he is able to view the act of surgery as "[*his*] deed." Blinded, voiceless, and paralyzed, the poet nevertheless presents himself at the center of the action as if he had performed surgery on himself. Snodgrass does away with the doctor who would diagnose him, open him up, and cut out his disease, who would, by interpreting, exposing, and invading him, violate his bodily privacy. The violation of male privacy remains, therefore, unimagined. Instead of forcing meaning from his body, the poem "offers" a sacrament of confession, like the schoolgirl of the first stanza. By eliminating the doctor, Snodgrass turns the operation into an act of self-disclosure rather than forced confession, implying that he has forfeited his own privacy rather than having had it taken from him.[14]

A reading of Sexton's "The Operation" in relation to that of Snodgrass reveals a fundamental principle of confession in these works: the male body, although forced to expose itself, never completely relinquishes its privacy, while the female body must expose itself in order to obtain a measure of its privacy. This phenomenon similarly animates the legal doctrine of privacy that became central to the notion of democratic citizenship in the cold war period. As the legal actors turned their attention away from questions of where privacy is "found" to the issue of contraception, the abstract individual who once functioned as the centerpiece of the emerging right to privacy became indisputably gendered. Once the right to privacy increasingly came to be applied in the context of reproductive rights, the private citizen—once implicitly understood as male—became, as in Snodgrass's poem, transgendered. And with the transformation of

the abstract or male body into a pregnant female body came new limitations of
the right to privacy and an emphasis on confession and testimony as necessary
to preserving the limited privacy rights awarded.

Prior to *Roe*, full privacy rights are imagined in contraception decisions that
are nongendered insofar as the body of the citizen remained an abstract rights-
bearer. *Griswold* had recognized that married couples had the right to make contraceptive decisions and that the bedroom was the place that such decisions were
taken. Nevertheless, this right inhered, according to the Court, in the "couple"
not the individual. Brennan revises this in *Eisenstadt v. Baird*:

> It is true that in *Griswold* the right of privacy in question inhered in the mar-
> ital relationship. Yet the marital couple is not an independent entity with a
> mind and heart of its own, but an association of two individuals each with
> separate intellectual and emotional makeup. If the right of privacy means any-
> thing, it is the right of the *individual*, married or single, to be free from unwar-
> ranted governmental intrusion into matters so fundamentally affecting a per-
> son as the decision whether to bear or beget a child. (452)

The phrase "an independent entity with a heart and mind of its own" describes
the abstract individual whose right to privacy the Court had consistently sought
to protect. Yet in deciding *Eisenstadt*, the Court began to distinguish the
"abstract individual" essential to American legal liberalism by reproductive ca-
pacity. Even as individuals were being protected in their difference—their capac-
ity to either bear or beget a child (if this can be understood as a distinction since
women both bear and beget)—*Eisenstadt v. Baird* remains focused on bodies
prior to conception, where men and women are still the "same" because they are
both not pregnant.

However, when the pregnant body comes before the court in *Roe*, the terms of
privacy change. The privacy of *Roe v. Wade*, as Justice Rehnquist noted, had
nothing whatever to do with the conception of privacy-as-withholding, what he
asserted as the "ordinary" concept of privacy. His dissent reads:

> I have difficulty in concluding, as the Court does, that the right of "privacy"
> is involved in this case. Texas, by the statute here challenged, bars the per-
> formance of a medical abortion by a licensed physician on a plaintiff such as
> Roe. *A transaction resulting in an operation such as this is not "private" in the*

ordinary usage of that word. Nor is the "privacy" that the Court finds here even
a distant relative of the freedom from search and seizures protected by the
Fourth Amendment to the Constitution, which the Court has referred to as
embodying a right to privacy [in] *Katz v. U.S.* (172; emphasis mine)

By characterizing the abortion procedure as a "transaction," a word whose economic connotation emphasizes the public and commercial nature of the doctor's
office, Rehnquist might appear to question whether the doctor's office is truly
"private," in the "ordinary" concept, for the pregnant woman. It might at first
appear that Rehnquist was arguing that the Court had not gone far enough, that
the privacy of the doctor's office was, indeed, no privacy at all. However, the
expansion of privacy to include women's complete autonomy from state or medical control is not Rehnquist's aim. By finding this "transaction" not even a "distant relative" of *Katz* (a case that affirmed the privacy of the public telephone,
even if that phone were being used to place illegal bets—clearly "transactions"
that are not " 'private' in the ordinary usage of the word"), Rehnquist ignores the
Court's gradual redefinition of privacy as autonomy because he cannot apply this
concept to the pregnant citizen.

Nevertheless, "transaction" accurately defines the exchange in *Roe* in which
information about the self and one's reasons for deciding to terminate a pregnancy are offered up to interpretation so that one's bodily privacy is maintained.
Indeed, a transaction of some sort must take place because the woman's bodily
integrity comes only through the doctor's permission. Anne Sexton's "The Operation" recognizes this kind of transactional privacy and denies the existence of
an a priori privacy. If privacy depends on a compact with the viewer/reader, the
doctor's agreement to the privacy of his patient is a promise that is always
already broken. The first stanza of Sexton's "The Operation" depicts the gynecologist and patient relationship, the very one *Roe* defines as private, as defined
by his violation of her body. The stirrups of the gynecologist epitomize the relationship of the woman to her doctor: on her back in an immobile position to
facilitate the doctor's access into her body.

> After the sweet promise,
> the summer's mild retreat
> from mother's cancer, the winter months of her death,
> I come to this white office, its sterile sheet,

its hard tablet, its stirrups, to hold my breath
while I, who must, allow the glove its oily rape,
to hear the almost mighty doctor over me equate
my ills with hers
and decide to operate. (*Complete Poems* 56)

The shape of the lines: "while I, who must, allow the glove its oily rape, / to hear the almost mighty doctor over me equate / my ills with hers / and decide to operate" emphasizes that the patient must permit the "oily rape" in order to be diagnosed. Diagnosis, the interpretation of her body, and rape, the invasion of her body, are bound together grammatically. At the same time Sexton accentuates her lack of choice in how she is examined by the "almost mighty doctor" who stands "over" her—"I, who must," which accentuates coercion, with the word, "allow," which indicates discretion, work together to exemplify the privacy of the doctor's office. "Must allow" expresses both the oxymoron of women's self-determination and the fictionality of any privacy that depends on being forced to grant permission for violation.

In the stanzas that relate her mother's death, Sexton gives an example of how privacy could exist between people. Rather than conceiving privacy as an essence enjoyed by an individual alone, she imagines a privacy that can be either withheld or bestowed. Her descriptions of her mother reveal her as

> . . . she grew frail.
> Frail, we say, remembering fear, that face we wear
> in the room of the special smells of dying, fear
> where the snoring mouth gapes
> and is not dear. (*Complete Poems* 56)

Sexton concludes with the physical presence of her mother, the dying patient—"the snoring mouth gapes / and is not dear"—to recall the indignities of illness. Her fascination with this aspect of her mother's death shows that as much as the operation signifies pain or possible death, it also reveals the loss of a public self. "That face we wear / in the room of the special smells of dying" is a performance that refuses to reflect back the "snoring mouth" or to acknowledge what "is not dear." For her dying mother, as for Sexton the patient, privacy is granted by the audience, which helps to maintain the fiction of a public self by refusing to acknowledge the self that would be, but cannot be, hidden. The audience must consent to preserve the mask for the fiction of privacy to be sustained.

"Pain: 1967," a poem from *The Nightmare Factory* (1970) by Maxine Kumin, Sexton's closest friend and most important interlocutor, shows from another angle the paradoxical relationship women have to the privacy of their bodies. Kumin's frustration with her ignorance about her body forces the speaker of "Pain: 1967" to invite the invasion of her privacy.

The lore of it is something they keep from you.
As with sex, the mechanics are little rehearsed.
Not even among grown men and women the specifics—
yes he unbuttoned her, yes she was a good lay
but how? and in exactly what circumstance?

The nurses will not tell you. They baste and simmer
tools in the autoclave. The doctors whisper
Demerol into their stethoscopes. And the interns,
that volleyball team still challenging its acne,
can only pump up the bag full of blood pressure.

Meanwhile the pain comes in dressed up like a spy.
A bearded spy wearing sneakers and murmuring eat!
Eat my quick poison. And of course I nibble the edges.
I eat my way to the center of his stem
because something inside it is secret.

At night rowing out to sea on drugs, rowing out
on my little oars, those carefully deployed spoons,
sometimes I think I catch a glimpse of that body
of knowledge. It is the fin of a flying fish.
It is a scrap of phosphorescent plankton
I would take hold of crying, wait!
Thinking, tell me.

Understand that by this time the man next door
is calling *police police police*—his pain

burgles him. *Police*, that kind of father.
Understand that on the other side an old lady
in the thin voice of a music teacher is calling
yoohoo, help me, am I alone in this house?
She is dying with the shades drawn in a deserted villa.

Meanwhile I continue putting out to sea
on my little wooden ice cream spoons.
Although I am not a Catholic, the priest has laid
his hands upon me. He has put God into my pain.
Somewhere in my pineal gland He sits and gloats.

As for the lore, I have learned nothing to hand on.
I go out nightly past these particular needles
and these knives. (*The Nightmare Factory* 73–74)

Because the medical community conceals its knowledge of the female body—
even "The nurses will not tell you"—Kumin figures her pain in the cold war
metaphor of "A bearded spy wearing sneakers and murmuring eat!" However,
Kumin inverts the spy's relationship to knowledge: instead of the spy infiltrating
in order to acquire knowledge, which would imply that the speaker possessed
it, Kumin's spy carries knowledge to the speaker. The spy, who is gendered male
by his beard, says "Eat my quick poison" and the speaker acquiesces, "I eat my
way to the center of his stem / Because something inside it is secret," a line
which hints at fellatio, a sexual image like Sexton's "oily rape," which implies
the indistinct line between coerced sex—she must "eat [her] way to the center
of his stem" because she needs his "secret" and medical power, "eat" being both
encouragement and command. So powerful is the lure of knowledge and so fran-
tic is the speaker to know her own body that she risks poisoning herself by doubly accepting the intruder into her body, once in the figure of the spy, once in the
ingestion of the spy's gift of poison. In contrast, the man next to her screams
"*police, police, police*" as "his pain / burgles him." In his case, "*Police*, that kind
of father," serve to protect the private space of the body because the intruder is
not welcome; the police will expel the intruder from the body, rendering it private once more. Unlike the speaker who must welcome invasion, the male
patient seeks to expel the intruder, pain, by appealing to patriarchal forces: the

doctors, the police, those kind of fathers. However, as Kumin shows, the doctor's overwhelming control of knowledge leaves the woman patient in the position of inviting his intrusion or inviting pain; Kumin welcomes pain rather than call on the doctor/policeman so that she might gain knowledge and achieve some control over her body.

Nevertheless, because the poet's lack of knowledge is related to her position in discourse, not her experience, the body of knowledge she seeks cannot be known through experience but only through the mastery of discourse, through learning the rules that dictate what the female body can mean. Kumin's poem equates medical diagnosis with locker-room sexual boasting where the rules of interpretation are left unspoken and inscrutable to women. Her questions: "yes he unbuttoned her, yes she was a good lay / but how? and in exactly what circumstance?" place her knowledge of her body at odds with coded male constructions of female sexuality, none of which she can decipher. In these questions, the woman's body lies at the center of an interpretation that is unknown to her, indicating that her relationship to her body is mediated—in this case obstructed—by male interpretation. Throughout the poem she searches for this "lore" in her body, twice "rowing out to sea on drugs, rowing out / on [her] little oars" where "sometimes [she thinks she catches] a glimpse of that body / of knowledge." The line break calls attention to the word "body," her physical body and the body of knowledge, both of which lie out of her reach, "the fin of a flying fish . . . [she] would take hold of crying, wait! / Thinking, tell me." Nevertheless, were she able to hook this fish, looking for the "body of knowledge" *in* her body guarantees that she will never find it. The poem, an attempt to penetrate the secrets of the medicalized body, closes with an admission of failure: "As for the lore, I have learned nothing to hand on," and a promise that the speaker will continue her search. All she can really "hand on" is the search, rowing out nightly in a seemingly futile quest for knowledge and mastery over her own body.

The paradox of privacy we find in both Sexton's and Kumin's poems returns us to *Roe v. Wade* and to the construction of privacy that situates the doctor's supervision at the heart of women's so-called autonomy. Blackmun boldly affirms that "The right of privacy . . . is broad enough to encompass a woman's decision whether or not to terminate her pregnancy" (*Roe v. Wade* 153) but then denies that this choice can be freely made: "This means . . . that, for the period of pregnancy prior to this 'compelling' point, *the attending physician*, in consultation with his patient, *is free to determine*, without regulation by the State, that, *in his medical judgment*, the patient's pregnancy should be terminated" (*Roe v. Wade* 163; emphasis mine). In this halting, qualified sentence, it is "the attending physician" who is "free" to determine whether or not to terminate the pregnancy of the woman, who is made adjunct to the decision by her status as consultant.[15] *Doe v. Bolton*, the case handed down with *Roe*, which overruled regulations imposed by the Georgia legislature on doctors performing abortions, further clarifies the doctor's status as decision maker. Blackmun states:

> *Roe v. Wade* sets forth our conclusion that a pregnant woman does not have an absolute constitutional right to an abortion on her demand. (189)

> We agree . . . that the medical judgment may be exercised in light of all factors—physical, emotional, psychological, familial, and the woman's age—relevant to the well-being of the patient. . . . This allows the attending physician the room he needs to make his best medical judgment. (192)

While "abortion on her demand" has become synonymous with an "extremist" prochoice position, from Blackmun's formulation it is evident that "abortion on demand" means independent of the doctor. Moreover, the "factors" essential to "his best medical judgment"—physical, emotional, psychological, familial— cannot be weighed by the doctor without complete and detailed storytelling by the woman.[16] To grant this woman privacy "in the ordinary sense," the doctor would have to leave her case history unfilled.

For Blackmun, it is precisely because he is viewing the pregnant woman as a citizen that he can imagine the abortion decision as a question of autonomy. However, because traditional notions of individual autonomy posit an antagonistic relationship between individuals, Blackmun inserts the doctor to referee what becomes defined as an adversarial relationship between the mother and the fetus. For Blackmun, it is not the woman's irrationality (though it will be for Justice White) that makes her incapable of deciding "between" herself and her fetus; it is in fact, her rationality. It is inherent in the model of autonomy he works with that privacy rights are competing rights, and so, *Roe* offers the doctor as judge in a juridical model of negotiation.[17]

Nevertheless, while *Roe* positions the doctor as listener and interpreter on the private decisions of women, *Doe v. Bolton* disallows just such a monitor on the *doctor's* judgment. In *Doe* the Court held unconstitutional the requirement that abortion decisions be ratified by two of the doctor's colleagues as well as a hospital review committee. This system, Justice Blackmun reasoned, improperly scrutinized the doctor's judgment, making little mention of the fact that it required the woman's story to be evaluated no fewer than six times. In addition he rejected the appellant's claim that "the Georgia system enables the committee members' personal views as to extramarital sex relations, and punishment therefore, to govern their decision" (*Doe v. Bolton* 196) by presenting a spirited defense of the good physician:

> The appellants' suggestion is necessarily somewhat degrading to the conscientious physician, particularly the obstetrician, whose professional activity is concerned with the physical and mental welfare, the woes, the emotions, and the concern of his female patients. He, perhaps more than anyone else, is knowledgeable in this area of patient care, and he is aware of human frailty, so-called "error," and needs. The good physician—despite the presence of rascals in the medical profession, as in all others, we trust that most physicians are "good"—will have sympathy and understanding for the pregnant patient that probably are not exceeded by those who participate in other areas of professional counseling. (196)

The physician's good judgment, his compassion, and most of all his objectivity are the foundation of the woman's right to privacy. Therefore, his ability to make decisions and his autonomy in making them cannot be questioned by the state.

Instead of the right to privacy guaranteeing a "right to silence," this right to privacy depends upon a forced confession. Not only must the woman confess the details of her life in order to establish a need to terminate her pregnancy, she must also be convincing. She must be rhetorically skilled in making her case before the doctor in order to achieve a decision purportedly made by herself. In other words, this right to privacy can only be effected by rhetoric, which means that the right to privacy, the autonomy celebrated by Justice Douglas, depends on the ability to make one's self-definition credible to others. In contrast to the a priori privacy of the abstract individual, the woman's privacy as defined in *Roe* has to be secured through rhetoric. This vision of women's privacy allows women to make decisions about themselves to the extent that they can persuade others that the decision is right: to the extent that they can reveal sufficient information about themselves to let others know them, but not so much that the decision is taken from them altogether.

The link between privacy and forced confession found in *Roe* is the subject of Anne Sexton's poem, "Unknown Girl in the Maternity Ward" (*To Bedlam and Part Way Back*, 1960) a work that revolves around a young woman's resistance to the doctors' pressure to confess the name of her child's father. Not only does resistance to confession mark this particular poem, but Sexton used the poem in an interview to obscure the confessionalism of her work as a whole. When William Heyen pressed her to answer, "to what extent are you fictionalizing Anne Sexton as you write some of these poems?" Sexton, like the speaker of her poem, refused in the terms that the questioner offered. Because Heyen was made anxious by the "shaky ground" between fiction and confession ("we feel sort of foolish. . . . It sort of makes us nervous"), he asked Sexton to clarify what the poems left ambiguous. In response, she explained that she wrote "Unknown Girl in the Maternity Ward" after reading Snodgrass's "Heart's Needle," the work she credited as her most important influence. At this crucial juncture in her career, she claimed she was "fictionalizing, but of course . . . so-called confessing" (Sexton, *No Evil Star* 136, 138). She then related that when Snodgrass read the poem, he told her to "tell the real story" (138), and so she wrote "The Double Image" (*To Bedlam and Part Way Back*), the poem that marked her arrival as a confessional poet but also one that fictionalized the account of her life. The answer, which only defers an answer, resists Heyen's pressure to explicate the lines of confession in her work, the indeterminacy of which thwarts forced confession. Moreover, Sexton's great insight into female privacy is that one guards it not through silence but through the multiplication of confession: she produces two versions of the same story, "Unknown Girl in a Maternity Ward" and "The Double Image," neither of which offers a full and complete account of her life— if such a thing could exist.

"Unknown Girl in the Maternity Ward" features the failure of silence to resist the power of doctors to compel confession, enacting a pre-*Roe* drama of self-determination. The doctor's quest for information and the mother's effort to maintain her silence compose the drama of the poem:

The doctors are enamel. They want to know
the facts. They guess about the man who left me,
some pendulum soul, going the way men go
and leave you full of child. But our case history
stays blank. All I did was let you grow.
Now we are here for all the ward to see.

They thought I was strange, although
I never spoke a word. I burst empty
of you, letting you learn how the air is so.
The doctors chart the riddle they ask of me
and I turn my head away. I do not know. (*Complete Poems* 24)

The doctors, covered by an impermeable surface of enamel, are resistant to penetration themselves, while in contrast the speaker, as a pregnant woman, has already been penetrated and punctured like a balloon ("I burst empty / of you"). Unable to leave the woman unfilled, the doctors supply their own interpretations of her predicament, putting words in her mouth by offering a generic story about women in her position, ". . . They guess about the man who left me, / some pendulum soul, going the way men go / and leave you full of child." This story she refuses to confirm *or* deny. She opposes the doctor's attempts to coerce a confession by initially remaining storyless—"our case history / stays blank"— refusing to answer, with truth or lies, because her defense, "All I did was let you grow," admits no crime to confess.

In the next stanza, however, the child's presence reminds her that her privacy is compromised by her relationship to someone else: "[her] funny kin, / . . . trouble[s] [her] silence."

. . . You blink in surprise
and I wonder what you can see, my funny kin,
as you trouble my silence. I am a shelter of lies.
Should I learn to speak again, or hopeless in
such sanity will I touch some face I recognize? (*Complete Poems* 24)

The question she poses in response to the perception of her new relational status: "Should I learn to speak again . . . ?" reminds us that her silence is only one of the hopelessly "sane" choices that she can make. Her eventual capitulation to the doctors is only partial, a reprieve from their insistent questioning, not an answer to their request for information.

. . . But the doctors return to scold
me. I speak. It is you my silence harms.
I should have known; I should have told

them something to write down. My voice alarms
my throat. "Name of father—none." I hold
you and name you bastard in my arms. (*Complete Poems* 25)

"I speak" appears to be her capitulation, and yet her regret, "I should have
known; I should have told / them something to write down," indicates that her
confession is incomplete and, more important, unsatisfactory to the doctors. In
refusing to name the father of the child, the one piece of information the doctors
repeatedly solicit in order to legitimate the birth, to place the child and identify
the mother, she names her child a bastard and herself disreputable.

In the final stanza she reveals the hopelessness of her act of choosing: "There
is nothing more / that I can say or lose." She has given everything away, including her child, by answering with no answer.

And now that's that. There is nothing more
that I can say or lose.
Others have traded life before
and could not speak. I tighten to refuse
your owling eyes, my fragile visitor.
I touch your cheeks, like flowers. You bruise
against me. We unlearn. I am a shore
rocking you off. You break from me. I choose
your only way, my small inheritor
and hand you off, trembling the selves we lose.
Go child, who is my sin and nothing more. (*Complete Poems* 25)

In this pre-*Roe* confessional moment, Sexton's poem does confess, but only to
the failure to confess. Refusing the demand for information that affirms masculine privilege and power does not eliminate the violation of the doctor, the image
of power, state sanction, and the invasion of her body. To see a doctor as *Roe*
imagines him as an affirmation of privacy is not possible in the terms of these
poems. Where Snodgrass eliminates the doctor's threat by simply eliminating his
presence from the poem, Sexton on the other hand contends with his presence
as one of the limitations on her choices. When privacy is situated "between a
woman and her doctor" as in *Roe*, confessional poetry shows that to give nothing away is to lose everything.

By reading these so-called confessional works against the backdrop of the emerging doctrine of privacy, we can see that what upholds privacy and autonomy is not the woman's withdrawal into silence but her perceived fitness for discourse. The question is, therefore, when the woman confesses to the doctor, what is the status of her testimony. In *Doe*, for example, if a woman's reason for requesting an abortion was rape, Georgia required that

> the woman make a written statement under oath, and subject to the penalties of false swearing, of the date, time and place of the rape and the name of the rapist, if known. There must be attached to this statement a certified copy of any report of the rape made by any law enforcement officer or agency and a statement by the solicitor general of judicial circuit where the rape occurred or allegedly occurred that, according to his best information, there is probable cause to believe that the rape did occur. (*Doe v. Bolton*, Georgia Statute Section 26–1202)

The woman's word here must be buttressed with two official certifications of its truthfulness, her statement alone being wholly unreliable. Moreover, in contrast to the assumed rationality of the doctor, women's judgment, what Justice White calls "caprice and convenience" in his dissent, is found wanting. Women's judgment, never addressed in Blackmun's opinion, though implicit in his curtailing of her right to privacy, is inherently untrustworthy. As Justice White states:

> The common claim before us is that for any one of such reasons, *or for no reason at all*, and without asserting or claiming any threat to life or health, any woman is entitled to an abortion at her request if she is able to find a medical advisor willing to undertake it. The Court for the most part sustains this position: During the period prior to the time the fetus becomes viable, [the Constitution] values *the convenience, whim or caprice of the putative mother* more than the life or potential life of the fetus. (*Doe v. Bolton* 221; emphasis mine)

The phrases I have emphasized—"for no reason at all" and "convenience, whim, or caprice"—indicate an irrationality that, in White's view, the state endorses in surrendering to a woman even a limited right to control her body. It follows therefore that granting privacy to women would bestow a right of citizenship on someone incapable of the rationality of public discourse. Because privacy might guard what the Court or even the doctor views as "no reason at all," the woman is not to be trusted with the right of privacy and its concomitant moral autonomy.

There is a circularity in this reasoning that doubly binds the pregnant citizen. The lack of rationality that makes a woman an unfit private decision maker also undermines her ability to testify on her own behalf. Though it was the de facto practice of the hospital to refuse to allow women to argue on their own behalf, this issue was rendered moot when Blackmun decided lack of access was not mandated by Georgia's statute. Furthermore, the pregnant woman's testimony had no credibility even in the "private" sphere of the doctor's office. This review process struck down by *Doe*, which at the time was a liberalization of abortion restrictions, took the woman's story from her and made it the doctor's. He gained control of her story not just to judge it for himself but to present it to a wider community of judges. The Court, by treating *Doe v. Bolton* as primarily an issue of the doctor's right to pursue his profession, could ignore the conflict between the privacy asserted in *Roe* and that confirmed in *Doe*.

Sylvia Plath wrestles with just this cooptation of the woman's voice by the doctor in "Lady Lazarus" (*Ariel* 1966) a poem that configures the medicalized confession as a striptease of gauze, bandages, and tissues. The private self is exposed layer by layer, and finally given away piece by piece, to the "Doktor." It is not the mass audience, but the intimate listener who would turn her relics into his "opus."[18]

There is a charge

For the eyeing of my scars, there is a charge
For the hearing of my heart—
It really goes.

And there is a charge, a very large charge,
For a word or a touch
Or a bit of blood

Or a piece of my hair or my clothes.
So, so Herr Doktor.
So, Herr Enemy.

I am your opus,
I am your valuable,
The pure gold baby

That melts into a shriek.
I turn and burn.
Do not think I underestimate your concern. (*Collected Poems* 246)

Plath's macabre exchange attempts to extract a return for her confession to the doctor. The "charge / For the hearing of [her] heart" can be read two ways—there is expense and there is excitement; there is a price to be paid but there is also an electric thrill for both her and her listener. The souvenirs of her body—blood, hair, clothes—are relics, totems of celebrity, while the "word" and "touch" speak of a more intimate exchange. Through the confession, which she characterizes as bits of herself, she is converted into "[his] opus . . . [his] valuable." The resistance to this process of appropriation, the "shriek," is inarticulateness and rage, which expresses her frustration, garbles his interpretation, and perhaps alerts the reader to danger. In both "Lady Lazarus" and *Doe*, the doctor—especially the "good doctor" whose "concern" Plath does not "underestimate," if only ironically—will take over the woman's confession, transfiguring her body into his "opus," and though Plath's shriek marks her as defiant, it fails to reclaim her self-determination. At the same time, exposing this private relationship in all its coercive danger subjects doctors to scrutiny and interpretation, which permits the woman to focus attention on the context of her self-revelation. We are forced to examine not only the woman's confession, but the circumstances of its production.

As Cynthia Daniels has so persuasively explained, the abortion debate changed substantially in the 1980s largely due to technological advances that made the fetus independent medically and visually from the mother (*At Women's Expense* 9). In addition, she argues, this independence has been enhanced by rhetoric that abstracts women's bodies into "hosts," transforming fetuses into "tiny citizens." Reproductive decisions are no longer "between a woman and her doctor"; instead the woman's body has been increasingly viewed as standing "between" the doctor and his "new patient," the fetus (41). Again, confessional poetry imagined this transformation several years before the Court would contend with it.

Robert Lowell's "Fetus" (*Day by Day* 1975) predicted the transformation of the pregnant body wrought by medical technologies in a post-*Roe* world. As the poem illustrates, the pregnant body fades to secondary significance; we no longer even see it, we see past it.

Lowell's poem, which offers an image of the fetus with "its shifty thumb in its mouth," demonstrates the power of metaphor in the debate over reproduction and women's bodies. The fetus is animated through paradox, vivified by the ironic denial of human qualities, a strategy that permits Lowell to use the arguments of abortion activists (the poem begins by evoking the "convicted abortion-surgeon") against them.

> When the black arrow arrives on the silver tray,
> the fetus has no past,
> not even an immovable wall of paintings—
> no room to stir its thoughts,
> no breathless servility
> overacting the last day,
> writhing like a worm
> under the contradicting rays of science—
> no scared eye on the audience.

Each verb, such as "overacting" or "writhing," gives the fetus not only movement but self-consciousness; each adjective, "scared" or "breathless," personifies. But Lowell's next move is the more powerful:

> How much we carry away with us
> before dying,
> learning we have nothing to take,
> like the fetus, the homunculus,
> already at four months one pound,
> with shifty thumb in mouth— (*Day by Day* 34–35)

The fetus is no longer an immature "us," we are "like the fetus" with every step we take toward death. As we grow older, we only become more, not less, like the fetus. This reversal inverts the court's compromise on abortion: as the fetus develops, the court increasingly restricts the woman's control over her body. In

Lowell's terms, there can be no point at which the fetus is anything less than fully mature.

Lowell then invokes a contrast through the word "model," comparing the fetus, "our little model," in a fragment stanza that links the "humunculus . . . with shifty thumb in mouth" to the "model" on the billboard in the last stanza.

> As I drive on, I lift my eyes;
> the focus is spidered
> with black winter branches
> and blackened concrete stores
> bonneted for Easter with billboards . . .
> Boston snow contracting
> like a yellow surgical bandage—
> the slut of struggle.
> The girl high on the billboard
> was ten years my senior in life;
> she would have teased my father—
> unkillable, unlaid,
> disused as the adolescent tan on my hand.
> She is a model, and cannot lose her looks,
> born a decade too soon for any buyer. (*Day by Day* 35)

At first glance, this stanza seems oddly unrelated to the meditations on mortality that precede it. And yet, if the first stanza invokes the "abortion-surgeon" and the others animate the fetus, the final stanza introduces the lost third party in this poem: the pregnant woman. While never naming her as such, the "yellow surgical bandage" and the "slut of struggle" introduce us to the image of a "girl high on the billboard." Almost subliminally in this juxtaposition of surgery and uncontrolled sexuality with the image of the "girl" (surely not the patient of the abortion-surgeon), Lowell manages to indict every woman because any woman will serve as a "model." By providing her with a mock immortality, "She is a model, and cannot lose her looks," Lowell implicitly contrasts this "unkillable" girl to the fetus who is animated, self-conscious, and mortal. The girl, now a woman (she was "ten years his senior in life"), is nothing more than a static image of debased sexuality, almost completely eclipsed by the fetus.

Can a notion of privacy that appears thoroughly paradoxical, be anything more than a limitation on female autonomy? Are there ways in which we can imagine the female body's "unbounded" privacy as a model for privacy in the postmodern world? That is, if the containment model of privacy has proved too anxious, is there a version of privacy that could be found in a formal territory— the metaphorics of the female body—that has historically been imagined as exposed, opened, porous, permeable, leaky, and penetrated? Can we imagine privacy in the model of the woman's body rather than against it? Can we imagine a privacy that is *not* contained and would we want to do so?

If *Roe* and the decisions that followed it split the terms of privacy for women—withdrawal from scrutiny *or* autonomy—is there anything to be gained by reforging their relationship? Though we might recognize that confessional poets were able to maintain privacy through the multiplication of confession or through positing a generous listener, one who agrees a priori to maintain the privacy of the confessor, this split remains a coercive construction. The burden of providing an adequate story remains the woman's, and this burden, though in the Court's reasoning not yet "undue," is increasingly onerous, especially for women most at the mercy of state regulation. However, at the same time, there are a number of problems in returning to an unreconstructed notion of withdrawal. By thinking through this reading of confessional poetry and legal privacy, the assumption that the private sphere exists prior to the public, that as citizens we enter and leave the public sphere from home base, seems untenable. The break down of the liberal notion of privacy was not simply a result of increased interest in fetal autonomy but, from the start, a consequence of women's precarious relationship to public speech and self-representation. What *Roe* made visible was that a woman's uncertain identity as a citizen undermined her status as a private decision maker. In other words, it is because men are a priori rational decision makers as citizens in the public sphere that they are assumed to be adequate decision makers in private. The Court's decision in *Roe* highlights the fact that the right to privacy is dependent on a secure public identity, which surely cannot be established by increased withdrawal into the private sphere.

If citizenship were reconstructed so that women were securely enfranchised, would that make the withdrawal into privacy possible? And if it were available, would it be valuable? As Jennifer Nedelsky ("Reconceiving Autonomy" 1989) and Lauren Berlant ("Live Sex Acts" 1985) have so persuasively argued, privacy as it is currently imagined is a fantasy. As Nedelsky has shown, defining autonomy as isolation from the community misrepresents the realities of interdependence that make autonomy possible.[19] In a somewhat different vein, Lauren

Berlant has explained that "a radical social theory of sexual citizenship in the United States must not aspire to reoccupy the dead identities of privacy," that the illusion of a normative and patriotic heterosexuality that privacy maintains can only be disrupted by often painful acts of self-disclosure ("Live Sex Acts" 402). And yet, given the continued intrusiveness of the state, particularly in regulating pregnant women, it remains crucial to imagine the possibility of refusing coerced confession without losing the opportunity of self-determination. As we have seen, confessional poets demanded not only that we hear their stories but that we attend to the production of their confessions. Without acknowledging the terms on which self-disclosure is made, it is impossible to maintain a viable distinction between voluntary self-disclosure and coerced confession. Privacy may simply be a mechanism of choosing what and how and to whom one reveals oneself; nothing more or less than the freedom of the speaker to refuse or embrace the confessional moment.

FIVE

Confessing the Ordinary

Paul Monette's *Love Alone* and *Bowers v. Hardwick*

An Epilogue

Borrowed Time and *Love Alone: Eighteen Elegies for Rog*, both published in March 1988, turned Paul Monette from a little-known writer of screenplays, light fiction, and "entertainments" into a "writer who humanized AIDS," as the *New York Times* would designate him in its 1995 obituary. Monette certainly caught the wave of increased media attention to AIDS with his twin publications, but it is equally clear that he propelled it by casting his protest in the form of autobiography. Monette's subject—his lover Roger's bewildering fight with AIDS and the rage and grief that followed Roger's death—reached across a curious divide. On the one hand, his work served as an important consolation as well as a source of information for gay men; at the same time, his image of the devoted—and monogamous—gay couple reassured a wary but increasingly concerned straight readership, many of whom were learning about AIDS for the first time. Monette's "human face" transformed body counts and dollar figures in all their staggering immensity into a drama of ordinary individuals. The shock of recognition produced in his readers catapulted him to national prominence.

Writing autobiography, however, was not as simple a choice for Monette as it might now seem. As he notes in his second autobiography, *Becoming a Man* (1992), the poems he wrote as a young man were obsessed with secrecy and self-camouflage, reflecting both his closeted homosexuality and his Yale literary training, which had taught him that poetry was necessarily impersonal. More important, his experience of AIDS had left him morbidly sensitive to invasions of privacy. He remarked in *Borrowed Time* that "The privacy issue surrounding AIDS engages vectors of the nightmare that make it different from every other medical crisis" (81). Playing variations on this theme throughout the memoir,

Monette points to the epidemiological surveillance of the disease, William F. Buckley's proposal to brand and quarantine those infected with HIV, and the daily psychic and bodily invasions of medical treatment. Still, in the face of this anxiety about privacy, Monette sought an outlet to express the extreme emotional states provoked by caring for a dying lover while negotiating the imminent breakdown of his own health. AIDS, we should therefore understand, produced in Monette not autobiography but an autobiographical tension, a desire for self-expression that was equaled only by the need to protect against self-revelation.[1]

This tension was relaxed by what he began to call "conspiracy poetry." With poet and friend Carol Muske, Monette

> wondered if it was possible to write a poem that never thought about being published at all, or about reaching an audience. But then who would you be speaking to, just yourself? I don't know which of us first proposed the idea, but I know the phrase was Carol's. What about a "conspiracy poem" that would pass back and forth like a secret between two voices. We played with the notion, at one point considering telegrams, at another using a code. (*Borrowed Time* 150)

Monette's question, perhaps ironic: "Who would you be speaking to, just yourself?" is, of course, the generic position of address in the Romantic and post-Romantic lyric tradition. It is precisely this condition of speaking to oneself that the lyric means to evoke. However, having no audience seemed not to liberate Monette to experience his own autonomy but to deepen the isolation the disease imposed upon him. Shunning this loneliness, Monette shifted away from an aesthetic tradition of lyric privacy and edged toward a politics of engagement, even if, initially, his address was intimate. His elegies would aspire to what J. S. Mill called eloquence: "feeling pouring itself out to other minds, courting their sympathy, or endeavoring to influence their belief, or move them to passion or to action" ("What Is Poetry" 12), precisely that which was *not* poetry.

The compromise Monette first struck can be viewed as a paranoid formulation of privacy, one that assumes the proximity of a hostile auditor but guards against it. This scenario, given the gestures toward espionage in his description (and in the first poems written in this arrangement, for example, "Buckley," with its "tales of Bucko Bill countercounter spy" [*West of Yesterday, East of Summer* 1994], indicates that Monette imagined privacy in cold war exigency, wrested out of a blanketing surveillance. "Conspiracy poetry" liberated him to confront his subject by incorporating his anxieties about privacy into his form of address. He claims that "[i]t wasn't exactly a conscious choice to write about AIDS, yet the privacy of the bargain with Carol gave me the freedom to close in on it" (*Borrowed Time* 152). Released from "the double closet of AIDS" with respect to a single, sympathetic reader, he "felt [his] way to a workable form of address, a courtly sort of confessional" in "couched terms" (152). This conspiracy then did *not* engender the confessional quality that we recognize in *Love Alone* and *Borrowed Time*, which achieved their notoriety precisely for their refusal of "couched terms" and "coded" revelations. This leaves us with the question: How did Monette move from the "conspiracy" of two voices to the double self-disclosure of the memoir and the poems?

Paradoxically, what finally spurred Monette to move beyond the refuge of conspiratorial intimacy was not AIDS but *Bowers v. Hardwick*, the 1986 Supreme Court decision that denied gay men the right to privacy. In his last collection of poetry, *West of Yesterday*, Monette tells a story about his development as a poet that pivots around *Hardwick*. He recalls that

the only [poem] that was more or less finished by the final weeks of Roger's life was "The Supreme Pork," in part because he'd been so appalled by the Court's 8–1 majority in *Bowers v. Hardwick*. Blind by then, he had me read to him from the *Times* the whole of Justice Blackmun's dissent. He talked about it for days whenever one of his lawyer friends would call. Roger was the one who made me understand that a great dissent could over the course of time acquire a moral force to alter bigoted laws that seemed impregnable. (xvi–xvii)

Reading Blackmun's dissent in the context of his own agitation sparked Monette's poetic dissent:

So ["The Supreme Pork"] was rather a gift of outrage to try to assuage the aggrieved honor of my beloved, who could not believe the Court had sunk so far. I read it to him one afternoon in bed, as he lay curled against the fever, facing the garden he could no longer see. . . . I ripped through my recitation with unpunctuated force and when I got to the end there was silence. . . . Then he spoke with a soft astonishment. "Sweetheart, that's terrific. How can you say you'll never write again?" . . . For that's exactly what I'd say. (xvii)

In placing *Hardwick* at this critical juncture in his return to poetry (though exaggerating the lopsidedness of the decision), Monette demands that his readers consider the Court's decision in relation to his transformation as a poet. While AIDS threatens to silence him—"How can you say you'll never write again?"—*Bowers v. Hardwick* incites Monette to break out of the conspiratorial relationship that had fostered his initial return to poetry.[2] But as he tells it, he emerged a completely different kind of poet, now a poet of "raw" not "courtly" confession. It would seem that losing the constitutional protection of privacy had elicited from Monette a poetics of candor.

We should not be surprised that this new crisis in privacy triggered a lyric meditation on the conditions of intimacy and publicity and the status of the sovereign domain—even if such a direct rejoinder to a Supreme Court decision is highly unusual.[3] As I have argued, both law and lyric respond to changing experiences of privacy because they are generically beholden to the concept. In the preface to *Love Alone*, when Monette broadcast his breach of social decorum—which he defined as "the contemptible pose of the politicians and preachers" and of the press, who suppressed the death of a generation of young men—he revealed a fascinating modification of confession wrought by the Court's decision. When Monette composed his elegies, critics and poets alike had already declared the 1980s a postconfessional era.[4] Nevertheless, Monette linked himself to the confessional poets, setting his work within a precedent of confrontational and scandalous self-revelation.[5] However, what makes *Hardwick* significant to this tradition of lyric confession is that very little of what Monette discloses in *Love Alone* could be called confessional in the terms used for Sexton, Plath, and Lowell. That is, if confessional poetry marked out the "too private," Monette's elegies are not confessional at all. One fact alone, his homosexuality, in the context of *Bowers v. Hardwick* rendered everything Monette disclosed a confession. While sharing with confessional poetry its emotional recklessness, his revelations are decidedly ordinary.

If we recall Monette's paranoid conception of privacy, which assumes the presence of a hostile listener but protects against it, we can understand *Hardwick*'s impact on not only his choice to go public with his story but also, on a formal level, his elaboration of a poetics of candor that, as we shall see, works simultaneously to reveal and protect from revelation. *Hardwick*'s shift in privacy doctrine breached a cold war compromise, most grievously for one group of citizens—gay men—but implicitly for all. If the right to privacy, "found" in the domain of sexuality under the pressure of cold war security excesses, provided limits on certain kinds of surveillance and intrusion, it did so recognizing that the technologies of invasion were not going to be dismantled. *Hardwick* represented the first time since the mid-sixties that the Court had opened its citizens to the surveillance of the bedroom, which was the image of totalitarianism most detested by the Court that had decided *Griswold v. Connecticut* twenty years earlier. This denial arose not only from the Court's hysterical response to homosexuality but also from its hostility to *Roe v. Wade*, as a number of legal scholars have suggested. *Hardwick* confirmed that privacy rights were not absolute, a fact that women fighting to protect *Roe* had long recognized but which came as a staggering blow to the gay men who invoked their rights to privacy in the battles over AIDS. Cold war privacy with all its complications was no longer available to Paul Monette and those who shared the anxieties about privacy that AIDS had stimulated.[6]

In the twenty years since *Griswold* had affirmed a constitutional right to privacy in the "zone of the home," a decision that from its origin excited controversy among legal scholars and historians, the American citizenry had come to imagine this constitutional protection as integral to their status *as* Americans. Gay men challenging epidemiological surveillance and state record keeping, the policing of commercial sex outlets, even proposals generated from within the gay community for tracking the spread of HIV, immediately reached for privacy rights to ground their opposition. That this should have seemed straightforward for so many gay men—who had been special targets of cold war security purges and for whom Supreme Court privacy rulings had made exception since the first attempts to rationalize a right to privacy in *Poe v. Ullman*—attests to the remarkable self-evidence and symbolic charge this right had acquired during the decades since *Griswold*, despite the backlash against *Roe v. Wade*. As Nan Hunter, founding director of the ACLU's project on lesbian and gay rights, lamented in the *Village Voice* shortly after the decision was handed down, even if *Hardwick* did not mean the overturning of *Roe* or the end of gay rights, "in its language and its social meaning as symbol, *Hardwick* [was] overpowering" because it was so openly contemptuous of claims by homosexuals to rights ("Banned in the USA" 81). Because AIDS had intensified desires for privacy and because rights to it had acquired such cultural capital during the cold war, *Hardwick*'s abrupt reversal of the expansion in privacy rights, as Deborah Gould points out, evoked a response like no single event of the AIDS crisis ("Sex Death" 222–35).

The expulsion from the rights of citizenship of these men, many of whom, like Paul Monette, were white and middle-class, was for many a novel experience of rights-less-ness, to borrow a term from Hannah Arendt, a previously unthinkable breach of the social contract.[7] In fact, *Borrowed Time* is punctuated by Monette's seemingly inexhaustible surprise at the vulnerability of his rights, an element of the autobiography that has dismayed many otherwise sympathetic readers who never enjoyed the same unalloyed confidence in their entitlements as citizens. Monette's poetic response to *Bowers v. Hardwick* derives from this double positioning as holder of the privileged status of citizen and, at the same time, sexual outlaw. In *Love Alone,* Monette seeks to repudiate *Hardwick's* notion of privacy without renouncing the right altogether. In fact, *Love Alone* employs many of the tropes and assumptions about privacy within the Court's tradition leading up to *Hardwick* but reworks them in order to claim privacy for gay men. In this sense *Love Alone* situates *Hardwick* as an anomaly in an otherwise workable liberal tradition of privacy rights. The exclusion enacted by *Hardwick* can be viewed as a developmental problem amenable to correction through exposure and education rather than as a categorical impasse. Monette's response to *Hardwick's* exclusion is not to abandon privacy but to reimagine it so that it returns to him transformed by his intervention.

This distinction between a developmental and a categorical impasse broadly maps the post-*Hardwick* privacy debate. On the one hand, gay rights activists followed a path similar to Monette's in lobbying for an expansion of privacy to include homosexuality. The arguments for gay marriage that dominated gay politics in the 1990s proceed from this basic faith in liberalism that, unsurprisingly, characterizes legal organizations such as LAMBDA. On the other, there also appeared in the domains of activism and the academy a deep skepticism of privacy as a concept. This postliberal critique did not seek to reclaim the right but to discard it as intractably heterosexist and too dangerously kin to the signature oppression of gay life: the closet. In this line falls much of ACT-UP's and, later, Queer Nation's politics of publicity, queer theory's critique of Anglo-American liberalism, and Sex Panic's efforts to protect and enlarge a queer public sphere.

Bowers v. Hardwick opened this debate over privacy and sexuality by attempting to foreclose it altogether. Bristling with what Eve Kosofsky Sedgwick described as the power of ignorance (*Epistemology of the Closet* 6–8), the Court imperiously defined for the nation at large not only gay privacy but a history of sexuality that it was contemptuously uninterested in knowing anything about.

Hardwick was far from the last word it was so clearly intended to be; instead it produced an enormous debate over the meaning and value of privacy within the gay community, which had first to come to terms with an image and a language that it had not chosen for itself. Monette's contribution to this debate is useful because it attempts through autobiography to wrest back control over the definitions of privacy that the Court had attempted to shut down. Monette discovered that his privacy was to be purchased not through silence, and not simply through publicity, but through a *studied* self-disclosure, one that instructs in the ambiguities of self-presentation. We might turn to Monette's work to think not only about the scandalous spectacle of gay visibility in American public culture but also about the banalities and fantasies of gay life, the ways in which homosexuality confuses the forms of American liberal politics and the ways in which gay people attempt to remake them.

However, in order to understand the transformation of privacy post-*Hardwick*, we need first to revisit the rhetoric and logic of the decision. Justice White presents the case of Michael Hardwick by reconfiguring Hardwick's claim to privacy in his home, what the Court had called "the zone of privacy" when it established the right in *Griswold v. Connecticut* in 1965. White says:

> This case does not require a judgment on whether laws against sodomy between consenting adults in general, or between homosexuals in particular, are wise or desirable. It raises no question about the right or propriety of state legislative decisions to repeal their laws that criminalize homosexual sodomy, or of state-court decisions invalidating those laws on state constitutional grounds. *The issue presented is whether the Federal Constitution confers a fundamental right upon homosexuals to engage in sodomy and hence invalidates the laws of the many States that still make such conduct illegal and have done so for a very long time....*
>
> We first register our disagreement with the Court of Appeals and with respondent that the Court's prior cases have construed the Constitution to confer a right of privacy that extends to homosexual sodomy and for all intents and purposes have decided this case. (190)

Ignoring the intrusion of the policeman in Hardwick's bedroom, White redefines Hardwick's "privacy" as the right to engage in a particular sexual act, which he will refer to ("obsessively," as Justice Blackmun notes in his dissent) as "homo-sexual sodomy."[8] Many legal commentators and literary critics alike have com-mented on this obsessive reference to homosexual sodomy, noting that the Court had singled out homosexuals for prosecution when Georgia's statute criminal-ized "any sexual act involving the sex organs of one person and the mouth or anus of another."[9] White might have taken a more direct path to his goal; in fact, privacy decisions such as *Griswold v. Connecticut* and its precursor, *Poe v. Ullman*, had expressly denied protection to nonheterosexual and extramarital sexual contact. But to rely on these precedents would have affirmed the legitimacy of constitutional privacy, which White was quite reluctant to do. Instead, White's reconfiguration of Hardwick's claim as a "fundamental right . . . to engage in sodomy" removed the case from a tradition of privacy that maintained a foothold in both domesticity and in the limits placed on state surveillance dur-ing the cold war.

We might note that privacy decisions exhibit a pattern of employing a terri-fying fantasy as a way of bolstering the arguments for the self-evidence of a deci-sion. Douglas's image of the policeman in the bedroom was one such fantasy. No policeman had entered a bedroom to pursue violators of Connecticut's statute forbidding the use of birth control. Nevertheless, Douglas conjures the specter of the police state—"would we allow the police to search the sacred precincts of marital bedrooms for tell-tale signs of the use of contraceptives?" (*Griswold* 485)—and this image provided such rhetorical force that it gave to the constitu-tional protection of privacy a quality of the taken-for-granted it did not yet pos-sess. Douglas's question, like all rhetorical questions, attests to the obviousness of his position.[10] In similar fashion, the Court's obsession with "homosexual sodomy" must also work against self-evidence—the very self-evidence that a right to privacy in the zone of the home had achieved in the twenty years since *Griswold*. The obsessive reference to sodomy distracts the presumptively het-erosexual reader/citizen from the real policeman who entered Michael Hard-wick's bedroom with an expired warrant. By the end of the decision we cannot see this invasion, we can only see Michael Hardwick's sexual practice.

If the Supreme Court's ruling makes homosexual sodomy coextensive with gay private life, the only activity that a zone of privacy could possibly harbor, many responses to *Hardwick*, including the first poem Monette wrote in response to the decision, immediately concluded that the decision had nothing whatsoever to say about the private life of gay men. "The Supreme Pork" mimics *Hardwick*'s obsession with sodomy—Monette keeps the reader tightly focused on it in terms as aggressively vulgar as the Supreme Court's are blunt— but with a distinct difference: the act may define his identity, but it is clearly not private.

The Supreme Pork
is not ready for dick which is bad news
for cowboys shroud the bunkhouse mirrors guys
shower room's off limits so is sweat
i.e. you can't eat it you can still sweat
but nicely and by yourself don't eat bupkes
is the general rule ride alone Injustice
Rehnquist speaking for the Pork neglects to
mention the seethe of maggots riced like a
wedding in his puffed Orwellian gown
he proposes the Rule of Thumb where dick is
contraindicated Cuban jails so deep
they debouch in China and no men kiss in
the bottommost cells their lips are shriven
away how else will they ever get straight
exactly where the thing does not belong
not to mention their butts nonfunctional
in highchurch whites where's the fag JDL
when you need it the exfundamentalists
ripple through the land like an underground
railway hiding up trees and gazing in
at the j.v. wrestlers pacing their bedrooms
can't talk to the coach can't leave it alone
how in hell does one man ever tag up
with his dream numero uno if it sucks and
bungs the wrong hole love is an outlaw thang
what did they do for fun you wonder in
Gomorrah sell Amway meanwhile why has
Georgia not passed a law against me I
freely admit I'd fuck the tanktop of
a dirt-blond over-the-hill Melrose waiter

my fly is an open book what's legal
in Georgia anyway high colonics Sherle
Wagner bidets with swan faucets baptist
Jockeys never show a proper shitline
oh even as I write let there be this
one poem banned in Georgia and bring all
the five injustices down for a burning books
and videorapes and the too long single
for piggly wiggly hogfat overflows
the inkwells of the Pork and Jesus is hetero
and not a hunk tiny figged-over peeny
and the fair state peaked on the brow of a hill
high on the ultramarine Aegean is still
and only a broken pediment ashed in the rain
being gotten wrong by shyster lawyers
scales all tipped and rusty it seems the Pork
will see us cowpokes hang by our balls to
keep the civilians in rubber shorts and bibs
justitia huic huac semper fi non homo
homo scored in Latin above the door
which no one now may open the only way to fuck
is straight up straight in the eyes shut tight (*West of Yesterday* 6–7)

By refusing euphemism's respectable camouflage, Monette, too, makes a spectacle of sodomy but places it in public and specifically male spaces. He begins by sending out a general alarm that performs a series of simultaneous reversals. First, *Hardwick* is "bad news for cowboys," those quintessentially masculine icons of the American frontier, the Marlboro men who ride the open ranges. Second, sodomy is not concealed in private spaces but is instead located within the most conventionally American spaces of male bonding; after *Hardwick*, "bunkhouses" and "shower rooms" will be off limits. The decision, according to the poem, does not expel sodomy from the sanctuary of privacy but, invading those areas that are private to men, creates an opposition to the private, domestic spaces of the home and "bunkhouses" and "shower rooms," homosocial spaces where, by implication, sodomy is a secret that men share.[11] Paradoxically, "The Supreme Pork" allows us to see that *Hardwick* drives sodomy *into* private domestic spaces.

What's more, since the state forces sodomy into private spaces so that it can watch, perversion is then displaced onto the state. In the interests of a decaying institution—the "maggots riced like a wedding" in Justice Rehnquist's "puffed Orwellian gown"—the state sponsors an erotic peepshow where "exfundamentalists . . . [hide] up trees and [gaze] in at j.v. wrestlers pacing their bedrooms." The invasion of privacy that *Hardwick* sanctions becomes the marker of the state's perverse erotic surveillance, which renders it morally incompetent to defend the private sphere against perversion.

"The Supreme Pork" circumvents the logic of *Hardwick* by undoing the link between domestic privacy and homosexuality that the decision seeks to forbid. When he asks, "why has Georgia not passed a law against me," Monette "freely admit[s] [he'd] fuck the tanktop of / a dirt-blond over-the-hill Melrose waiter" and declares "[his] fly . . . an open book." Instead of retreating from *Hardwick*'s criminalization of sodomy, Monette adopts the most strident and public terms of his career. Another poem written during the burst of outrage provoked by *Hardwick*, "Buckley," observes the same reversals of public and private sexuality. The conservative pundit's solution to AIDS transmission, "a small / tattoo on the upper thigh in the thick-haired / swirl by the balls," is linked to the "tales of Bucko Bill countercounterspy," a cold war fable of endlessly refracted spying. Together these images establish Buckley's marking of homosexuals within the confusion over the enemy created by the end of the cold war. Monette embraces his status as the "enemy within," that rhetorically flexible image that coded both homosexuals and communists as the enemies that were unmarked, imperceptible except by surveillance and confession. Monette will take Buckley one step further, however, just as he does the Court, by adopting the stigma—the "scarlet letter F" meant to make the HIV-positive man a pariah—as a symbol of his own, a label that he will use to make the hidden visible: "I want my f for fag of course on the left / bicep twined with a Navy anchor." In his self-marking, Monette inverts Buckley's public/private symbolism. Instead of a private sign, hidden in the hair of the balls, which is meant to perform a public humiliation like the "scarlet F," Monette wears his "f for fag of course," calling attention to the symbol's "hidden" meaning by interpreting it within the line of the poem and emblazoning it on a visible part of his body, "the left bicep," exposed by the pack of cigarettes rolled in his sleeve. Entwining this "f" with a symbol of American military might—the Navy anchor—that is also a gay erotic cliché works to queer the nation even as it ironically Americanizes the queer. This reclamation of stigma, the self-disclosure of that which should be secret, is a distinctively confessional move that aligns Monette with an earlier generation of confessional poets.

Just as in Monette's reading the Court's ruling drives sodomy into the private sphere, so too does it threaten to force gay identity under the mantle of privacy. Monette is daring the Court to enforce the law it upheld, opening himself not only to seduction but also to the capricious prosecution of the sodomy laws that Michael Hardwick experienced. In pleading "oh even as I write let there be this / one poem banned in Georgia and bring all / the five injustices down for a burning of books," he draws a connection between the symbolic violence done to his self-presentation and the physical violence that, as Kendall Thomas has argued in "Beyond the Privacy Principle" (1992), *Hardwick* implicitly endorses. If Michael Hardwick can be "read" as gay when he throws out the garbage behind a gay nightclub, any and all self-presentation is at risk, not just the erotic but the mundane. Monette is not concerned with the fit of the closet, whether or not he can retreat to a privately homosexual identity. His assumption in "The Supreme Pork" is that *Hardwick* has made all access to the closet precarious. His answer is not to reclaim the closet but instead to bust it wide open.

In one sense then, we can see in the evolution of Monette's poetry after *Hardwick* that publicity is the necessary precondition of the privacy he will claim in *Love Alone*. Nevertheless, in figuring himself as an "open book," Monette offers a kind of legibility in these earlier poems that the later elegies will take back as he resists the force of the law to render any self-disclosure a confession. Like "The Supreme Pork" and "Buckley," *Love Alone* shares the emphasis on reading; in countless poems, Monette, Roger, and their relationship are figured as books or the pages of a book. Yet, where "The Supreme Pork" seems to promise an instantly recognizable self-presentation—the "open book"—the elegies begin where this exhibition of open sexuality leaves off: by using the form of Monette's poem as a pedagogy of reading, a complication of hyperlegibility that restores some notion of privacy. Because *Hardwick* has made erotic self-disclosure unavoidable, Monette can dispense with the question of the privacy of his sexual identity or practice. Instead, the challenges of reading gay identity in *Love Alone*, as opposed to "The Supreme Pork," begin *after* the fly has been read, which is not the end but the beginning of self-disclosure. In other words, the elegies confront the post-*Hardwick* dilemma of publicity by reclaiming a formal privacy, which is not a retreat to the closet, based as it is on publicity, but an attempt to formulate a poetics to instruct in the nuances of publicity. Therefore, *Love Alone* attempts to manage information, to make disclosures on its own terms, which places Monette's work squarely within a tradition of informational privacy that extends back to Brandeis and Warren's tort defined in the pages of the *Harvard Law Review* in 1890. However, if self-disclosure nullified privacy rights in their argument, it will legitimate them in Monette's.

In the preface to *Love Alone* Monette comments on the form he discovered when *Hardwick* provoked him into writing.[12] He says, "I let [the poems] stand as raw as they came" and that "I don't mean them to be impregnable, though I admit I want them to allow no escape, like a hospital room, or indeed, a mortal illness" (*Love Alone* xii). What this explanation suggests is that Monette had worked out a poetics in response to *Hardwick*, one that attempted a complex parallel move: to open himself to being read while resisting the force of the law to set the terms of self-revelation by compelling confession. However, this poetics of privacy is self-canceling because candor produces a kind of illegibility. In describing the poems as unedited and raw, Monette is calling his work a full disclosure. We are meant to understand that he is unmasked, fully present to us, resolutely public. But at the same time, the form he uses creates an experience of reading that complicates this unmasking. By eliminating punctuation and conventional line breaks, he forces the reader to reread. Grouping words to make sense of a line must always be a retrospective act, the result not of a first impression but of some sort of earned intimacy. The reader must constantly start over, retrace steps, reformulate the line to make sense of Monette's disclosure. While the first reading gives the impression of careening furiously out of control, it is the second and third readings that open the work to legibility. His form thus rewards sustained engagement while it frustrates a facile or cursory encounter. Thus the surface candor of the work *prevents* the reader from "knowing" him or Roger or their relationship at first glance. I don't mean to suggest that Monette is technically obscure; he wanted his work "filed under AIDS" (xi) not poetry, which suggests a political intervention, not a literary one. Still, this makes his resistance all the more compelling because he kept in place the "impregnability"—that is, the resistance to force—even with readers he knew to be most sympathetic to and familiar with his story, those "mad with loss" to whom he dedicated the elegies.

While "The Supreme Pork" reaches for scandalous publicity, *Love Alone* works from constitutional privacy doctrine's important precedents. Monette's most direct confrontation with *Hardwick*'s denial of privacy comes in "The House on King's Road," a poem that evokes privacy doctrine's central metaphor—a "man's home is his castle"—the zone that the Court's decision rendered invisible by focusing on homosexual sodomy. In this poem Monette permits us to read from yet another book, one that promises access to the most intimate self: the diary. Monette plays with the generic guarantee of this book by unveiling it only to reveal *nothing*. Instead of the secrets of individual idiosyncrasy, we are offered "fixed roof skimmed pool pasta for dinner." If private life had been defended as the locus of individual autonomy and self-governance, Monette has offered us a privacy that is, in his words, "stuff you wouldn't suppose worth the ink."

And yet, this moment of reading the dead lover's diary is both the most banal and the most vital revelation of the poem. It is precisely the ordinariness of the diary's disclosures that makes Monette's grief intolerable. He argues for its centrality to his poetics by claiming for it an extraordinary evocative power—"it breaches the wall / within the wall more than memory more than / the pivot of event." To return to one of Monette's key terms, "impregnability"—he uses it to describe his poems as well as "bigoted laws"—the diary breaches the wall, rendering Monette defenseless. We have finally gotten to him. But what have we got? It is the banality of private life—"casual embraces unremarkable / as sky no set like Juliet's balcony / no histrionic star turns curtain calls / just putting a house in order"—that makes privacy valuable to him. The invasiveness of *Hardwick* does not threaten to reveal the exceptional, the spectacular, or the traumatic, nor to expose the real, deep, or true individual self sheltered by the sovereign domain but, rather, to make vulnerable the common experiences of everyday life. Unlike his confessional precursors, Monette produces emotional extremity in the revelation of "pasta for dinner," hardly the "too private" terrain of Sexton, Plath, or Lowell or the much maligned overexposure of talk-show television. His information management, therefore, knows no boundaries. When you have no right to privacy, everything becomes a confession.

"The House on Kings Road" goes further, though, to suggest why the home was so important an image for Monette. In this poem, the home functions as the *antidote* to the closet—precisely that which the gay man "must" desire—"you have to crave your own room"—which is not the room with "the merit badges / pinned in a row on a chest of drawers"—but the "place and the friend with the key." This craving might paradoxically leave one home-*less*—in a "refrigerator crate under 101" or a "heating vent on eighth and Olive"—but in Monette's terms this homelessness does not undermine the "vision," it attests to its power. Monette never questions that "Visioning the place and the friend with the key" will draw legions of gay youth—"some just out of high school some in the army"—to leave their closets and enter into the adult world, which is imagined as the gay couple, who form the final image of the home in the poem.

This emphasis on the couple rather than the "zone of the home" as the location of both maturity and sexual autonomy is, ironically, strikingly similar to Harlan's in *Poe v. Ullman*, where marriage underwrote moral autonomy. The house on King's Road becomes a reward for maturity, which is the point at which Monette's embrace of privacy's traditions ensnares him in its limitations. Monette wants to claim his relationship to Rog as a marriage, but at the same time his terms create a new set of exclusions, which has been amplified more recently by Michael Warner in *The Trouble with Normal* (1999). Warner argues that rights to marriage always work as privilege; even if this privilege extends to gay people, it still leaves a large class of unmarried individuals without the benefits that accrue to the married couple, chief among which is sexual autonomy.[13] Monette's vision in "The House on King's Road" adds to these exclusions the closeted individual who is disqualified from the advantages of marriage and maturity. A profit of self-disclosure, privacy rights become not only the obverse of the closet, they are explicitly denied to those who cannot or will not make their sexuality a part of their public identity. To those who imagine that a right to privacy is merely the self-erasure of the closet, Monette argues that privacy only belongs to those who have already left its brittle security.

The representation of the gay couple in *Love Alone* also responds to the Court's determination to limit privacy rights to marriage, procreation, and family. Justice White pointedly, even flippantly, argued that "[n]o connection between family, marriage, or procreation on the one hand and homosexual activity on the other has been demonstrated, either by the Court of Appeals or by respondent" (190). In attempting to meet this objection, Blackmun's dissent looks to identify a principle encompassed by—but broader than—the "family" in the precedents White cites:

> While it is true that these cases may be characterized by their connection to protection of the family, . . . the Court's conclusion that they extend no further than this boundary ignores the warning in *Moore v. East Cleveland* (plurality opinion) against "[closing] our eyes to the basic reasons why certain

rights associated with the family have been accorded shelter under the Fourteenth Amendment's Due Process Clause." We protect these rights not because they contribute, in some direct and material way, to the general public welfare, but because they form so central a part of an individual's life. (205)

Blackmun classifies privacy's protection of family as a foundation of *individual* liberty, distinguishing it from "public welfare," which is indirectly the "public morality" that had traditionally been viewed as threatened by private homosexual relationships. However generously Blackmun conceives of the Court's intention to protect a "central part of an individual's life," he nevertheless implicitly agrees that family is not an operative rubric for thinking about homosexuality.

Monette, who, it should be noted, greatly admired Blackmun's dissent, traces the connection between the gay couple and the extended, intergenerational, and even traditional family in his poem "Three Rings." The first ring connects Monette to Roger and to the larger circle of their family:

before I left you I slipped off the ring
the nurse had taped to your finger so it
wouldn't get lost the last day you think I'd
forget I forget nothing was there the day
Dad gave it to you Chestnut St. a continent
ago there when you said in the bathtub ten
years later sobbed really *If something happens*
to me I guess this should go to your brother
then your nephew still our best hope with his
sister of a future that will call us back
unencumbered just for love (*Love Alone* 29)

While tracing the passage of the ring from father to lover to brother, a transfer that in itself unites the couple with the extended family, Monette confuses family membership by blending his voice with Roger's. Roger's voice, identified by italics, begins to bequeath the ring, but Monette breaks off the italics to complete Roger's thought. In this merging of their voices, "your brother" becomes ambiguous, identified with Monette's family as the completion of Roger's sentence and Roger's family as Monette's interruption. Instead of attributing the brother, the poem makes him emblematic of the two families' union: he is neither Paul's nor Roger's brother but both at once. This merging of families completes the circle of relationship that the ring and its journey signify. Moreover, the poem's formal structure—line endings and beginnings running together—also creates a circle that will not permit the two families to be distinguished. Because the prose companion to *Love Alone*, Monette's memoir *Borrowed Time*, explains clearly to whom Roger meant the ring to go, the poem's ambiguity is all the more meaningful.

Like the joining of families in "Three Rings," the elegies constantly work to identify links between the couple and the circles of relationship that interpenetrate their private union. Throughout the poems Monette refers to his relationship with Roger as a marriage, and yet, unlike the legal conception of marriage as the most private of relationships, Monette defines his marriage as a relationship that can never be uncoupled from a larger community. The last of the elegies, "Brother on the Mount of Olives," expands their marriage to include a third party:

and the picture he saved three years for me . . .
. . . turned out to hold our wedding portrait
the innocent are so brief and the rigid world
doesn't marry its pagans any more but John
didn't care what nothing we professed he joined
us to him a ritual not in the book
but his secret heart . . . (*Love Alone* 64)

Their marriage becomes a chain of engagement, connecting Paul to Roger, then to a third man, "Brother John," who in witnessing their union "joined / [them] to him." More than embracing three individuals, however, the union of the two men expands horizontally and vertically: the couple links Brother John to the current generation of gay men while at the same time Brother John links Monette and Roger to a lineage of gay priests, whose history is denied by the Church. Rather than severing the couple from community in a bond of wholly private affiliation, Monette's marriage ceremony symbolically joins the larger community with their marriage partnership. Brotherhood becomes a relationship as binding as family, forming a social configuration that borrows from the powerful associations of the private nuclear family and the equally powerful political tradition that bases the free society on bonds of fraternity. Monette uses a fraternal metaphor for marriage to attach the private union between the two men to a political relationship that will stand behind the private union. In other words, he embeds the private union of gay marriage in the liberal democratic polity, the bonds of fraternal political obligation strengthening the commitment of marriage and marriage sustaining and enriching the bonds of fraternity. This is Monette's homosocial utopia.

If the prolonged controversy over *Roe* suggested the gendered asymmetry of privacy rights, *Hardwick* quickly came to signify the sexual inequality at the heart of liberal privacy. For many, *Hardwick* confirmed a categorical impasse rather than a developmental (and therefore only temporary) glitch. Critics such as Janet Halley, Kendall Thomas, Eve Kosofsky Sedgwick, Jonathan Goldberg, Lauren Berlant, and Michael Warner recognized immediately that the criminalization of sodomy posed excruciating questions about self-representation, identity, public discourse, and political action.[14] Queer theory in the United States finds at least some of its origin and much of its urgency in *Bowers v. Hardwick*, which is not to say that *Hardwick* occasioned queer theory but that the decision condensed a set of questions that queer theory was beginning to articulate. Critical to the "epistemology of the closet," *Hardwick* was taken by many theorists and activists to mark the pernicious end point of that epistemology. The solution to *Bowers v. Hardwick*'s crisis of privacy for gay people would lie, therefore, not in a reconceptualization of privacy but in the formation of queer publics. Only in transformed public space where identities form, communities are built, and individuals are recognized in new ways[15] can anything like sexual autonomy be imagined. This, of course, inverts the expectations of the privacy debate because sexual autonomy is not imagined as developing in private but, rather, in the public sphere.

The question I want to ask more than a decade and a half after *Bowers v. Hardwick* is: must we decide between the developmental and the categorical impasse? Indeed, the emergence of a vigorous championing of queer publicity and the ascent to the top of the gay rights agenda of marriage in the post–cold-war 1990s imply that publicity and privacy remain open questions. The intensity and duration of the difficulties presented by *Roe* and *Hardwick* suggest that the developmental model is inadequate. The structure of liberal privacy has made it difficult to accommodate to new bodies, new subjectivities. Likewise, as Eric O. Clarke has argued in a symmetrical debate, the utopian promise of the public sphere is limited by many of the same structural contradictions. Publicity is not simply, as Habermas would have it, "self-correcting"; the cost of inclusion—the normalizing, even heteronormalizing of queer life—demands a careful attention to its forms of publicity, not just their presence in the public sphere (*Virtuous Vice* 2000).

Though less obvious than the transformation of the public sphere in the past forty years, privacy has also changed more than the categorical impasse would predict. The concept is protean enough to adapt to new ideas about the experience of privacy, as Reva Siegel claims in "Abortion as a Sex Equality Right" of the Court's decision to uphold *Roe* in *Planned Parenthood of Southeastern Pennsylvania v. Casey* (1992).[16] Privacy "as we have always known it," however, is not adequate to challenges from technology, bureaucracy, medicine, mass media, etc., and to appeals from excluded citizens/subjects. No matter how often the media tell us otherwise, "we" never had and do not want to "return" to a genteel, patriarchal, and property-based norm of privacy. But that doesn't mean that privacy is something we can do without. Rather, it suggests that we learn to recognize the ways in which debate, redescription, and formal experimentation replenish the concept so that we can be released from the anxiety that privacy is dying. Only by understanding how vital the concept really is can we build new forms of privacy that will not suffocate us but offer a fluid relationship with the public world.

Notes

INTRODUCTION

1. See Foucault, *Discipline and Punish* (1979) and *The History of Sexuality*, vol.1, *An Introduction* (1978).

2. 381 U.S. 479 (1965).

3. 410 U.S. 113 (1973).

4. 478 U.S. 186 (1986).

5. 116 U.S. 616 (1886).

6. See W. R. Johnson's *The Idea of Lyric* (1982).

7. See George Chauncey, *The Strange Career of the Closet*, forthcoming.

8. See Dimock, *Residues of Justice* (1996).

1. REINVENTING PRIVACY

1. 359 U.S. 360 (1959).

2. Legal histories of the Supreme Court's privacy doctrine have had little to say about the intersections between wiretapping and surveillance cases and cases dealing with rights of sexual or domestic privacy. For example, David Garrow's monumental study, *Liberty and Sexuality* (1994), treats in impressive depth the cases of sexual autonomy but makes no reference to the wiretapping cases that lie adjacent to them. Very few law review articles treat the cold war context of privacy doctrine or its relationship to totalitarianism. Richard Primus contends in "A Brooding Omnipresence" (1996) that antitotalitarianism underwrote a major shift in constitutional interpretation in the postwar. Primus interprets the "emanations" and "penumbras" of Douglas's *Griswold* opinion, as well as the extremely rare invocation of the Ninth Amendment by all five concurring justices (it is invoked in only three cases prior to *Griswold*), as evidence of an anxiety about the positivistic legal

reasoning that was associated with totalitarianism. In providing a more capacious reading of constitutional rights, the justices, he argues, were protecting civil liberties such as
the right to travel, which is inferred from the Fifth and Fourteenth Amendments but not
explicit in them. Seth Kreimer's "Sunlight, Secrets, and Scarlet Letters" (1991) situates
changes in First Amendment rulings in relation to McCarthyism but relegates most of its
discussion of privacy law to the footnotes. Finally, Jed Rubenfeld's "The Right to Privacy"
(1989) makes broad conceptual links to totalitarianism but focuses on the special attention to sexuality in privacy law.

3. Michael Rogin's *Ronald Reagan, The Movie* (1987), Robert Corber's *Homosexuality in
Cold War America* (1997), and Elaine Tyler May's *Homeward Bound* (1988) have in different
ways argued that the relationship of private to public in containment logic is deeply paradoxical. To use Rogin's formulation, "the cold war politicized privacy in the name of protecting it" (245).

4. Torts, like libel and trespass, regulate conflicts between citizens. Constitutional law
adjudicates conflicts between the citizen and the state.

5. Peter Brooks in *Troubling Confessions* (2000) examines the ambivalence surrounding
confession that resides in the problem of voluntariness. The law, he explains, works to
assure the voluntary confession even while sanctioning methods of procuring these confessions under pressure. The coercion of confession goes beyond the juridical, bleeding
into the "tyranny of the requirement to confess" in a culture that exhibits a "generalized
demand for transparency" (4). This general demand is a large part of the backlash against
confessional culture. Richard Sennett's *The Fall of Public Man* (1974) also registered this
sort of generalized coercion.

6. Readings of Brandeis and Warren's "The Right to Privacy" by cultural historians—
for example, Brook Thomas's "The Construction of Privacy" (1992), Philip Fisher's
"Appearing and Disappearing in Public" (1986) and Milette Shamir's "Hawthorne's Romance" (1997), carefully distinguish this tort from more familiar contemporary debates
on constitutional privacy. Examining the use of Brandeis and Warren in early 1960s debates over constitutional rights to privacy, however, shows traces of this formulation in
constitutional privacy and sharpens our sense of how dramatically privacy itself changed
when it shifted from the tort to the constitutional domain.

7. Even though they sought to maintain privacy as a "spiritual" right by locating it in
artistic or literary production, copyright anchored privacy as a right of property. See Brook
Thomas in "The Construction of Privacy."

8. 202 F.2d 866 (1953).

9. 114 U.S.P.Q. 314 (Pa.Ct.C.P.Phil.Cy.) (1957).

10. See Morris Ernst's discussion of this evolution in Ernst and Schwartz, *Privacy*
(1962), 192–202.

11. 277 U.S. 438 (1928).

12. For example, in *Wolf v. Colorado* (338 U.S. 25) in 1949 the Court permitted the states to use evidence obtained in violation of the Fourth Amendment, refusing to intervene in state court rules of evidence. In *On Lee v. U.S.* (343 U.S. 747) in 1952 the Court upheld a narcotics conviction, arguing that an agent wearing a recording device was not "wiretapping" and that since the agent was invited into the laundry (he had been an acquaintance of the defendant), there had been no illegal trespass. Moreover, the laundry where the recording took place, though also the home of the defendant, was not viewed as a private space.

13. 367 U.S. 643 (1961).

14. 367 U.S. 497 (1961).

15. Only clinic operators and their staff doctors had been arrested under this statute, which had been in effect since 1879.

16. Mark Seltzer locates the advent of what he calls "wound culture"—the fascination with insides and outsides—at roughly this historical juncture. See *Serial Killers* (1998), 109–10.

17. Since the late nineteenth century, there have been periodic warnings about the death of privacy. However, the intensity of privacy's visibility is incomparably greater in the early 1960s, touching virtually every domain of American political, social, psychological, and cultural life.

18. Abbott Gleason in *Totalitarianism* (1995) links Arendt and Orwell as the two great popularizers of the concept of totalitarianism, and the two whose visions were particularly apocalyptic and "demonic." If as Gleason says, "totalitarianism was the great mobilizing and unifying concept of the cold war" (3), and if, as he argues, the totalitarian regime "obliterated the distinction between public and private, which even the most brutal of older dictatorships had respected" (4), then naturally even minor incursions into private spaces or infringements on individual privacy were to be feared as a step toward eroding all private space, all democratic freedom, all self-sovereignty and autonomy.

19. In 1962, after Soviet and U.S. satellites had been launched with the express purpose of surveying the globe in minute detail, Arthur C. Clarke in *Life Magazine* ("Telstar" 1962) mixed his praise of telecommunications technology with fears about the loss of privacy. The satellite immediately found its way into television as a manifestation of overpowering surveillance. See Jeffrey Sconce's "The 'Outer Limits' of Oblivion" (1997).

20. Brenton might have been imitating Packard's successful formula, but his book was actually conceived before Packard's. See Daniel Horowitz's *Vance Packard and American Social Criticism* (1994), 227.

21. The FBI also had a program to monitor libraries. As early as 1962, the FBI monitored the withdrawal of unclassified information from libraries because the Soviet State

Committee on Science and Technology had a "shopping list" of information that they needed and could find via diplomats and others such as agents, students, and librarians. However, in typically overzealous manner, the FBI had rather broad criteria for its surveillance—the usual expansion from espionage to "subversive activities and related matters"—which broadened its reach. This program began to be scrutinized in 1990 at the end of the cold war. Congress was reexamining its mandate, but it had been upheld by the Subcommittee on Civil and Constitutional Rights as late as 1988. See Erika Ault's "The FBI's Library Awareness Program" (1990).

22. The opportunity to withdraw from the test is a costly sort of privacy for it could very well have meant unemployment. If in 1956, C. Wright Mills wonders in a review of William Whyte's *The Organization Man* in the *New York Times*, why Whyte tells his readers to "cheat on personality tests" rather than "refuse—if possible as a group—to take the silly things," eight years later these tests would seem far more menacing than absurd.

23. See John D'Emilio's "The Homosexual Menace" (1989).

24. It is currently impossible to talk about the cold war without employing the word "containment," a term taken from an essay called "The Sources of Soviet Conduct" (1947) by George Kennan, the director of policy planning for Secretary of State George Marshall. Beginning with the work of John Lewis Gaddis (*Strategies of Containment* 1982), the strategies Kennan outlined for containing the spread of Soviet military and ideological influence became central to accounts of American history and culture in the late twentieth century. After Gaddis, cultural historians, many from the field of cultural studies, extended the term to describe the peculiar social formations, aesthetic innovations, and mass cultural inventions of the cold war. Alan Nadel has defined "containment culture" broadly as follows:

> Containment was the name of a privileged American narrative during the cold war. Although technically referring to U.S. foreign policy from 1948 to at least the mid-60s, it also describes American life in numerous venues and under sundry rubrics during the period: to the extent that corporate production and biological reproduction, military deployment and industrial technology, televised hearings and filmed teleplays, the cult of domesticity and the fetishizing of domestic security, the arms race and atoms for peace all contributed to the containment of communism, the disparate acts performed in the name of these practices joined the legible agenda of American history as aspects of containment culture. (*Containment Culture* 2–3)

As the history of the cold war has developed, then, containment as a foreign policy objective has come to depend, not exclusively but significantly, on containing the internal divisions within American society itself. The United States would stymie Soviet expansion and defuse the threat of nuclear annihilation by rendering mute political dissent, non-procreative sexual energy, gender nonconformity, racial unrest, and artistic expression within its own borders.

25. For example, cold war cultural critic Robert Corber in "*Rear Window* and the Postwar Settlement" (1994) reads *Rear Window* as an attempt to rescue scopophilic pleasure from the taint of its abuse—its politicization—in McCarthyite national security paranoia. He argues that the general collapse of public and private boundaries that structured McCarthyism and cold war paranoia had contaminated film's innocent erotic play with voyeurism. Pleasure in looking, Corber notes, quickly transfers from the erotic to the juridical. In this shift, the gaze of the state and the private citizen converge in the surveillance of private space. This collapse of forms of surveillance is, however, paranoid reading because it finds a root cause for the proliferation of violation, which indicates how the cold war continues to organize breakdowns between public and private in our histories of the period.

26. Koestler's *The God that Failed* (1949) is a series of conversion narratives, in which, like Whittaker Chambers's *Witness* (1952), the protagonist looks back at his "conversion" to communism and his disillusioned second conversion to anticommunism. Mary McCarthy disparages both these memoirs as prurient but then goes on to provide an account of her own brush with communism called "My Confession" (*On the Contrary* 75).

27. 357 U.S. 449 (1958).

28. Alabama had accused the NAACP of causing irreparable damage to the citizens of the state—by, for example, organizing boycotts of the bus lines in protest of Jim Crow restrictions—and therefore sought to identify members of the organization. When identified, these members were harassed by both state and private citizens.

29. See Randall Kennedy's "Contrasting Fates of Repression" (1995).

30. 354 U.S. 178 (1957).

31. The career of Robert Harrison, a fervent, even fanatical anticommunist, and his scandal magazine, which in addition to trafficking in sex and infidelity also relied heavily on the exposure of "communist tendencies" in the era's most famous celebrities (for example, Lucille Ball), suggests the ways in which the cold war shades our discussion of the loss of privacy and the move from a culture of gossip to one of confession. See Neal Gabler, *Winchell* (1994).

32. Of course, Mailer also suggests that inept self-expression devolves into mere therapy (*Advertisements* 283).

33. He begins by saying that "few values so fundamental to society as privacy have been left so undefined in social theory or have been the subject of such vague and confused writing by social scientists" (*Privacy and Freedom* 7).

34. 388 U.S. 1817 (1967).

35. 389 U.S. 347 (1967).

36. 392 U.S. 1 (1968).

37. 394 U.S. 557 (1969).

38. 405 U.S. 438 (1972).

39. 410 U.S. 179 (1973).

40. Richard Nixon's involvement in Watergate takes on an additional irony if we recall that he had made himself an expert on U.S. privacy law. Nixon's first appearance in an appellate court came in oral argument before the Supreme Court in a landmark tort privacy case, *Time, Inc. v. Hill*, 385 U.S. 374 (1967). As Leonard Garment, Nixon's cocounsel, wrote in *The New Yorker* in 1989, Nixon "began by reading and virtually committing to memory not only the trial record . . . but copious quantities of additional background material, including federal and state case law, law-review articles, and philosophical writings on libel and privacy" ("The Hill Case" 94). Among the articles Nixon consulted were those written by Thomas Emerson (counsel for Planned Parenthood in the *Griswold v. Connecticut* case), as well as by William Prosser and Edward Bloustein, whose accounts of tort and constitutional privacy law will be the focus of the next chapter.

41. James Rule, Douglas McAdam, Linda Stearns, and David Uglow, *The Politics of Privacy* (1980).

42. See Frank J. Donner, *The Age of Surveillance* (1980) for a full account of this shift.

43. South Carolina started to compile a master list of HIV-positive people in 1986. In 1988 California weighed Proposition 102, which would have required reporting of those "reasonably believed" to be HIV-positive. "Reasonable belief" obviously implicated lifestyles—drug use, homosexuality, etc.

44. Heterosexuals who joined the case were declared to have no standing. Lesbians had been exempted from sodomy rulings by a Georgia court in the late 1960s even though the statute's definition of sodomy does not make any such distinction.

45. The best description of this replaying of cold war rhetoric in the AIDS discourse is Susan Sontag's "AIDS and Its Metaphors" (*Illness as Metaphor* 1989). As Cindy Patton (*Inventing AIDS* 1990) has argued, no matter what form of protest AIDS activism took, it could not avoid the terms and metaphors in which the disease had already been cast, no matter how politically debilitating these might be.

46. See Deborah Gould's "Sex, Death," 222–35.

47. Television as a medium both participated in and broadcast the death of privacy. *The Outer Limits*'s memorable opening—an ominous voice narrating over a test pattern commanded: "Do not attempt to adjust the picture. *We* are controlling transmission . . . *we* will control all that you see and hear"—exploited a long-existing fear about TV: the possible two-directional gaze of the medium, George Orwell's "Big Brother." As Jeffrey Sconce has explained in "The 'Outer Limits' of Oblivion," this penetration of the private home

by the watchful eye of an unknown outsider played upon fears of the breakdown of public and private space that television had from its inception provoked in myriad ways. In addition to its ability to intrude the camera into private life, television had long been viewed as one of the important institutions of late-twentieth-century American life to introduce new pressures on the boundaries of public and private. Television's endless recycling of domestic interiors would erode the public's interest in the grander stage of world politics. Television's live reporting of events would preclude judicious and restrained editing, thus exposing the subjects of a story to unwanted and injurious intrusion, or exposing the viewers to unseemly displays of emotion or self-exhibition. The mere witnessing of public life from the living room would abrade the clear distinction between private and public life. Journalists, media experts, bureaucrats at the FCC, and public intellectuals worried that television's blurring of private and public could have disastrous implications for American democracy, whose bedrock was implicitly the stable and unambiguous distinction between public and private life.

The Outer Limits worked within the conventions of a TV genre that was developed the 1960s, the "fantastic family sitcom," which, as Lynn Spigel defines it, explored "the homogenizing conformity demanded by suburban living" (as quoted in Sconce 24). The fear of exposure and the perpetual, but informal, invasion of privacy drives the plots of 60s sitcoms such as *Bewitched*, *My Favorite Martian*, the *Addams Family*, and *The Munsters*, in which the deviance of the main character is continually discovered by snooping neighbors and then covered over again. As the work of Sconce and Spigel suggests, television and suburbia were both stirring new and very public debates over privacy. Spigel has argued that early television metaphorized its obsessions with privacy in the figure of the window, the transparent boundary between inside and out (*Make Room for TV* 1992). This metaphor is, too, a central one for discourses about suburbia in the 1950s and 1960s where the large plate-glass picture window of the suburban home created an ambiguity between public and private. If as Spigel suggests, "television meshed perfectly with the aesthetics of modern suburban architecture" (103), we should not be surprised to find the privacy concerns of one overlapping the other. It is precisely this ambiguity that is so troubling, this inability to identify confidently, much less defend, the boundaries of private space.

Like television, one of the key elements of commentary on suburban life suggested that this social space, newly available with the mass production of housing in the Levittown model, troubled conventional boundaries of privacy. In contrast, as privacy was ostensibly disappearing in traditional realms like the home, it was dispersed across American social life into other spaces such as movie theaters or automobiles, which became a new—and very transportable—private space for teenagers to explore sexuality unsupervised by adults. Taken together, postwar American social life had produced too little privacy—the prying eye of the television camera and the suburban neighbor—and too much—the withdrawal into the interior of the home from the complicated public world of a heterogeneous society and the unchaperoned spaces of young adult courtship. This dilemma of having *both* too little and too much privacy accounts for the relentlessness of the privacy debate, since not only was it difficult to assign stability to these increasingly mobile or penetrated private spaces but the calibration of the appropriate measure of privacy was rendered impossible.

48. Timothy Melley (*Empire of Conspiracy* 2000) finds a similar type of anxiety at the core of postwar paranoia, what he calls "agency panic": "the troubled defense of an old but increasingly beleaguered concept of personhood—the idea that the individual is a rational, motivated agent with a protected interior core of beliefs, desires, and memories" (viii). This anxiety moves up levels of abstraction from the individual to things that resemble tropologically this structure of personhood.

49. Landmark works of social criticism pivoted around this impasse, which on the one hand evokes the mourning for and the desire to reclaim privacy and on the other the suffocation and derangement by it. For example, Betty Friedan's *The Feminine Mystique* (1963) signaled the gendered asymmetry of expectations of privacy in the early 1960s. Friedan understood the move to the suburbs to have created a privacy double bind for women: a crippling lack of engagement in the public world of work, politics, and community, combined with an equally disabling lack of solitude within the home itself. She argued for the necessity of privacy but, unlike other critics of suburban life, called attention to the paradoxical ways that privacy was gendered. Women suffered the deprivations of the private sphere without being compensated by the autonomy it was supposed to ensure. Suburbs were not the only postwar spaces to elicit "death of privacy warnings." Jane Jacobs's seminal critique of city planning, *The Death and Life of Great American Cities* (1961), also rested on the indispensability of clearly marked borders between public and private life. As Jacobs describes it, cities are uniquely impersonal, full of strangers with whom an individual shares a complex and public relationship that entails minor duties of civic responsibility but crucially *no* expectation of intimacy and the obligations that it entails. Jacobs indicts city planners for having focused unnecessarily and detrimentally on fostering the expansion of privacy, which in her analysis pressures people into a burdensome expansion of intimate acquaintance and responsibility or, because this burden often feels overwhelming, cuts people off from casual informal human contact. In other words, cities were becoming too much like suburbs, with their vacillation between too little and too much privacy.

Social spaces, however, were not the only ones to have lost clearly drawn boundaries between public and private; so, too, were psychic spaces thought to be vulnerable to penetration by the external world, whether that was defined as a political, social, or commercial world. *The Manchurian Candidate*, which appeared in the mid-sixties, followed a brainwashed soldier who becomes the dupe of McCarthyite politicians, who are really communists (and also his parents, but that's another story). The film plays with one of the most alarming lines of debate over privacy at the end of the 1950s, "brainwashing," a technique of invading the mind that was linked not only to cold war and fascist propaganda but, in the United States, to the ever-expanding promotional industries. Packard's *The Hidden Persuaders*, his bestseller defining subliminal advertising, represents a first step in the acceleration of the privacy debate. Here ordinary consumers are bombarded with messages that infiltrate their subconsciouses and determine their behavior at a later date. Since advertising can by-pass the gatekeeping structures of the conscious mind by appealing directly to the drives of the unconscious, the mind is envisioned as a porous container. The languages of commerce and mass media and the techniques of psychoanalysis collapse into one another in the growing anxiety about the instability of public and private.

50. One of the most well-worn phrases of the privacy crisis: "a man's home is his castle," registers the privacy crisis as a crisis of sovereignty. As Allen Grossman (*The Sighted Singer*, 1992) suggests, this sovereignty is the same as the lyric's: "Since the self-representation of the poet in history is authenticated as a residue of the privileged speech acts of kings, the mimetic enfranchisement of the nonpractic consciousness will never be complete. The chorus is still a slave collectivity even when the king and queen are wholly and nothing but their dream. There is no poetry but the creative acts of kings and gods and of the servile dreamers whom they hallucinate" (272).

51. The development of constitutionally guaranteed self-sovereignty, most powerfully articulated in the constitutional revolution in the United States, coincided with a paradigm shift in the lyric. W. R. Johnson (*The Idea of Lyric*) suggests this somewhat obliquely in his discussion of the transformation of the lyric in the nineteenth century. Of course, Adorno ("On Lyric Poetry and Society" 1991) also makes the equation between the lyric and the sovereign subject of liberalism, though he's more concerned with the "shadow side" of lyric autonomy, which is the self-as-commodity in the free market. This paradigm shift coincides with the elevation of lyric as a genre. M. H. Abrams suggested this change in status for the lyric in the 1950s with his *Mirror and the Lamp* (1953). See also the difference between English and American literature in terms of sovereignty as a national project in Sacvan Bercovitch's *Rites of Assent* (1993)

52. Mill is utterly emphatic about the privacy of poetic (lyric) expression. His definition is as follows:

Eloquence supposes an audience; the peculiarity of poetry appears to us to lie in the poet's utter unconsciousness of a listener. Poetry is feeling, confessing itself to itself in moments of solitude, and embodying itself in symbols, which are the nearest possible representations of feeling in the exact shape in which it exists in the poet's mind. Eloquence is feeling pouring itself out to other minds, courting their sympathy, or endeavoring to influence their belief, or move them to passion or to action. All poetry is of the nature of soliloquy. It may be said that poetry which is printed on hot-pressed paper and sold at a bookseller's shop, is a soliloquy in full dress, and on stage. It is so; but there is nothing absurd in the idea of such a mode of soliloquizing. What we have said to ourselves, we may tell to others afterwards; what we have said or done in solitude, we may voluntarily reproduce when we know that other eyes are upon us. *But no trace of consciousness that any eyes are upon us must be visible in the work itself.* ("What Is Poetry" 12; emphasis mine)

For Mill, like Adorno, the "shadow side" of liberal subjectivity is also the lyric self on "hot-pressed paper . . . sold at a booksellers shop," which is the very exchange that lyric is meant to deny. Mill does not seem to believe that the lyric is detached from market exchange, but rather that the lyric is meant to create the fiction of autonomy from that market. Mill is describing a lyric poem that offers itself as a fantasy of radical autonomy, disguised as a mimetic representation of it. He is especially careful to assert the transparency of poetic expression, the "nearest possible representations of feeling in the exact shape," which assures the reader's access to the very heart of liberty per se: "the inward domain of consciousness; demanding liberty of conscience, in the most comprehensive sense; liberty of thought and feeling; absolute freedom of opinion and sentiment on all subjects, practical or speculative, scientific, moral, or theological" (*On Liberty* 264). This transparency, only possible because of the poet's complete withdrawal from scrutiny, presents us with an autonomy that is socially impossible. It is only poetically conceivable, which makes it a fantasy all the more powerful because it looks mimetic. In other words, even Mill does not believe that absolute privacy—no trace of the eyes of the world—is possible. But he does believe that lyric poetry's function is to make it *look* possible. The uncanny version of this autonomy is the automated and mechanical, what Daniel Tiffany calls the "toy medium" of lyric poetry. See his *Toy Medium* (2000).

53. Walter Kalaidjian (*Languages of Liberation* 1989), who sees confessionalism as an extension of bourgeois individualism underwriting the poetic autonomy championed by New Criticism, is an important exception to the rule. In a sense he recognizes a shift but disputes its severity and its real "revolutionary" significance.

54. The class politics of confessional writing have been an important part of these debates. Diane Levertov, for example, writing about Sexton's suicide in 1973, disparaged confessional poetry as *apolitical* and limited. Addressed to a complacent public concerned

only with its narrow concerns, confessional poetry was in her view easily pigeonholed as the anguish of the comfortable and narcissistic middle class. See "Light Up the Cave" (1981).

55. Take for example what might be—but is not—an anxiety about privacy in the poetry of Nikki Giovanni, writing from and for the Black Panthers in the late 1960s (*Black Feeling* 1970). Grounded in a politics of racial identity, her response provides an alternative to the poetics of privacy. In a poem called "A Short Essay on Affirmation Explaining Why (With Apologies to the Federal Bureau of Investigation)," "that little microphone / In our teeth / Between our thighs / Or anyplace / that may have needed medical attention recently" provides a concrete image of state invasion at the most intimate level possible. Instead of exhibiting an anxiety about privacy, however, Giovanni casually brushes it off: "They ain't getting / Inside / My bang/ or / My brain / I'm into my Black Thing / And it's filling all / My empty spots / Sorry 'bout that / Miss Hoover." What is interesting here is that Giovanni disables surveillance not by reinforcing her protective covering but by doing away with the container model of selfhood that depends upon the inside/outside distinction. She is "filling all / [her] empty spots" with a body politics and so, unlike "Miss Hoover," does not need to protect a hidden "real" self that is vulnerable to disclosure.

56. "Poetry, Politics, and Intellectuals" (1995).

57. This argument had resonance in the United States, too, in debates over mass culture. As Dwight MacDonald argued in his essay "Masscult and Midcult," even an inept work of High Culture "is an expression of feelings, ideas, tastes, visions that are idiosyncratic and the audience similarly responds to them as individuals" (5). In contrast, "mass man," the product and target of mass culture, would have "no private life, no personal desires, hobbies, aspirations, or aversions that are not shared by everyone else" (11). The lyric, as the almost paradigmatic work of high culture, therefore represents the last stronghold of the private individual in mass society.

58. See Michael Davidson's *Ghostlier Demarcations* (1998).

59. There is one somewhat incoherent moment of intersection in Kalaidjian's *Languages of Liberation*. He cheers Sandra Gilbert's embrace of confessional writing even though his introduction generally derides the politics and poetics of self-revelation.

60. Gilbert, *Shakespeare's Sisters* (1979).

61. Tobin Siebers has a somewhat similar argument though he does not characterize the lyric as sovereign. He does suggest how the lyric was meant to provide a rhetorical form uncorrupted by the dangers of persuasion and propaganda. See "Cold War Criticism" (1993).

62. One of the reasons that form and formalism in both law and literature were so disrupted by the privacy crisis is that form conceptually mirrors the structural problems of

privacy. As Jeffrey Malkan says in "Literary Formalism" (1998) says, form is often conceived as a container, and formalism is the theory by which one understands what belongs inside and what must be excluded from the container.

63. In 1928 in *Olmstead*, the Supreme Court ruled that wiretapping did not violate the Fourth Amendment because telephone wires are not inside the home and the conversations these wires carry are not properly private. No trespass of the home can occur. In 1967 in *Katz v. U.S.*, the Court ruled that even public payphones carried with them a "reasonable expectation of privacy," so tapping these phones would constitute a violation of privacy. Finally, in 2000 the White House recommended using the telephone system as a metaphor for privacy on the Internet. The use of precedent is not static but dynamic and deeply enmeshed in experience. It is both a conceptual and an experiential shift that changes the terms of privacy.

64. See Jeffrey Malkan, "Literary Formalism" and Kenji Yoshino, "What's Past is Prologue" (1994). Unfortunately, matters of genre in literature are of some indifference to them.

65. Alicia Ostriker, " 'Fact' as Style" (1968).

66. 385 U.S. 323, 87 S. Ct. 439 (1966).

2. "THIRSTING FOR THE HIERARCHIC PRIVACY OF QUEEN VICTORIA'S CENTURY": ROBERT LOWELL AND THE TRANSFORMATIONS OF PRIVACY

1. Myron Brenton uses this phrase in *The Privacy Invaders*, as do so many other legal and journalistic accounts of privacy in the early 1960s. This reference is casual and not intended to mark specificity; rather, it is a unifying national generality.

2. While Brandeis and Warren's "The Right to Privacy" is generally acknowledged to be the most influential law review article ever written, Prosser's article is thought to rival it. As Bloustein argues, in the 1960s Prosser's account had supplanted Brandeis and Warren's as the most influential exploration of the tort.

3. Bloustein is somewhat overstating the coherence of Brandeis and Warren's concept of privacy, as I explain later. This overestimation of the coherence and stability of lost forms of privacy is characteristic of the latter half of the twentieth century.

4. The Lowell household was acutely sensitive to the culture of Boston in the late 1950s, and its waning influence on American politics and letters that was linked to a certain claustrophobic conception of privacy. Lowell's wife, Elizabeth Hardwick, published an essay called "Boston" (*A View of My Own*, 1962) the same year as Lowell published *Life Studies*. Hardwick's scathing reflections on Boston's place in American culture emphasized the link between privacy and social standing, what she refers to as the Boston obsession

with being "well-born." She describes local social interaction as essentially private—"nearly every Bostonian is in his own house or in someone else's house, dining at the home board, enjoying domestic and social privacy" (150). This kind of social world suggests the lack of a public sphere and the contented insularity of inherited connections. Moreover, she further derides the hierarchic social privacy of Boston's Brahmin class because it denied its superfluity, its lack of real political power or influence. As Hardwick notes, the Irish and the Italians ran Boston. Cultural or social power becomes increasingly a fantasy protected by the failure of the "well-born" to engage in a public world beyond their drawing rooms.

5. Lowell gave many reasons for this shift: reading the poetry of Elizabeth Bishop and W. D. Snodgrass, experimenting with prose, undergoing psychoanalysis after his mother's death, reading his work with Beat poets in San Francisco.

6. Allen Tate commented on his own advice to Lowell not to publish the autobiographical poems in *Life Studies*: "It seemed to me that the personal poems were a little morbid, private, and unorganized; and I was not put off because they were not *like* your old work; rather because they lacked the concentration and power, lacking as they seemed to lack, the highly formalistic organization of the old" (Letter to Robert Lowell, January 31, 1958).

7. See Lowell's *Paris Review* interview in Van Wyck Brooks, ed., *Writers at Work* (1963), 346.

8. James Merrill, commenting on the conventionality of confessional poetry, remarked that whether or not the revelation exposed the "real Robert Lowell," it had to give "the illusion of a True Confession" (as quoted in Marjorie Perloff's *Poetic Art* 80).

9. Lowell, Autobiographical Prose, "I Take Thee, Bob," undated.

10. In *Private Poets, Worldly Acts* (1996) Kevin Stein, like most of Lowell's critics, finds that "Skunk Hour," and *Life Studies* more generally, offer "implicit parallels between modern culture's slow motion ruin and that of his family and himself" (21). In this line of criticism, Lowell is the representative sufferer and public life is mirrored in the private travails of Lowell and his family. The relationship of private to public is one of condensation; the private is a metaphor of public life, which is to say that it is no different except in scale. Lowell's mental illness in this reading is actually the psychosis of society at large. In *The Psycho-Political Muse* Paul Breslin disputes this mirroring of the public and private and finds in "Skunk Hour" a perfect instance of the limitations of confessional poetry: the poet overestimates his ability to act as representative. This failure to assess the incommensurability of private experience with public event is for Paul Breslin the chief failing of confessional poetry and the primary failing of American political thinking on the relationship between the two spheres during this moment in American history. He argues that without a closer connection of public world and private illness, we're given no way—but

by mere assertion—to accept the poet as representative sufferer. While these two critics disagree about the ability of private experience to stand for public, they measure the relationship between the two spheres in precisely the same way.

11. Bishop is known for this reserve, both in personal relations and in her poetry. Her admiration for Lowell's confessions, a subgenre of poetry toward which she exhibited a pronounced hostility, derived not only from her respect for his technical brilliance; she also felt he was the one poet she knew whose family history gave him a universal relevance. "Whereas all you have to do is put down the names!" she wrote to Lowell in 1957, "And the fact that it seems significant, illustrative, American, etc. gives you, I think, the confidence you display about tackling any idea or theme, *seriously*, in both writing and conversation" (*One Art* 351).

12. In *Enlarging the Temple* Charles Altieri also reads "Skunk Hour" as a "final interpretation of the confessional process leading up to it" (64).

13. Jerome Mazzaro's essay, "Robert Lowell's Early Politics of Apocalypse," in *Modern American Poetry* (1970), shows how well acquainted Lowell was with accounts of the modern state's interventions in private life. Religious writers such as Christopher Dawson and T. S. Eliot, whom Lowell read while an undergraduate and before his conversion to Catholicism, decried the influence of the secular state in the private life of the citizen of a democracy. In Dawson's view, fascism, communism, *and* democracy marked the decline of Western civilization that began with the French Revolution. An influence on Dawson was the promonarchist journal *Commonweal*, in which one writer declared in 1942: "For my part I prefer an authoritarian 'I' who is competent only to build roads to a democratic 'we' who is competent to decide whom I must marry, what profession I must follow, what city I must live in and to what school I must send my children" (as quoted in *Modern American Poetry* 340). This link between democratic and totalitarian states was a visible but far less influential account of totalitarianism than Arendt's, which distinguishes totalitarianism not only from other forms of tyranny but also from democracy.

14. See Don Pember's account of this social and journalistic context in *Privacy and the Press* (1972). Pember says: "The Warren-Brandeis proposal was essentially a rich man's plea to the press to stop its gossiping and snooping, not an argument for the improvement of general journalistic standards" (23). He argues that Prosser's eminence as a legal scholar explains why the wedding story has had such currency, despite the fact that it is entirely fabricated. Warren's daughter was not married until 1905, fifteen years after the appearance of the article.

15. In researching her subject, Diane Middlebrook used tape recordings that Sexton had made of her therapy sessions, which were provided to the biographer by Sexton's psychoanalyst, Dr. Martin Orne.

16. Lowell, letter to Harriet Winslow, July 29, 1960.

17. Here as voyeur to family illness, Lowell is like Agrippina, a witness and then betrayer of a decaying empire. Similarly in "Grandparents," "[doodling] handlebar mustaches / on the last Russian Czar," Lowell is defacing the last in an imperial line.

18. Critics have frequently noted this voyeurism, but generally treated it as evidence of a general breakdown—"my mind's not right"—a generic mental illness rather than a particular set of symptoms.

19. Lowell, drafts of "Skunk Hour," undated. The version—"I am the visionary, the voyeur"—is found on the back of sheet 10 in the drafts of "Commander Lowell" (2195).

20. Lowell, drafts of "Skunk Hour," undated.

21. Privacy rights were not simply the juridical forms of a social good, they were increasingly and soon to be conceived as a juridical form of a political good. In the early 1960s the right to privacy was a tort that governed the interactions between private citizens or institutions. When the anxieties about privacy accelerated as the decade wore on, the driving force of the privacy debate was increasingly the state's infringement of individual autonomy. In the shift from a social to a juridical right, privacy also underwent another shift from a social to a political right.

22. Bloustein was working from a paper he had presented at a conference on the "Impact of Technological Advances on the Law of Privacy" convened by the New York City Bar Association's Special Committee on Science and Law. Among others who worked with Bloustein on the article was Allan Westin, who also served on this committee and from its findings produced his influential book *Privacy and Freedom*.

23. This phrase was repeated widely in legal scholarship on privacy during the late fifties and early sixties. Before *Griswold*, the incoherence of privacy law was the primary obstacle for deciding its legal standing. Strangely, this incoherence follows privacy throughout the late twentieth century. Jed Rubenfeld makes a similar judgment in "The Right to Privacy" in 1989.

24. 46 Mich. 160, 9 N.W. 146 (1881). Caroline Danielson, in "The Gender of Privacy" (1999), also treats *DeMay v. Roberts* to argue that this case "incorporates both Roberts's claims to her experience and the assertion of a conception of 'woman' and stabilizes them as privacy" (313).

25. This is an argument most fully developed in the field of domestic violence. See Martha Fineman, Nancy Thomadsen, and Roxanne Mykitiuk, eds., *Public Nature of Private Violence* (1994).

26. In fact, the first cases to produce a "right to privacy" were about publicity. The New York Court of Appeals refused in 1902 to grant the privacy claim of a plaintiff whose picture was used to advertise a product without her permission. In response to public outcry

following the decision, the New York legislature enacted the country's first privacy law to protect against this sort of intrusion. Still, it is easy to see that this case was essentially about who profited from publicity. It is not, strictly speaking, the kind of intrusion Brandeis and Warren imagined, nor the kind that worried late-twentieth-century legal scholars concerned with technological intrusion by the state.

27. There is ample evidence of this search in *Life Studies*. For example, Lowell "wished [he] were an older girl . . . wrote Santa Claus for a field hockey stick" and claimed that "to be a boy at Brimmer was to be small, denied, and weak" (27). He asks "with the egotistic, slightly paranoid apprehensions of an only child . . . what became of boys graduating from Brimmer's fourth grade. . . . And to judge from [his] father, men between the ages of six and sixty did nothing but meet new challenges, take on heavier responsibilities, and lose all freedom to explode" (28).

28. Lowell, Autobiographical Prose, "Rock," undated.

29. As quoted in Ian Hamilton's *Robert Lowell* (1982), 422–23.

30. Ibid.

31. Lowell, letter to Elizabeth Hardwick, May 26, 1970.

32. Adrienne Rich, "Carytid," 42.

33. Donald Hall, "Knock, Knock," 44.

34. As Paul Mariani claims in *Lost Puritan* (1994), Lowell thought that *The Dolphin* was a work of major social significance since it dealt with what he considered one of his era's most visible social transformations, which was the growing number of divorces and remarriages (Mariani 407).

35. This republication was itself a cause of some consternation among Lowell's readers. In fact, the two central criticisms in reviews of the three volumes were first, the ethical transgression of using Hardwick's letters in *The Dolphin* and second, the literary and ethical complications of republishing his work. Which of the two was the greater problem depended on the critic, and there is no consistent point of view.

36. Jean Cohen makes the point that *Roe* does not defend patriarchal privacy precisely because women become autonomous from their husbands. See her "Rethinking Privacy" (521).

37. Robert Giroux has pointed out that Lowell used Hardwick's letters in *Life Studies* too. See Hamilton, 434. However, nothing in this poem comes close to the specificity of attribution in *The Dolphin*. Though we "know" this is Lowell's wife, there is not the same "documentable" presence. This is a later innovation.

38. The drafts of Lowell's poems are available at the Harry Ransom Humanities Research Center but the letters themselves are not. I have inferred the trajectory of Lowell's rewriting from the drafts of the poems.

39. Lowell, drafts of poems from *The Dolphin*, box 4, folder 3. By permission from the Harry Ransom Humanities Research Center, The University of Texas at Austin.

3. PENETRATING PRIVACY: CONFESSIONAL POETRY, *Griswold v. Connecticut,* AND CONTAINMENT IDEOLOGY

1. While we enter Lowell's confessional project through the door of his boyhood home, "91 Revere Street," the address is no longer a "straightforward, immutable residential fact." In one sense the house of Lowell is difficult to locate because the world around it was changing: "Houses, changing hands, changed their language and nationality." The house symbolizes social mobility, upward and downward, instead of social position. Moreover, within the surrounding social flux, the "house of Lowell" is itself in eclipse, though in a rather understated way. Lowell's ironic twist—that his parents' purchase of 91 Revere Street constitutes a *recovery* of status, a reclaiming of ground lost to "lace curtain Irish"—at the same time suggests just how silly is his mother's sense of vertiginous decline. The Lowells remain only "fifty yards" from the "Hub of the Hub of the Universe" though they stare out at their uncertain future: "the unbuttoned part of Beacon Hill" and the north end slums. Metaphorically, the Lowells are facing their own decline, but at their backs remains the solid Brahmin gentility that anchors them to Boston's elite (*Life Studies* 14–15).

2. This exceptional and paradoxical status of the home in cold war politics is much like the "sovereign exception" in Giorgio Agamben's *Homo Sacer* (1998). Agamben asks "what is the relation between politics and life, if life presents itself as what is included by means of an exclusion?" (7). In other words, the home of cold war ideology was included in politics, indeed was the ground of politics in so many ways, by being imagined as exempt and distinct from politics. As Agamben suggests, this exclusion does not relieve but intensifies the confusion between inside and outside, state and self, public and private.

3. Diane Middlebrook in "What Was Confessional Poetry?" has a similar perspective: "Confessional poems sought to expose the poverty of the ideology of family that dominated postwar culture and to draw poetic truth from the actual pain given and taken in the context of family life, especially as experienced by children" (648).

4. In *Osborn*, the question related to hidden recording devices, in *Hoffa*, to the inducement of a friend to act as the eyes and ears of the government in Hoffa's circle, and in *Lewis*, the breach of the home by an agent posing as someone else to enter a home.

5. This encyclopedic approach continues long after the American public was supposed (according to Allen Westin) to have fully assimilated the loss of privacy.

6. It is well known that Plath's selections for *Ariel* were amended and reordered after her death by her husband/editor, Ted Hughes, omitting, as Marjorie Perloff has argued in *Poetic License* (1991), poems that revealed Plath's anger over his infidelity. While I find Perloff's reading persuasive, these poems also have intriguing political readings. Furthermore, there are indications throughout her work that Plath was sensitive to her political context. The introduction to *The Haunting of Sylvia Plath* (1991) by Jacqueline

Rose is perhaps the most complex working through of Plath's political and historical awareness.

7. 232 U.S. 383, (1914).

8. See Norman Redlich, "Are There 'Certain Rights . . . Retained by the People'?" A number of cases that traversed the line between Fourth and Fifth Amendment violation were associated with HUAC and more generally with red-hunting, for example, *Slowchower v. N.Y.* (350 U.S. 551) in 1956 and *Cohen v. Hurley* (366 U.S. 117) in 1961.

9. 342 U.S. 165 (1952).

10. This is a much noted pattern in FBI investigations. The fewer communists the FBI located, the more money, manpower, and resources it requested to press the investigation forward. The sheer fact that communists could not be found intensified the FBI's belief in their masterful disguise. See Fred J. Cook in *The FBI Nobody Knows* and Frank Donner in *The Age of Surveillance.*

11. Numerous accounts in addition to Whyte's and Friedan's note both the appeal of privacy to suburban home buyers and the extraordinary "visibility," as William Dobriner called it in *Class in Suburbia* (1963), that defined suburban living (11). That is, many couples were understood to be leaving cities for suburbs to enjoy larger private space. At the same time these new suburbanites often complained that what defined their experience of suburban life was the extent to which their neighbors knew their business. See also Dobriner's edited collection, *The Suburban Community* (1958), Mark Baldassare's *Trouble in Paradise* (1986), Kenneth T. Jackson's *The Crabgrass Frontier* (1985), and more recently Roger Silverstone's collection *Visions of Suburbia* (1997).

12. Joanne Meyerowitz acknowledges Friedan's inestimable influence on postwar historiography but disputes the accuracy of her depiction of middle-class women and the popular culture they consumed. See Meyerowitz, "Beyond the Feminine Mystique."

13. Following Foucault, critics now routinely portray the confessional act as always already solicited, coerced by the powerful listener who interprets, sanctions, and legitimizes the confessional subject. This insight has been especially fruitful in feminist theories of autobiography and women's confessional writing where Susan Bernstein (*Confessional Subjects,* 1997) and Leigh Gilmore (*Autobiographics,* 1994) have demonstrated that the female confessional subject is already caught in a system of surveillance. Both these critics also acknowledge their debt to Rita Felski (*Beyond Feminist Aesthetics*) in rethinking the confessionalism of women's writing. This does not mean, nor do they suggest, that women writers simply submit to this coercion or surveillance but that they are not able to set the terms of their self-disclosure.

14. As White acknowledges, the strategies the Court produced to evade the property restrictions have been less than "eminently successful." See his explanation of the relationship of property to privacy in *Justice as Translation,* 204–07.

15. 262 U.S. 390 (1923).

16. 365 U.S. 505 (1961).

17. The dissenters in this case—Harlan, Frankfurter, and Whittaker—wished not to violate stare decisis and instead would have overturned the obscenity law in Ohio, which had been the grounds of Mapp's arrest. They are not sure that privacy exists as a coherent right though Harlan will write that very same year his crucial dissent in *Poe v. Ullman*, where the invasion is much less literal. It's instructive to note along with Norman Redlich that Harlan dissented from *Mapp*, which did protect privacy, and dissented in *Poe*, arguing that privacy was not protected enough. Redlich can't explain this through any consistency of legal reasoning, which suggests that legal reasoning is not the source of Harlan's difference of opinion. I would suggest that the reason that Harlan finds the privacy of *Poe* so persuasive is that it concerns *marital* privacy, which becomes a special category for him.

18. Brief for Planned Parenthood of Connecticut at 32–36, 40–47, 49–54, 62–65, *Griswold v. Connecticut*.

19. This language is extremely close to the summary dismissal in *Bowers v. Hardwick* of the claim by Michael Hardwick, a gay man, of a right to sexual intimacy. The Court treats each as an outrageous affront to common sense and national traditions.

20. Sexton is troping two poems from *Life Studies*, "Man and Wife" and "To Speak of Woe that Is in Marriage."

21. Perhaps no one is more associated with the split between autonomous privacy and the deprivations of privacy than Hannah Arendt in *The Human Condition* (1958). Margaret Canovan suggests that we look to *The Origins of Totalitarianism* to understand the urgency behind Arendt's mapping of terms, in this case especially, public, private, and that slippery category, the social. See Canovan, *Hannah Arendt* (1992).

22. Lowell, too, has used the image of "suffocating for privacy" ("For the Union Dead"), which, as Meredith McGill has suggested, is inherently unreadable: Colonel Shaw either sacrifices for his privacy or is sacrificed to it. In either case, both Sexton and Lowell suggest that privacy is unspeakable because it has no language. See McGill, "Enlistment and Refusal," 144–49.

23. Women in Connecticut were able to procure birth control by going out of state or by appealing to private doctors, many of whom would provide it. However, this meant that there was a disproportionate impact on poor women who relied on the clinic for basic reproductive services.

24. Roraback consistently tried to clear the courtroom when these women were to give testimony. The judges did not always permit it.

4. CONFESSIONS BETWEEN A WOMAN AND HER DOCTOR:
Roe v. Wade AND THE GENDER OF PRIVACY

1. *Katz v. U.S.* established two important precedents: (1) that a "reasonable expectation" of privacy was sufficient to protect citizens from surveillance in public places such as pay phones, and, (2) that language could be seized. *Terry v. Ohio* affirmed the bodily privacy of individuals in public by restricting police searches for weapons. In *Loving v. Virginia* the Supreme Court struck down Virginia's miscegenation laws, claiming for individuals the right of association in marriage that had been defined in *Griswold. Eisenstadt v. Baird* disconnected privacy from the marital relationship by allowing unmarried individuals access to birth control.

2. My argument about the Court's limitation of state intrusion on individuals should not be construed to apply to post-*Roe* privacy decisions for two reasons: first and most obviously, the Court that decided the important privacy decisions of the 1980s and early 1990s—*Bowers v. Hardwick* in 1986, *Webster v. Reproductive Health Services* (492 U.S. 490) in 1989, and *Planned Parenthood of Southeastern Pennsylvania v. Casey* (112 S.Ct. 2791) in 1992—was substantially altered from the Warren Court of the sixties that initially "found" the right to privacy in *Griswold v. Connecticut* and developed this right through *Roe*. Not only had the Court grown more conservative in its principles of interpretation, but this interpretive strategy was a direct result of the appointment of justices presumed to be hostile to *Roe*. Second, as I argue later in the chapter, *Roe* itself reshaped the legal and political direction of privacy rights by transforming privacy from a right symbolically associated in the cold war with protection from totalitarianism to a woman's right of bodily selfsovereignty.

3. My thanks to Scarlett Higgins for elaborating these connections.

4. Timothy Melley argues that the forces of social control in the dominant narrative modes of the period—conspiracy and paranoia—are consistently represented as feminizing. See *Empire of Conspiracy*, 32.

5. As W. R. Johnson argues in *The Idea of Lyric* (1982), the "rebirth of lyric vitality" derives from a renewed attention to the speaker's relationship to audience, found in the "restoration of the pronomial form" (22). For a critique of the overuse of "pronomial forms," see Jonathan Holden *The Rhetoric of Contemporary Lyric* (1980) for his chapter, "The Abuse of the Second-Person Pronoun." Alicia Ostriker describes this attention to audience as a "poetics of empathy" in "Anne Sexton and the Seduction of Audience." This attention to the structure of address in postwar lyric poetry has been extensive. My suggestion derives from this criticism but also proposes that there is something more threatening in confessional poetry.

6. Both Diane Middlebrook's *Anne Sexton* and Ian Hamilton's *Robert Lowell* suggest the importance of psychoanalysis to their subjects' poetry. Though Lowell himself notes a

variety of influences—reading Snodgrass's *Heart's Needle*, hearing Allen Ginsberg in San Francisco, and writing prose—Hamilton also suggests that Lowell's psychoanalysis in the mid-fifties influenced his turn to the self-revelations of *Life Studies*. Responding to a similar prompt, Anne Sexton began to write poetry at the urging of her psychoanalyst, Dr. Martin Orne, who became a controversial figure for readers of Sexton when he released her tapes of their sessions. James E. B. Breslin makes a similar comment about Lowell assuming psychoanalysis as the "frame" for *Life Studies*. See Breslin, *From Modern to Contemporary*, 141.

7. In Sylvia Plath's *The Collected Poems* (1981) the poem directly after "The Courage of Shutting-Up" called "The Bee Meeting" also features a surgeon and a kind of inquisition; other medicalized poems by Plath are "Face Lift," "In Plaster," and "The Surgeon at 2AM" from *Crossing the Water* (written between 1960–1961) and "Lady Lazarus," "Tulips," and "Fever 103°" from *Ariel*. Other examples of this kind of poem are Snodgrass's "The Operation" from *Heart's Needle* and "The Examination," "A Character," "Inquest," and "A Flat One" from *After Experience* (1968) and too many poems to list in Anne Sexton's *The Complete Poems* (1981).

8. In this questioning, confessional poetry unveiled the relationship between confession and the medicalization of the body that has become so familiar to us through volume 1 of Michel Foucault's *The History of Sexuality*.

9. Rosalind Petchesky has observed that medical technologies have troubled "the very definition, as traditionally understood, of 'inside' and 'outside' a woman's body" (as quoted in Cynthia Daniels, *At Women's Expense* 17). I agree, but simply note that this questioning has a long history.

10. As Susan Bernstein suggests, it is not merely revelation but the attention to the conditions and effects of revelation that make confessional writing political. Though her article, "What's 'I' Got to Do With It?" (1992) limits itself to feminist literary critics and their confessional writing, her questioning of a too easy connection between confession and political engagement can be useful in other genres.

11. Brook Thomas's article "The Construction of Privacy in and around *The Bostonians*" has been very important to the development of my work. In fact, this chapter is in some sense a response to Thomas's article. I would, however, like to distinguish my conception of privacy from his. He says: "A private personality for [Henry] James does not result from protecting a self that preexists social relations. Nor does it result from the union of two selves into one that underlies the so-called sanctity of the domestic sphere. It does not even result from disappearance from the public. Instead, it has to do with the creation of a space *between*, a space that establishes connection while simultaneously helping to define the parties involved as individuals" (734). In Thomas's model, both individuals construct their privacy in relation to one another. In the *Roe* model of privacy, only one

individual's privacy is at stake, the woman patient's. To create a privacy on her own terms, perhaps in excess of what the doctor will be willing to grant her, she must enter discourse, use language, in a very real sense give up a measure of her privacy. There is no parallel compulsion for the doctor or even for the male patient.

12. The label "confessional" might now be more associated with women than with men. Robert Lowell's ability to both define "confessional" and remain undefined by it points to a central problem with the gendering of the label. While M. L. Rosenthal derived his definition of confessional poetry from Lowell's work, he maintained that Lowell would never be "a 'confessional' poet only" (*The New Poets* 4). Those poets who are deemed "only" confessional poets tend to be women poets, specifically Sexton and Plath, because critics have found their work more transgressive and because feminist critics have embraced rather than fled from the label.

13. In *Unbearable Weight* (1993) Susan Bordo studies Court responses to the invasion of the body and concludes that the inviolability of the body, the right to "personal security" that has a long tradition in American law, extends only to male bodies. Pregnant women are the exception to this sanctity of the body because their bodies are perceived as inhabited. Snodgrass's poem illustrates that inviolability and maleness are so interconnected that the violation of the male body does away with the category of maleness altogether.

14. Critics have generally underestimated how generically the invasion of privacy is represented through the invasion of women's rather than men's bodies. Michel Foucault, though mindful of the power differential in the medicalized confession, nevertheless ignores the gendered gaze. Similarly, Peter Brooks's *Body Work* (1993), which explores the paradox that privacy is always represented through its invasion, fails to acknowledge the extent to which this defining paradox is always displayed through the revelation of women's private lives. Likewise, in his article "Appearing and Disappearing in Public" (1986), Philip Fisher reads Thomas Eakin's painting, "The Agnew Clinic," as an "exhibition of privacy" where the scalpel's penetration of the female breast offers a glimpse of the "most intimate and private physical self" (162). The invasion of the woman's body, and more specifically, the invasion of the most visible marker of femininity, her breast, is precisely *not* the signifier of the "most private self" because it is the site of a history of representations of its violation. Instead, we might see this history as the portrayal of women's categorical lack of privacy.

15. Is this medical procedure different from any others—such as cosmetic surgery or sterilization—which also require women to justify their wishes to doctors? Yes and no. I would argue that by 1973 the difficulties of abortion were moral and only occasionally medical, which is not to say that other types of surgery do not have moral dimensions. Nevertheless, it is the moral, not the medical issues, that complicate abortion and to rule that doctors are better moral decision makers than pregnant women is precisely the problem of *Roe*.

16. Several readers have noted that the doctor is merely grammatically male. While I think that it matters little to my argument whether the doctor is biologically male or female, it is more than likely that the Court imagined a male physician in their deliberations. Though I have no direct evidence of this, the generic maleness of doctors is nearly a given in 1973. I remind you of the episode from the third season of *All in the Family* (1972–73) in which Gloria stumps both conservative Archie and liberal Mike with the riddle about the boy and his doctor. It goes like this: a man and his son are badly injured in a car accident. When they are taken to the hospital and the boy is wheeled into surgery, the surgeon takes one look at him and says, "I can't operate. This boy is my son." An entire episode is devoted to unraveling this mystery. (Moreover, this same riddle reappeared in a sitcom in 1996.)

17. As Jennifer Nedelsky has argued in "Reconceiving Autonomy" (1989), the liberal individualism that produces the notion of autonomy and privacy the court deals with may never truly exist in isolation for any citizen; privacy is always a relational right, she argues, though permission may be granted in ways so invisible or so deeply habitual that we fail to see them. She proposes reconceiving autonomy as a relational right to more accurately reflect the necessary interdependence of individuals striving for autonomy.

18. Like Jahan Ramazani in *The Poetry of Mourning* (1994) I read Plath's "Lady Lazarus" as a critique of the confessional project. Ramazani brilliantly analyzes Plath's accounting of the costs of the commercialized confession though I see the doctor's presence as more dangerous to the speaker than the "peanut-crunching crowd."

19. As Nedelsky says, "our political tradition has virtually identified freedom and autonomy with the private sphere, and posed them in opposition to the public sphere of state power." Moreover, she continues: "there is virtually nothing in Federalist thought which treats political participation as an important component of individual autonomy, as a dimension of self-determination with intrinsic value" ("Reconceiving Autonomy" 15–16).

5. CONFESSING THE ORDINARY:
PAUL MONETTE'S *Love Alone* AND *Bowers v. Hardwick*: AN EPILOGUE

1. This tension radiates all through the response to AIDS. On the one hand, as the ACT-UP slogan "Silence = Death" suggests, AIDS provoked a collective coming out of the closet. At the same time, as Gregory Woods has noted, AIDS was returning many to secrecy, especially older gay men who were "most at home" in the closet ("AIDS to Remembrance" 158).

2. Lee Edelman says that "Silence = Death" translates "Action = Live" but that this "action" nearly always takes the form of speech, discourse. See "The Plague of Discourse" (1989). Jason Tougaw suggests that the central ambivalence of AIDS memoirs like

Monette's is their "devotion to and skepticism about the value of AIDS writing as a combatant to the collective trauma of the epidemic" ("Testimony" 235).

3. Sexton did write a poem about *Roe v. Wade*, "Is it True?" (*The Awful Rowing Towards God* 1975). Lowell began "Fetus" (*Day by Day* 1977) on the steps of a courthouse. More recently, Susan Hahn set a number of poems in *Confession* (1997) in a juridical frame.

4. See, for example, Earl G. Ingersoll, et al., eds., *The Post-Confessionals* (1989).

5. He invokes Sexton in *West of Yesterday, East of Summer* and makes a pilgrimage to her house in *Borrowed Time*, and he is compared to Plath in the blurbs for *Love Alone*.

6. Nan Hunter immediately linked *Hardwick* to McCarthyism in her 1986 essay "Banned in the USA," which argues: "[J]ust as the Supreme Court suspended the First Amendment to silence Communists 35 years ago, it has now rendered homosexuals, as a class, outlaws in the eyes of America" (80).

7. In " 'All They Needed' " (1997), Peter Cohen describes this phenomenon as "class dislocation." He identifies the "rude shock" these men experienced when they confronted a contradiction: "their possession of a tremendous amount of class privilege combined with their inability to fully mobilize this privilege in the absence of a cure" (86). He argues that the experience of privilege of white middle-class men was a double-edged sword in AIDS activism. On the one hand, the sense of entitlement raised expectations of what activism could effect; on the other, the embrace of institutions could at times create a reformist, and perhaps more limited, agenda.

8. Harlan was moved to dissent in *Poe* because he thought that the machinery of prosecution would be too intrusive for married couples. It is the problem of how to prosecute Connecticut's birth control statues that made the law unconstitutional to him not the prohibition against birth control.

9. White declares that the coplaintiffs, a heterosexual couple, have no standing because they are not in danger of prosecution. On these grounds, it could have been argued that this discriminatory prosecution itself should invalidate the law against sodomy. This problem of selective prosecution was part of the original complaint in *Poe v. Ullman*.

10. Justice Hugo Black felt himself obliged to answer "yes" to Douglas's question because he felt privacy was not stipulated by the framers in the language of the Constitution or the Bill of Rights. Nor did he find due process a sufficiently compelling rationale for the right to privacy.

11. The most obvious revelation of this "secret" is of course the Kinsey Report in the 1940s. But the secret keeps being revealed, though in ever more trivial forms. For example, in the 1960s Lenny Bruce declared that "if faggot means ever involved with a homosexual, active or passive, then I just *know* I'm looking at a room full of fags. Isn't that weird? Whether you were two years old or six years old, any time that scoutmaster or gym coach jacked you off to a Tillie and Mack book, your uncle Donald wanted to kiss

you, or that truck driver that jacked you off when you were hitchhiking on Merrick Road, or you were experimenting and playing doctor—that's it Jim: you're a sometimes fag" (*The Essential Lenny Bruce* 180). In the 1990s Michael J. Fox can ask on a prime-time sit-com, *Spin City*: "Who here is gay? Ok, who here has ever had any kind of gay experience? Ok, who here has been to summer camp?"

12. Joseph Cady in "Immersive and Counterimmersive Writing About AIDS" (1993) argues that the most important feature of Monette's "immersive" writing, that is, writing that squarely confronts the denial of the disease, is the elegies' "chaotic form." This form "disrupts all traditional notions of focus, sequence, tone, and structure" (247). Deborah Landau also comments on the shape of these lines, arguing that they refuse distance and control, "saturat[ing]" themselves in rage and anguish. See " 'How to Live. What to Do.' " (1996).

13. Warner is also talking about the numerous material benefits of marriage—tax relief, inheritance, health benefits, etc.—that gay rights groups have worked hard to procure for gay couples.

14. See of course *The Epistemology of the Closet* (1990). See also two articles by Janet Halley: "The Politics of the Closet" (1989) and "Reasoning about Sodomy" (1993); Jonathan Goldberg *Sodometries* (1992); Kendall Thomas, "Beyond the Privacy Principle"; Lauren Berlant's "Live Sex Acts"; Michael Warner's introduction to *Fear of a Queer Planet* (1993); and Berlant and Elizabeth Freeman's "Queer Nationality."

15. I'm suggesting a social use of Jessica Benjamin's psychoanalytic model of mutual recognition as the basis of subjectivity in her *Like Subjects* (1995).

16. Reva Siegel observes that in this case what the Court imagined contained by priva-cy had changed dramatically because of feminist rethinking of the public/private binary since *Roe v. Wade*. *Casey* upheld the privacy doctrine of *Roe* but what precisely constitut-ed privacy had mutated. It was not the exact same privacy of the earlier decision. See "Abortion as a Sex Equality Right," 66–68.

Works Cited

Abrams, M. H. *The Mirror and the Lamp: Romantic Theory and the Critical Tradition*. New York: Oxford University Press, 1953.

Adorno, Theodor W. "On Lyric Poetry and Society." In Shierry Weber Nicolson, trans., *Notes to Literature: Volume One*. New York: Columbia University Press, 1991.

Agamben, Giorgio. *Homo Sacer: Sovereign Power and Bare Life*. Trans. Daniel Heller-Roazen. Stanford: Stanford University Press, 1998.

Allen, Anita L. *Uneasy Access: Privacy for Women in a Free Society*. New Jersey: Rowman and Littlefield, 1988.

Altieri, Charles. *Enlarging the Temple*. Lewisburg: Bucknell University Press, 1979.

——. *Self and Sensibility in Contemporary American Poetry*. Cambridge: Cambridge University Press, 1984.

Anderson, Quentin. *The Imperial Self: An Essay in American Literary and Cultural History*. New York: Knopf, 1971.

Arendt, Hannah. "The Concentration Camps." *Partisan Review* (July 1948).

——. *The Human Condition*. Chicago: University of Chicago Press, 1958.

——. *Totalitarianism: Part Three of the Origins of Totalitarianism*. New York: Harcourt Brace, 1966.

Ault, Erika. "The FBI's Library Awareness Program: Is Big Brother Reading Over Your Shoulder." *New York University Law Review* 65, no. 6 (December 1990): 1532–1565.

Baldassare, Mark. *Trouble in Paradise: The Suburban Transformation in America*. New York: Columbia University Press, 1986.

Benjamin, Jessica. *Like Subjects, Love Objects: Essays on Recognition and Sexual Difference*. New Haven: Yale University Press, 1995.

Bercovitch, Sacvan. *The Rites of Assent: Transformations in the Symbolic Construction of America*. New York: Routledge, 1993.

Berlant, Lauren. "Live Sex Acts." *Feminist Studies* 21, no. 2 (Summer 1995): 379–404.

Berlant, Lauren and Elizabeth Freeman. "Queer Nationality." In Michael Warner, ed., *Fear of a Queer Planet: Queer Politics and Social Theory*, 193–229. Minnesota: University of Minnesota Press, 1993.

Bernstein, Susan. "What's 'I' Got to Do With It?" *Hypatia* 7, no. 2 (Spring 1992): 120–47.

——. *Confessional Subjects: Revelations of Gender and Power in Victorian Literature and Culture*. Chapel Hill: University of North Carolina Press, 1997.

Berryman, John. *77 Dream Songs*. New York: Farrar, Straus and Giroux, 1964.

——. *Love and Fame*. New York: Farrar, Straus and Giroux, 1970.

Bishop, Elizabeth. *One Art: Letters*. Robert Giroux, ed. New York: Farrar, Straus and Giroux, 1994.

Bloustein, Edward. "Privacy as an Aspect of Human Dignity: An Answer to Dean Prosser." *New York University Law Review* 39 (1964): 962–1007.

Bordo, Susan. *Unbearable Weight*. Berkeley: University of California Press, 1993.

Brandeis, Louis and Samuel Warren. "The Right to Privacy." *Harvard Law Review* 4, no. 5 (December 1890): 193–220.

Brenton, Myron. *The Privacy Invaders*. New York: Coward-McGann, 1964.

Breslin, James E. B. *From Modern to Contemporary: American Poetry, 1945–1965*. Chicago: University of Chicago Press, 1984.

Breslin, Paul. *The Psycho-Political Muse: American Poetry Since the Fifties*. Chicago: University of Chicago Press, 1987.

Brooks, Peter. *Body Work: Objects of Desire in Modern Narrative*. Cambridge: Harvard University Press, 1993.

——. *Troubling Confessions: Speaking Guilt in Law and Literature*. Chicago: University of Chicago Press, 2000.

Brooks, Van Wyck, ed. *Writers at Work:* The Paris Review *Interviews Second Series*. New York: Viking, 1963.

Bruce, Lenny. *The Essential Lenny Bruce*. John Cohen, ed. New York: Douglas Books, 1970.

Cady, Joseph. "Immersive and Counterimmersive Writing About AIDS: The Achievement of Paul Monette's *Love Alone*." In Timothy F. Murphy and Suzanne Poirier, eds., *Writing AIDS: Gay Literature, Language, and Analysis*, 244–64. New York: Columbia University Press, 1993.

Canovan, Margaret. *Hannah Arendt: A Reinterpretation of Her Political Thought*. Cambridge: Cambridge University Press, 1992.

Carson, Anne. *Men in the Off Hours*. New York: Knopf, 2000.

Chambers, Whittaker. *Witness*. New York: Random House, 1952.

Chauncey, George. *The Strange Career of the Closet: Gay Culture, Politics, and Consciousness from the Second World War to the Stonewall Era*. Basic Books, forthcoming.

Clarke, Arthur C. "Telstar, Telstar . . . Burning Bright." *Life*, August 3, 1962, 4.

Clarke, Eric O. *Virtuous Vice: Homoeroticism and the Public Sphere*. Durham, N.C.: Duke University Press, 2000.

Clausen, Jan. *A Movement of Poets: Thoughts on Poetry and Feminism*. Brooklyn, N.Y.: Long Haul Press, 1982.

Cohen, Jean L. "Rethinking Privacy: Autonomy, Identity, and the Abortion Controversy." In Jeff Weintraub and Krishan Kumar, eds. *Public and Private in Thought and Practice*, 133–65. Chicago: University of Chicago Press, 1997.

Cohen, Peter. " 'All They Needed': AIDS, Consumption, and the Politics of Class." *Journal of the History of Sexuality* 8, no. 1 (July 1997): 86–115.

Cook, Fred. *The FBI Nobody Knows*. New York: Pyramid Books, 1964.

Corber, Robert J. *Homosexuality in Cold War America*. Durham, N.C.: Duke University Press, 1997.

——. "Rear Window and the Postwar Settlement." In Donald Pease, ed., *National Identities and Post-Americanist Narratives*, 121–48. Durham, N.C.: Duke University Press, 1994.

D'Emilio, John. "The Homosexual Menace: The Politics of Sexuality in Cold War America." In Kathy Peiss and Christina Simmons, eds., *Passion and Power: Sexuality in History*, 226–40. Philadelphia: Temple University Press, 1989.

Daniels, Cynthia. *At Women's Expense: State Power and the Politics of Fetal Rights*. Cambridge: Harvard University Press, 1993.

Danielson, Caroline. "The Gender of Privacy and the Embodied Self: Examining the Origins of the Right to Privacy in U.S. Law." *Feminist Studies* 25, no. 2 (Summer 1999): 311–44.

Dash, Samuel. *The Eavesdroppers*. New Brunswick, N.J.: Rutgers University Press, 1959.

Davidson, Michael. *Ghostlier Demarcations: Modern Poetry and the Material Word*. Berkeley: University of California Press, 1998.

Davison, Peter. *The Fading Smile: Poets in Boston, from Robert Frost to Robert Lowell to Sylvia Plath, 1955–1960*. New York: Knopf, 1994.

Dimock, Wai Chee. *Residues of Justice: Literature, Law, Philosophy*. Berkeley: University of California Press, 1996.

Dobriner, William. *Class in Suburbia*. Englewood Cliffs, N.J.: Prentice-Hall, 1963.

——. *The Suburban Community*. New York: Putnam, 1958.

Donner, Frank. *The Age Of Surveillance: The Aims and Methods Of America's Political Intelligence System*. New York: Knopf, 1980.

Doty, Mark. "The 'Forbidden Planet' of Character: The Revolutions of the 1950s." In Jack Meyers and David Wojahn, eds., *A Profile of Twentieth-Century American Poetry*, 131–57. Carbondale: Southern Illinois University Press, 1991.

Douglas, William O. *The Right of the People*. New York: Doubleday, 1958.

DuPlessis, Rachel. *The Pink Guitar: Writing as Feminist Practice*. New York: Routledge, 1990.

Edelman, Lee. "The Plague of Discourse: Politics, Literary Theory, and AIDS." In
Ronald Butters, John Clum, and Michael Moon, eds., *Displacing Homophobia: Gay
Male Perspectives on Literature and Culture*. Durham, N.C.: Duke University Press,
1989.

———. *Homographesis*. New York: Routledge, 1994.

Ellis, Edward Robb. *The Traitor Within*. Garden City, N.Y.: Doubleday, 1961.

Ernst, Morris L. and Alan U. Schwartz. *Privacy: The Right to Be Let Alone*. New York:
Macmillan, 1962.

Fein, Esther B. Obituary for Paul Monette. *New York Times*, February 13, 1995, B7.

Felski, Rita. *Beyond Feminist Aesthetics: Feminist Literature and Social Change*.
Cambridge: Harvard University Press, 1989.

Fineman, Martha and Nancy Sweet Thomadsen, eds. *At the Boundaries of Law: Feminism
and Legal Theory*. New York: Routledge, 1991.

Fineman, Martha, Nancy Sweet Thomadsen, and Roxanne Mykitiuk, eds. *The Public
Nature of Private Violence: The Discovery of Domestic Abuse*. New York: Routledge,
1994.

Fisher, Phillip. "Appearing and Disappearing in Public: Social Space in Late
Nineteenth-Century Literature and Culture." In Sacvan Bercovitch, ed.,
Reconstructing American Literary History, 155–88. Cambridge: Harvard University
Press, 1986.

Foucault, Michel. *Discipline and Punish: The Birth of the Prison*. Trans. Alan Sheridan.
New York: Vintage, 1978.

———. *The History of Sexuality*, vol. 1, *An Introduction*. Trans. Robert Hurley. New York:
Vintage, 1978.

Friedan, Betty. *The Feminine Mystique*. 1963; reprint, New York: Dell, 1983.

Gabler, Neal. *Winchell: Gossip, Power, and the Culture of Celebrity*. New York: Knopf,
1994.

Gaddis, John Lewis. *Strategies of Containment: A Critical Appraisal of Postwar American
National Security Policy*. New York: Oxford University Press, 1982.

Garber, Marjorie, Paul B. Franklin, and Rebecca L. Walkowitz, eds., *Field Work: Sites In
Literary and Cultural Studies*. New York: Routledge, 1996.

Garber, Marjorie and Rebecca Walkowitz, eds. *Secret Agents: The Rosenberg Case,
McCarthyism, and Fifties America*. New York: Routledge, 1995.

Garment, Leonard. "Annals of Law: The Hill Case." *The New Yorker*, April 17, 1989,
90–110.

Garrow, David. *The FBI and Martin Luther King Jr.: From "Solo" to Memphis*. New York:
Norton, 1981.

———. *Liberty and Sexuality: The Right to Privacy and the Making of Roe v. Wade, 1923–1973*.
New York: Maxwell Macmillan International, 1994.

Gewanter, David. "Child of Collaboration: Robert Lowell's *The Dolphin*." *Modern Philology* 93, no. 2 (November 1995): 179–203.

Gilbert, Sandra. "My Name is Darkness: The Poetry of Self-Definition." *Tendril Magazine* 18 (1984): 98–110.

Gilbert, Sandra and Susan Gubar, eds. *Shakespeare's Sisters: Feminist Essays on Women Poets*. Bloomington: Indiana University Press, 1979.

Gilmore, Leigh. *Autobiographics: A Feminist Theory of Women's Self-Representation*. Ithaca, N.Y.: Cornell University Press, 1994.

Ginsberg, Allen. *Howl and Other Poems*. San Francisco: City Lights Books, 1956.

——. *Kaddish, and Other Poems, 1958–1960*. San Francisco: City Lights Books, 1961.

Giovanni, Nikki. *Black Feeling, Black Talk, Black Judgement*. New York: Morrow Quill Paperbacks, 1970.

Gleason, Abbott. *Totalitarianism: The Inner History of the Cold War*. New York: Oxford University Press, 1995.

Goldberg, Jonathan. *Sodometries: Renaissance Texts and Modern Sexualities*. Stanford: Stanford University Press, 1993.

Gould, Deborah. *Sex, Death, and the Politics of Anger: Emotions and Reason in Act Up's Fight Against AIDS*. Ph.D. Dissertation, University of Chicago, 2000.

Grossman, Allen. *The Sighted Singer: Two Works on Poetry for Readers and Writers*. Baltimore: Johns Hopkins University Press, 1992.

Habermas, Jürgen. *The Structural Transformation of the Public Sphere: An Inquiry into a Category of Bourgeois Society*. Trans. Thomas Burger. Cambridge: MIT Press, 1993.

Hahn, Susan. *Confession*. Chicago: University of Chicago Press, 1997.

Hall, Donald. "Knock, Knock." *American Poetry Review* 2 (November/December 1973): 44.

Halley, Janet. "Reasoning About Sodomy: Act and Identity in and After *Bowers v. Hardwick*." *Virginia Law Review* 79 (October 1993): 1721–1780.

——. "The Politics of the Closet: Towards Equal Protection for Gay, Lesbian, and Bisexual Identity." *UCLA Law Review* 36 (June 1989): 915–76.

Halperin, David M. *Saint Foucault: Towards a Gay Hagiography*. New York: Oxford University Press, 1995.

Hamilton, Ian. *Robert Lowell: A Biography*. New York: Vintage, 1982.

Hardwick, Elizabeth. *A View of My Own: Essays in Literature and Society*. New York: Farrar, Straus and Cudahy, 1962.

——. *Bartleby in Manhattan and Other Essays*. New York: Random House, 1983.

Hass, Robert. *Twentieth Century Pleasures: Prose on Poetry*. New York: Ecco Press, 1984.

Holden, Jonathan. *The Rhetoric of Contemporary Lyric*. Bloomington: Indiana University Press, 1980.

——. *Style and Authenticity in Postmodern Poetry*. Columbia: University of Missouri Press, 1986.

Horowitz, Daniel. *Vance Packard and American Social Criticism*. Chapel Hill: University of North Carolina Press, 1994.

Howe, Florence and Ellen Bass, eds. *No More Masks! An Anthology of Poems by Women*. Garden City, N.Y.: Anchor Press, 1973.

Hunter, Nan. "Banned in the USA." In Lisa Duggan and Nan D. Hunter, eds., *Sex Wars: Sexual Dissent and Political Culture*, 80–84. New York: Routledge, 1995.

Ingersoll, Earl G., Judith Kitchen, and Stan Sanvel Rubin, eds. *The Post-Confessionals: Conversations with American Poets of the Eighties*. Rutherford, N.J.: Associated University Presses, 1989.

Inness, Julie C. *Privacy, Intimacy, and Isolation*. New York: Oxford University Press, 1992.

Jackson, Kenneth T. *Crabgrass Frontier: The Suburbanization of the United States*. New York: Oxford University Press, 1985.

Jacobs, Jane. *The Death and Life of Great American Cities*. New York: Vintage, 1961.

Johnson, W. R. *The Idea of Lyric: Lyric Modes in Ancient and Modern Poetry*. Berkeley: University of California Press, 1982.

Juhasz, Suzanne. *Naked and Fiery Forms: A New Tradition*. New York: Harper Colophon, 1976.

Kalaidjian, Walter. *Languages of Liberation: The Social Text in Contemporary American Poetry*. New York: Columbia University Press, 1989.

Kalstone, David. *Five Temperaments*. New York: Oxford University Press, 1977.

Kamisar, Yale. "Searches and Seizures: Drugs, AIDS, and the Threat to Privacy." *New York Times Magazine*, September 13, 1987, 109.

Kennan, George. "The Sources of Soviet Conduct." *Foreign Affairs* 25 (1947): 556–82.

Kennedy, Randall. "Contrasting Fates of Repression: A Comment on *Gibson v. Florida Legislative Investigation Committee*." In Marjorie Garber and Rebecca Walkowitz, eds., *Secret Agents: The Rosenberg Case, McCarthyism, and Fifties America*, 265–74. New York: Routledge: 1995.

Kennedy, Robert. *The Enemy Within*. New York: Harper-Collins, 1960.

Koestler, Arthur. *The God That Failed*. Richard Crossman, ed. New York: Harper, 1949.

Kreimer, Seth. "Sunlight, Secrets, and Scarlet Letters: The Tension Between Privacy and Disclosure in Constitutional Law." *University of Pennsylvania Law Review* 140 (November 1991): 1–147.

Kumin, Maxine. *The Nightmare Factory*. New York: Harper and Row, 1970.

Kushner, Tony. *Angels in America: A Gay Fantasia on National Themes*. New York: Theatre Communications Group, 1993.

Lacey, Paul A. *The Inner War: Forms and Themes in Recent American Poetry*. Philadelphia: Fortress Press, 1972.

Laing, R. D. *The Divided Self: an Existential Study in Sanity and Madness*. New York: Penguin, 1965.

Lakoff, George and Mark Johnson. *Metaphors We Live By*. Chicago: University of Chicago Press, 1980.

Landau, Deborah. " 'How to Live. What to Do.': The Poetics and Politics of AIDS." *American Literature* 68, no. 1 (March 1996): 193–225.

Lerner, Laurence. "What is Confessional Poetry?" *Critical Quarterly* 29, no. 2 (Summer 1987): 46–66.

Levertov, Diane. *Light Up the Cave*. New York: New Directions, 1981.

Levinson, Sanford and Steven Mailloux, eds. *Interpreting Law and Literature*. Evanston: Northwestern University Press, 1988.

Lieberman, Laurence. *Unassigned Frequencies: American Poetry in Review, 1964–1977*. Urbana: University of Illinois Press, 1977.

Lowell, Robert. Drafts of "Skunk Hour," undated. Robert Lowell Papers, 73M 90 bMS Am 1905 (2206). Houghton Library, Harvard University.

——. Letter to Elizabeth Hardwick, May 26, 1970. Box 5, Folder 5. By permission of the Harry Ransom Humanities Research Center, The University of Texas at Austin.

——. Letter to Harriet Winslow, July 29, 1960. Robert Lowell Papers, 73M 90 bMS Am 1905 (1613–1676). Houghton Library, Harvard University.

——. Autobiographical Prose, "I Take Thee, Bob," undated. Robert Lowell Papers, 73M 90 bMS Am 1905 (2211). Houghton Library, Harvard University.

——. Autobiographical Prose, "Rock," undated. Robert Lowell Papers, 73M 90 bMS Am 1905 (2220) sheet 17. Houghton Library, Harvard University.

——. *Collected Prose*. New York: Farrar, Straus, and Giroux, 1987.

——. *Day by Day*. New York: Farrar, Straus, and Giroux, 1977.

——. *For Lizzie and Harriet*. London: Faber and Faber, 1973.

——. *For the Union Dead*. New York: Farrar, Straus, and Giroux, 1964.

——. *History*. London: Faber and Faber, 1973.

——. *Life Studies*. New York: Farrar, Straus, and Giroux, 1959.

——. *Notebook 1967–1968*. New York: Farrar, Straus, and Giroux, 1969.

——. *Notebook*. New York: Farrar, Straus and Giroux, 1970.

——. *The Dolphin*. London: Faber and Faber, 1973.

MacDonald, Dwight. *Against the American Grain*. New York: Random House, 1962.

——. "Masscult and Midcult." In Dwight MacDonald, ed., *Against the American Grain*, 3–75. New York: Random House, 1962.

Mailer, Norman. *Advertisements For Myself*. New York: Putnam, 1959.

Malkan, Jeffrey. "Literary Formalism, Legal Formalism." *Cardozo Law Review* 19 (March 1998): 1393–1439.

Malkoff, Karl. *Escape from the Self: A Study in Contemporary American Poetry*. New York: Columbia University Press, 1977.

Marcuse, Herbert. *One Dimensional Man: Studies in the Ideology of Advanced Industrial Society*. Boston: Beacon Press, 1964.

Mariani, Paul. *Lost Puritan: A Life of Robert Lowell*. New York: Norton, 1994.

May, Elaine Tyler. *Homeward Bound: American Families in the Cold War Era*. New York: Basic Books, 1988.

May, Lary. ed. *Recasting America: Culture and Politics in the Age of the Cold War*. Chicago: University of Chicago Press, 1989.

Mazzaro, Jerome. *The Achievement of Robert Lowell, 1939–1959*. Detroit: University of Detroit Press, 1960.

——. ed. *Modern American Poetry: Essays in Criticism*. New York: David McKay, 1970.

——. *The Poetic Themes of Robert Lowell*. Ann Arbor: University of Michigan Press, 1965.

——. *Postmodern American Poetry*. Urbana: University of Illinois Press, 1980.

——. "Robert Lowell's Early Politics of Apocalypse." In Jerome Mazzaro, ed., *Modern American Poetry: Essays in Criticism*, 321–50. New York: David McKay, 1970.

McCarthy, Mary. *On the Contrary: Articles of Belief, 1946–1961*. New York: Farrar, Straus and Cudahy, 1961.

McGill, Meredith. "Enlistment and Refusal: The Task of Public Poetry." In Marjorie Garber, Paul B. Franklin, and Rebecca L. Walkowitz, eds., *Field Work: Sites In Literary and Cultural Studies*, 144–49. New York: Routledge, 1996.

Melley, Timothy. *Empire of Conspiracy: The Culture of Paranoia in Postwar America*. Ithaca, N.Y.: Cornell University Press, 2000.

Meyerowitz, Joanne. "Beyond the Feminine Mystique: A Reassessment of Postwar Mass Culture, 1946–1958." In Joanne Meyerowitz, ed. *Not June Cleaver: Women and Gender in Postwar America, 1945–1960*, 229–62. Philadelphia: Temple University Press, 1994.

Meyerowitz, Joanne, ed. *Not June Cleaver: Women and Gender in Postwar America, 1945–1960*. Philadelphia: Temple University Press, 1994.

Meyers, Jeffrey, ed. *Robert Lowell: Interviews and Memoirs*. Ann Arbor: University of Michigan Press, 1988.

Middlebrook, Diane Wood. *Anne Sexton: A Biography*. New York: Vintage Books, 1991.

——. "What Was Confessional Poetry?" In Jay Parini, ed., *Columbia History of American Poetry*, 632–49. New York: Columbia University Press, 1993.

Miles, Barry. *Ginsberg: A Biography*. New York: Harper Collins, 1989.

Mill, John Stuart. *On Liberty*. 1859; reprint, John Gray, ed., New York: Oxford University Press, 1991.

——. "What Is Poetry."; reprinted in F. Parvin Sharpless, ed., *Essays on Poetry*. Columbia: University of South Carolina Press, 1976.

Millett, Kate. *Sexual Politics*. Garden City: Doubleday, 1970.

Mills, C. Wright. *White Collar: The American Middle Classes*. New York: Oxford University Press, 1951.

——. Review of William Whyte's *The Organization Man*, *New York Times*, December 9, 1956, 6.

Mills, Ralph J. Jr. *The Cry of the Human: Essays on Contemporary American Poetry*. Urbana: University of Illinois Press, 1975.

Molesworth, Charles. *The Fierce Embrace*. Columbia: University of Missouri Press, 1979.

Monette, Paul. *Becoming a Man: Half a Life Story*. New York: Harcourt Brace Jovanovich, 1992.

——. *Borrowed Time: An AIDS Memoir*. New York: Avon Books, 1988.

——. *Love Alone: Eighteen Elegies for Rog*. New York: St. Martin's Press, 1988.

——. *West of Yesterday, East of Summer*. New York: St. Martin's Press, 1994.

Montefiore, Jan. *Feminism and Poetry: Language, Experience, and Identity in Women's Writing*. New York: Pandora, 1987.

Nadel, Alan. *Containment Culture: American Narratives, Postmodernism, and the Atomic Age*. Durham, N.C.: Duke University Press, 1995.

Nedelsky, Jennifer. "Reconceiving Autonomy: Sources, Thoughts, and Possibilities." *Yale Journal of Law and Feminism* 1, no. 1 (Spring 1989): 7–36.

Nelson, Emmanuel, ed. *AIDS: The Literary Response*. New York: Twayne, 1992.

Orwell, George. *Nineteen Eighty-Four*. New York: Harcourt, Brace, 1949.

Ostriker, Alicia "Anne Sexton and the Seduction of Audience." In Diane Hunter ed., *Seduction and Theory*, 154–69. Urbana: University of Illinois Press, 1989.

——. " 'Fact' as Style: The Americanization of Sylvia." *Language and Style: An International Journal* 1, no. 3 (Summer 1968): 201–12.

——. *Stealing the Language: The Emergence of Women's Poetry in America*. Boston: Beacon Press, 1986.

Packard, Vance. *The Hidden Persuaders*. New York: David McKay, 1957.

——. *The Naked Society*. New York: David McKay, 1962.

——. *The Status Seekers: An Exploration of Class Behavior in America and the Hidden Barriers That Affect You, Your Community, Your Future*. New York: David McKay, 1959.

——. *The Waste Makers*. New York: David McKay, 1960.

Parkinson, Thomas Francis. *Robert Lowell: A Collection of Critical Essays*. Englewood Cliffs, N.J.: Prentice-Hall, 1968.

Patton, Cindy. *Inventing AIDS*. New York: Routledge, 1990.

Pearson, Gabriel. "*For Lizzie and Harriet*: Robert Lowell's Domestic Apocalypse." In R. W. Butterfield ed., *Modern American Poetry*, 187–203. New York: Vision Press, 1984.

Pease, Donald. "National Identities, Postmodern Artifacts, and Postnational Narratives." In Donald Pease, ed., *National Identities and Post-Americanist Narratives*, 1–13. Durham, N.C.: Duke University Press, 1994.

Pease, Donald, ed. *National Identities and Post-Americanist Narratives*. Durham, N.C.: Duke University Press, 1994.

Pember, Don. *Privacy and the Press: The Law, the Mass Media, and the First Amendment*. Seattle: University of Washington Press, 1972.

Perloff, Marjorie. *The Poetic Art of Robert Lowell*. Ithaca, N.Y.: Cornell University Press, 1973.

———. *Poetic License*. Evanston: Northwestern University Press, 1990.

———. *Radical Artifice: Writing Poetry in the Age of Media*. Chicago: University of Chicago Press, 1991.

Phillips, Robert. *The Confessional Poets*. Carbondale: Southern Illinois University Press, 1973.

Pinsky, Robert. *Poetry and the World*. New York: Ecco Press, 1988.

———. *The Situation of Poetry: Contemporary Poetry and Its Traditions*. Princeton: Princeton University Press, 1976.

Plath, Sylvia. *Ariel*. New York: Harper and Row, 1966.

———. *The Collected Poems*. New York: Harper and Row, 1981.

———. *The Colossus and Other Poems*. New York: Knopf, 1967.

———. *Crossing the Water: Transitional Poems*. New York: Harper and Row, 1971.

———. *Winter Trees*. New York: Harper and Row, 1972.

Poirier, Richard. *A World Elsewhere: The Place of Style in American Literature*. New York: Oxford University Press, 1966.

Pomeroy, Wardell B. *Dr. Kinsey and the Institute for Sex Research*. New York: Harper and Row, 1972.

Price, Jonathan. *Critics on Robert Lowell*. Coral Gables: University of Miami Press, 1972.

Primus, Richard. "A Brooding Omnipresence: Totalitarianism in Postwar Constitutional Thought." *Yale Law Review* 106 (November 1996): 423–57.

Procopiow, Norma. *Robert Lowell: The Poet and His Critics*. Chicago: American Library Association, 1984.

Prosser, William L. "Privacy." *California Law Review* 48 (1960): 383–423.

Purnik, Joyce. "First, Call a Doctor, Then a News Conference; Politicians Open Up About What Ails Them." *New York Times*, April 30, 2000, 35.

Ramazani, Jahan. *The Poetry of Mourning*. Chicago: University of Chicago Press, 1994.

Ransom, John Crowe. "Criticism as Pure Speculation." In Donald A. Stauffer, ed., *The Intent of the Critic*, 91–124. Princeton: Princeton University Press, 1941.

Redlich, Norman. "Are There 'Certain Rights . . . Retained by the People'?" *New York University Law Review* 37 (1962): 787–812.

Rich, Adrienne. Review of Robert Lowell's *The Dolphin* in column "Carytid." *American Poetry Review* (September/October, 1973): 42.

———. *Snapshots of a Daughter-in-Law: Poems, 1954–1962*. New York: Norton, 1967.

Riesman, David. *The Lonely Crowd: A Study of the Changing American Character*. New Haven: Yale University Press, 1961.

Roche, George. *The Bewildered Society*. New Rochelle, N.Y.: Arlington House, 1972.

Rogin, Michael. *Ronald Reagan, The Movie and Other Episodes in Political Demonology*. Berkeley: University of California Press, 1987.

Roraback, Catherine. "*Griswold v. Connecticut*: A Brief Case History." *Ohio Northern University Law Review* 16, no. 3 (1989): 395–401.

Rose, Jacqueline. *The Haunting of Sylvia Plath*. Cambridge: Harvard University Press, 1991.

Rosenberg, Jerome. *The Death of Privacy*. New York: Random House, 1969.

Rosenberg, Norman. "Gideon's Trumpet: Sounding the Retreat from Legal Realism." In Lary May, ed., *Recasting America: Culture and Politics in the Age of the Cold War*, 107–24. Chicago: University of Chicago Press, 1989.

Rosenthal, M. L. *The Modern Poets: A Critical Introduction*. New York: Oxford University Press, 1960.

——. *The New Poets: American and British Poetry Since World War II*. New York: Oxford University Press, 1967.

——. *Our Life in Poetry*. New York: Persea Press, 1991.

Ross, Andrew. *No Respect: Intellectuals and Popular Culture*. New York: Routledge, 1989.

Rubenfeld, Jed. "The Right to Privacy." *The Harvard Law Review* 102, no. 4 (February 1989): 737–807.

Rule, James, Douglas McAdam, Linda Stearns, and David Uglow. *The Politics of Privacy: Planning for Personal Data Systems as Powerful Technologies*. New York: Elsevier Press, 1980.

Sconce, Jeffrey. "The 'Outer Limits' of Oblivion." In Lynn Spigel and Michael Curtin, eds., *The Revolution Wasn't Televised: Sixties Television and Social Conflict*, 21–46. New York: Routledge, 1997.

Sedgwick, Eve Kosofsky. *The Epistemology of the Closet*. Berkeley: University of California Press, 1990.

——. *Novel Gazing: Queer Readings in Fiction*. Durham, N.C.: Duke University Press, 1997.

Seltzer, Mark. *Serial Killers: Death and Life in America's Wound Culture*. New York: Routledge, 1998.

Sennett, Richard. *The Fall of Public Man*. New York: Norton, 1974.

Sexton, Anne. *All My Pretty Ones*. Boston: Houghton Mifflin, 1962.

——. *The Awful Rowing Toward God*. Boston: Houghton Mifflin, 1975.

——. *The Complete Poems*. Boston: Houghton Mifflin, 1981.

——. *The Death Notebooks*. Boston: Houghton Mifflin, 1974.

——. *Live or Die*. Boston: Houghton Mifflin, 1966.

——. *Love Poems*. Boston: Houghton Mifflin, 1969.

——. *No Evil Star: Selected Essays, Interviews, and Prose*. Steven Colburn, ed. Ann Arbor: University of Michigan Press, 1985.

——. *To Bedlam and Part Way Back*. Boston: Houghton Mifflin, 1960.

Shamir, Milette. "Hawthorne's Romance and the Right to Privacy." *American Quarterly* 49, no. 4 (1997): 746–79.

Shilts, Randy. *And the Band Played on: Politics, People, and the AIDS Epidemic*. New York: St. Martin's Press, 1987.

Siebers, Tobin. *Cold War Criticism and the Politics of Skepticism*. New York: Oxford University Press, 1993.

Siegel, Reva. "Abortion as a Sex Equality Right: Its Basis in Feminist Theory." In Martha Albertson Fineman and Isabel Karpin, eds., *Mothers in Law*, 66–68. New York: Columbia University Press, 1995.

Silverstone, Roger, ed. *Visions of Suburbia*. New York: Routledge, 1997.

Snodgrass, W. D. *Heart's Needle*. New York: Knopf, 1959.

Sontag, Susan. *Illness as Metaphor and AIDS and Its Metaphors*. New York: Doubleday, 1989.

Spigel, Lynn. *Make Room for TV: Television and the Family Ideal in Postwar America*. Chicago: University of Chicago Press, 1992.

Spigel, Lynn and Michael Curtin, eds. *The Revolution That Wasn't Televised: Sixties Television and Social Conflict*. New York: Routledge, 1997.

Spindel, Bernard. *The Ominous Ear*. New York: Award House, 1968.

Stein, Kevin. *Private Poets, Worldly Acts: Public and Private History in Contemporary American Poetry*. Athens: Ohio University Press, 1996.

Strong, William. "The Grave's a Fine and Private Place." *Society* (January/February 1992): 5–8.

Talmon, J. L. *The Origins of Totalitarian Democracy*. London: Secker and Warburg, 1952.

Tate, Allen. Letter to Robert Lowell, January 31, 1958. Lowell Papers, 73M 90 bMS Am 1905 (1205–1266). Houghton Library, Harvard University.

Thomas, Brook. *Cross-Examinations of Law and Literature*. New York: Cambridge University Press, 1987.

——. "The Construction of Privacy in and around *The Bostonians*." *American Literature* 64 (December 1992): 719–47.

Thomas, Kendall. "Beyond the Privacy Principle." *Columbia Law Review* 92, no. 6 (October 1992): 1431–1516.

Tiffany, Daniel. *Toy Medium: Materialism and Modern Lyric*. Berkeley: University of California Press, 2000.

Tougaw, Jason. "Testimony and the Subjects of AIDS Memoirs." *a/b: Auto/Biography Studies* 13, no. 2 (Winter 1998): 235–56.

Tucker, Herbert. "Dramatic Monologue and the Overhearing of Lyric." In Chaviva Hosek and Patricia Parker, eds., *Lyric Poetry: Beyond New Criticism*, 229–243. Ithaca, N.Y.: Cornell University Press, 1985.

Vendler, Helen. "Reading a Poem." In Marjorie Garber, Paul B. Franklin, and Rebecca L. Walkowitz, eds., *Field Work: Sites in Literary and Cultural Studies*. New York: Routledge, 1996.

Von Hallberg, Robert. "Poetry, Politics, and Intellectuals." In Sacvan Bercovitch, ed., *The Cambridge History of American Literature*, vol. 8, *Poetry and Criticism 1940–1995*, 1–159. New York: Cambridge University Press, 1996.

————. *American Poetry and Culture 1945–1980*. Cambridge: Harvard University Press, 1985.

Wagner-Martin, Linda. ed. *Critical Essays on Anne Sexton*. Boston: G. K. Hall, 1989.

Warner, Michael, ed. *Fear of a Queer Planet: Queer Politics and Social Theory*. Minneapolis: University of Minnesota Press, 1993.

————. Introduction to Michael Warner, ed., *Fear of a Queer Planet: Queer Politics and Social Theory*, vii–xxxi. Minnesota: University of Minnesota Press, 1993.

————. *The Trouble With Normal: Sex, Politics, and The Ethics of Queer Life*. New York: The Free Press, 1999.

Westin, Alan. *Privacy and Freedom*. New York: Atheneum, 1967.

Wheeler, Stanton, ed. *On Record: Files and Dossiers in American Life*. New York: Russell Sage Foundation, 1969.

White, James Boyd. *Justice as Translation: An Essay in Cultural and Legal Criticism*. Chicago: University of Chicago Press, 1990.

Whitehead, Kim. *The Feminist Poetry Movement*. Jackson: University Press of Mississippi, 1996.

Whyte, William Hollingsworth. *The Organization Man*. New York: Simon and Schuster, 1956.

Wigley, Mark. "Untitled: The Housing of Gender." In Beatriz Columina, ed., *Sexuality and Space*, 327–89. New York: Princeton Architectural Press, 1992.

Williamson, Alan. *Introspection and Contemporary Poetry*. Cambridge: Harvard University Press, 1987.

————. *Pity the Monsters: The Political Vision of Robert Lowell*. New Haven: Yale University Press, 1974.

Wolfe, Thomas. *The Kandy-Kolored Tangerine-Flake Streamline Baby*. New York: Pocket Books, 1966.

Woods, Gregory. "AIDS to Remembrance: The Uses of Elegy." In Emmanuel Nelson, ed., *AIDS: The Literary Response*, 155–66. New York: Twayne, 1992.

Yoshino, Kenji. "What's Past Is Prologue: Precedent in Literature and Law." *Yale Law Journal* 104 (November 1994): 471–510.

Zinn, Howard. *Postwar America: 1945–1971*. Indianapolis: Bobbs-Merrill, 1973.

RELEVANT CASES (BY YEAR)

DeMay v. Roberts, 146 Mich. 160, 9 N.W. 146 (1881)

Boyd v. U.S., 116 U.S. 616 (1886)

Weeks v. U.S., 232 U.S. 383 (1914)

Meyer v. Nebraska, 262 U.S. 390 (1923)

Olmstead v. U.S., 277 U.S. 438 (1928)

Wolf v. Colorado, 338 U.S. 25 (1949)

On Lee v. U.S., 343 U.S. 747 (1952)

Rochin v. California, 342 U.S. 165 (1952)

Haelan's Laboratories Inc, v. Topps Chewing Gum, 202 F.2d 866 (1953)

Slowchower v. N.Y., 350 U.S. 551 (1956)

Hogan v. A. S. Barnes and Co., 114 U.S.P.Q. 314 (Pa.Ct.Phil.Cy.) (1957)

Watkins v. U.S., 354 U.S. 178 (1957)

N.A.A.C.P. v. Alabama, 357 U.S. 449 (1958)

Frank v. Maryland, 359 U.S. 360 (1959)

Cohen v. Hurley, 336 U.S. 117 (1961)

Silverman v. U.S., 365 U.S. 505 (1961)

Mapp v. Ohio, 367 U.S. 643 (1961)

Poe v. Ullman, 367 U.S. 497 (1961)

Griswold v. Connecticut, 381 U.S. 479 (1965)

Osborn v. U.S., Lewis v. U.S., Hoffa v. U.S., 385 U.S. 323, 87 S. Ct. 439 (1966)

Time, Inc. v. Hill, 385 U.S. 374 (1967)

Loving v. Virginia, 388 U.S. 1817 (1967)

Katz v. U.S., 389 U.S. 347 (1967)

Terry v. Ohio, 392 U.S. 1 (1968)

Stanley v. Georgia, 394 U.S. 557 (1969)

Eisenstadt v. Baird, 405 U.S. 438 (1972)

Roe v. Wade, 410 U.S. 113 (1973)

Doe v. Bolton, 410 U.S. 179 (1973)

Bowers v. Hardwick, 478 U.S. 186 (1986)

Webster v. Reproductive Health Services, 492 U.S. 490 (1989)

Planned Parenthood of Southeastern Pennsylvania v. Casey, 112 S.Ct. 2791 (1992)

Index

abortion. *See* reproductive rights; *Roe v. Wade*

"Abortion as a Sex Equality Right" (Siegel), 159

ACT UP, 25–26, 146

Advertisements for Myself (Mailer), 19

Agamben, Giorgio, 177

agency panic, 168

AIDS, 24–25; *Bowers v. Hardwick* and, 24; deprivatization of sex and, 25; Monette and, 141–59

Allen, Anita, 22–23

All My Pretty Ones (Sexton), 29, 119

Altieri, Charles, 33

ambivalence, xiv–xv

America, as private space, 107

Angels in America, 25

anticommunism: House Un-American Activities Committee, 15, 16; in mass culture, 14; surveillance and, 11–12, 84–85

Arendt, Hannah, 9, 55, 109, 146, 163

"Are there 'Certain Rights . . . Retained By the People?' " (Redlich), 80

Ariel (Plath), 29, 40, 177–78

autonomy: doctors and women's, 126–30; feminist criticism on, 33–37; of Hardwick in *The Dolphin*, 65–73; home as, 106–8; lyric poetry and, 32–34; marriage and, 68–70; patriarchal control and, 59–64;

Roe v. Wade on, 112–13; self-sovereignty as, 28, 169; wiretapping and, 161–62; women poets on, 109–11

Bass, Ellen, 34

Benjamin, Jessica, xix

Berlant, Lauren, 69, 139–40, 158

"Beyond the Privacy Principle" (Thomas, Kendall), 152

Bill of Rights: coercion of confession and, 4; penumbra of, 2

birth control. *See Griswold v. Connecticut; Poe v. Ullman*

Bishop, Elizabeth, 47, 64, 174

Blackwood, Carolyn, 64

Bloustein, Edward, 43, 55–57; on manhood, 62–63

bodies, privacy of, 112–40, 182; doctors and, 116–23

Bordo, Susan, 182

Boston, privacy in, 42–44, 48–49, 172–73

boundaries of privacy, 31–33; voyeurism and, 52–55; women's bodies and, 114–40

Bowers v. Hardwick, xv, 24–26, 141–59; Monette on, xviii–xix, 143–45

Boyd v. U.S., xvi, 7

brainwashing, 169

Brandeis, Louis; dissent in *Olmstead*, 5–8; on inviolate personality, 5, 58–59;

201